Jedi Knight™
Dark Forces® II

Official Strategy Guide

Rick Barba

Prima Publishing
Rocklin, California
916-632-4400
www.primagames.com

 ® is a registered trademark of Prima Publishing, a division of Prima Communications, Inc.

P ® and Prima Publishing® are registered trademarks of Prima Communications, Inc.

PRIMA

Important:
Prima Publishing has made every effort to determine that the information contained in this book is accurate. However, the publisher makes no warranty, either expressed or implied, as to the accuracy, effectiveness, or completeness of the material in this book; nor does the publisher assume liability for damages, either incidental or consequential, that may result from using the information in this book. The publisher cannot provide information regarding game play, hints and strategies, or problems with hardware or software. Questions should be directed to the support numbers provided by the game and device manufacturers in their documentation. Some game tricks require precise timing and may require repeated attempts before the desired result is achieved.

Edited by Allan Kausch and Cara Evangelista (Lucasfilm), Mollie Boero (LucasArts), and Chris Balmain (Prima).

ISBN: 7615-0922-4
Library of Congress Catalog Card Number: 96-70082
Printed in the United States of America

97 98 99 00 BB 10 9 8 7 6 5 4 3 2 1

Table of Contents

Part II: Jedi Walkthrough (Hard Difficulty Mode)   60

INTRODUCTION

WELCOME TO THE OFFICIAL STRATEGY GUIDE FOR JEDI KNIGHT: DARK FORCES II, ONE OF THE MOST ANTICIPATED GAMES IN INDUSTRY HISTORY. WHEN WE SAY "OFFICIAL" GUIDE, WE MEAN EXACTLY THAT. THIS BOOK WAS CREATED WITH THE HANDS-ON HELP OF THE JEDI KNIGHT DESIGN AND TESTING TEAMS. IN FACT, WE SPENT A GIDDY WEEK AT OUR OWN DESK IN THE HALLOWED JEDI KNIGHT DESIGN DOMAIN AT LUCASARTS—A BIZARRE, TWISTED ARCHITECTURE OF DARK CUBICLES RIGHT OUT OF NAR SHADDAA. SURE, IT WAS FUN, BUT MORE IMPORTANTLY, OUR EXTENDED VISIT ALLOWED US TO SIT DOWN WITH EACH OF THE LEVEL DESIGNERS, PLAY THROUGH THEIR MISSIONS, AND FIND EVERY NOOK AND CRANNY, EVERY WANDERING MOUSEBOT, EVERYTHING.

SO BEFORE WE GO ANY FURTHER, WE'D LIKE TO EXTEND OUR WARMEST THANKS TO JEDI KNIGHT PROJECT LEADER JUSTIN CHIN AND THE DESIGN CREW, A BUNCH OF NICE GUYS WHO ALSO HAPPEN TO BE MORE TALENTED THAN ANYBODY I KNOW.

How to Use This Book

Gamers seeking guidance have various needs, so *Jedi Knight: Dark Forces II, The Official Strategy Guide* provides various levels of help for lost or frustrated players.

▼ Part 1 offers general information, charts, tables, tips, and strategies you can apply to pertinent situations throughout the game.
▼ Part 2 features detailed maps and step-by-step walkthroughs for each mission in the single-player game played at the Hard difficulty level.

How the Maps Work

For a game like Jedi Knight, maps are important. Strategy guide users tend to consult the maps and map legends first, and, if they're still stymied, read the accompanying sections of the walkthrough later. We designed the maps to make it easy to use this approach. Numbers mark key locations on each map.

These map numbers correspond to a variety of things, including:

▼ important objects (keys, weapons, power-up items);
▼ notable situations (tough battles, good vantage points, tricky maneuvers);
▼ secret areas (*very* important in Jedi Knight);
▼ doors, turbolifts, elevators;
▼ hard-to-find passages.

Map Legends

Check out each map legend—that is, the numbered list near each set of maps—for a quick reference to what the numbers on the maps represent. Each number lists significant items or situations located at the corresponding number on the map. Note that there is only *one legend* for each mission, no matter how many maps we've created for that mission. In some cases, maps overlap; you may find the same number on two maps for a particular mission.

Maps and the Walkthroughs

Each map number also corresponds to a numbered entry in the mission walkthrough. Walkthrough entries give you a more detailed description of what you encounter at each map location. Example: Suppose you find a locked room. The map legend may list only the items available *inside* the room, or say "need red key" and nothing more. Consult the entry for the corresponding number in the walkthrough to learn exactly what you must do to unlock (or bypass) the door.

Jedi Knight Cheat Codes

Sure, we call ourselves a "strategy guide." But we're big enough to admit a popular identity as a "cheat book." So let's get the basic cheats right up front. Here's a list of cheat codes for Jedi Knight: Dark Forces II.

To enter any of the following cheat codes, first hit the T key to bring up the command line at the top of the screen. Then type the code, including any spaces indicated:

Type	To activate code
JEDIWANNABE 1	Invulnerability on.
JEDIWANNABE 0	Invulnerability off.
RED5	All Weapons.
BACTAME	Full health/shields.
ERIAMJH	Fly mode on/off.
PINOTNOIR [mission number]	Go to mission number.
IMAYODA	"Lightmaster" (Acquire all Neutral and Light Side Force Powers at one star).
SITHLORD	"Darkmaster" (Acquire all Neutral and Dark Side Force Powers at one star).
RACCOONKING	"Uberjedi" (Acquire *all* Force Powers at one star).
DEEZNUTS	Add one star to all available Force Powers.
YODAJAMMIES	Replenish Force Energy.
5858LVR	Show full map with enemies/items.
WAMPRAT	Get all items.

PART I

General
Strategies and Statistics

IN THIS SECTION, WE OFFER BASIC GAMEPLAY TIPS; notes and statistics for the game's various characters and weapons; charts and tables full of good, hard Force Power information, and an invaluable set of multiplayer tips. Most of this handy info comes straight from the crack team of LucasArts game testers, folks who've been playing Jedi Knight day and (mostly) night for many months.

Tim Miller and Matthew Azeveda were the spokesmen for the Jedi Knight testing team, generally recognized as the best and brightest in the business. We at Prima, as well as the Jedi Knight design team led by Justin Chin, want to acknowledge and thank the entire testing crew, who helped make Jedi Knight a surefire candidate for game of the year, and who provided much of the critical information for this strategy guide.

Chapter 1

General Tips and Tactics

Here's a short list of wisdom culled from common sense, many hours of Imperial entanglements, and conversations with the Jedi Knight design and testing groups at LucasArts. Be sure to check the excellent starter list of playing tips and strategies on page 34 of the Jedi Knight game manual, as well.

In combat, keep moving.

This may seem obvious, but we'll say it anyway: A moving target is harder to hit. In any exchange of gunfire, we recommend the basic strafe-and-shoot tactic—that is, slide side to side while keeping your target centered in your crosshairs

But after you clear all enemies from an area, slow down and take your time.

After combat's over, relax. Take a break. Look around. Smell the roses. There are good reasons to do this. First, you may have expended your Force Energy using Force Powers in the battle, and only time will replenish it. (For more on this, see Replenishing

Force Energy in Chapter 4, "Force Powers.") Second, you should do a quick health assessment, and then some careful exploration and puzzle-solving. When exploring, it's always best to be slow and methodical, so you don't miss cleverly hidden power-ups or passages.

Keep a low profile.

When we watched LucasArts testers play Jedi Knight, we noticed they play much of the game with a finger planted on the Ⓒ key (or whatever key they've programmed for the Crouch function). Why? Because crouching is always good though it slows you down. Anytime you're under fire or you approach a new area or you just feel uncertain, seek cover and travel in a crouch. It makes you a much smaller target.

Play the angles.

Combat in Jedi Knight can be nerve-racking at times, as combat *should* be. Nothing extracts the saliva from your mouth quite like the knowledge that a vicious bounty hunter or a highly-trained Imperial assassin lurks just around the corner. But the game gives you one slight advantage: Most of the time, you can see him before he sees you. If you inch *very* slowly around the corner, you can often target a piece of him—an arm or a leg, usually—in your crosshairs. Then take him out before he knows what's hit him.

Make your Force connection work for you.

One of the coolest things in Jedi Knight is your access to the Force. Once you obtain Force Powers, you suddenly have a serious advantage over the

regular bad guys. You can speed past them, jump over them, blind them, pull their guns away, make yourself invisible, and, in general, set up situations where you can hit them, but they can't hit you. Whenever possible, exploit this ability. It may seem unfair, but remember, in this game, the bad guys outnumber you about a bazillion to one.

Think vertically.

When in doubt, look up, look down. Jedi Knight is the most exquisitely layered game we've ever played. Missions require a lot of vertical movement. Snipers abound, both high and low. Look for lifts, ramps, high and low ledges, grates and ducts leading through ceilings and floors, and jumps and drops of all kinds.

Look skyward in rising elevators.

Imperial guard units are taught to ambush unwary elevator riders. So as you ride up in an elevator or turbolift, look up to learn in advance which way the doorway exits. Then turn to face that way, pointing your chosen weapon into the snout of any imminent threat at the top, and get ready to open fire.

Send a calling card down elevator shafts.

Moving vertically is often quite hazardous in Jedi Knight. Riding down an elevator shaft can be particularly dangerous; elevator movement often triggers an "awareness event" that draws enemies to investigate. When you arrive, an Imperial greeting party may be waiting, grinning, and looking to ventilate the inner you.

You can use this AI awareness to your advantage, however. Send the lift down without you; in some cases, you must step aboard to activate the lift and hop off quickly. Then clank a few thermal detonators down the open shaft. Enemies who congregate to check out the elevator arrival will get a face full of heat.

But don't stop there. When the lift comes back up, send it back down again. Why? Because troopers who survived the thermal attack sometimes investigate further by moving directly under the lift platform. When the platform goes back down, make sure you're not on it, you may hear the amusing *"Arg! Arg! Arg! Arg!"* of some Imperial fool getting crushed.

Another tactic: When you send down a lift, use secondary fire (the Z key) to place a sequencer charge on the lift's floor. Chances are good that some enemy below will approach the elevator and get a nice proximity mine in the snout. However, if no enemy detonates the sequencer, you face a minor dilemma. When you call the lift back up, you must move back a safe distance and detonate the mine yourself.

Always let your weapons precede you into new areas.

Did we mention the "awareness event" concept? Jedi Knight enemies respond to sound, among other things. When they hear something funny, they check it out. So if you see a new room or area up ahead, fire a few blaster rounds through the doorway at a far wall. This draws Imperials like flies to a bantha road apple. And then you can see what you're up against.

"For example, in Mission 10, there's the room with two red key doors, and it's full of bad guys," notes LucasArts tester Matthew Azeveda. "I fire a single blaster shot against the far wall. All the guys congregate near the shot. Then I launch a rail charge right into the pile. I often take them all out with one shot."

This is a great technique if you're low on ammo or facing levels with wild melee situations: Get troopers to congregate so you can eliminate lots of them with a single shot of your big guns (rail detonator or concussion rifle).

Roll your greetings into suspect rooms.

Better yet, if you have a good supply of thermal detonators, be like a bomb squad and use the Z key (secondary fire) to roll them ahead of you into suspect areas. Not only will you draw out lurking enemies, you'll hurt some of them, too. You'll hear few things as satisfying as the death scream of an unseen commando in the next room. Of course, in areas with high civilian concentrations, this tactic loses some luster. Don't condemn yourself to the dark side with indiscriminate bomb-tossing on the streets of Barons Hed, for example.

Assassinate enemies from afar whenever possible.

Some people consider sniper tactics to be cowardly. Then again, some people like to march in straight lines and wear bright red coats while guys behind trees kill them. Who wins in the long run? (Hint: Check your local government flagpole.) In any case, it's kind of fun to pick off a stormtrooper from a hundred yards and watch his buddies scurry around in a daze because you're so far away you haven't triggered the "sound awareness event" that prompts them to attack you.

Be smart about consuming health and shield items.

The game manual mentions this one, but it's so important we reiterate it here. Waste is as evil as Emperor Palpatine, so if you're only a few points low on your health meter and you find a health pack, *don't grab it*. Note the pack's location, and then return when your health is in a more deplet-ed condition. The same holds true with your shields. Leave shield recharges for when you really need them.

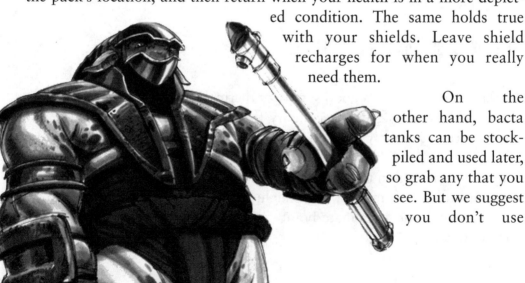

On the other hand, bacta tanks can be stock-piled and used later, so grab any that you see. But we suggest you don't use

them until you get dangerously low on health. When your health meter drops below 80, look for health packs first. If health drops below 50 and health packs seem scarce, then consider a quick bacta infusion.

Use smart door tactics.

Be wary of doors. Something's usually on the other side, hungry for its first Jedi kill. Most doors in Jedi Knight simply slide open when you nudge them with the spacebar or push a nearby wall button. This action alerts enemies to your presence. We suggest you immediately crouch, squeeze off a few shots, and slide sideways, if possible. (If not, backpedal.) Let the door close. Most enemies in Jedi Knight can open doors, so they'll follow you through. Camp at an angle to the door and pick off attackers one by one as they rush through.

Chapter 2
Jedi Knight Characters: Tips & Stats

TRUE TO THE SPIRIT OF THE *STAR WARS* UNIVERSE, Jedi Knight is populated by a wild menagerie of aliens, creatures, droids, and Imperial shock troops. Each species and rank offers a different combat experience; the game manual mentions some. But we managed to penetrate the LucasArts inner sanctum in San Rafael, California, to spend a few days peppering the Jedi creative team with pertinent questions.

Here are some inside tips, observations, and statistics on Jedi Knight's diverse cast of characters, courtesy of the design and testing groups. Our primary contact (and source of quotes) was Matthew Azeveda, who provided the point of view of the LucasArts testers. Special thanks also to Christopher Ross (Jedi Knight's enemy placement and game tuning specialist), who compiled the stats that follow.

Notes and Definitions

The following character statistics apply to the Medium difficulty setting. To see if or how they adjust for Easy and Hard modes, consult these notes:

Health

Health is a measure of the number of hit points a character can suffer before expiring. Each weapon hit scored against an enemy subtracts hit points from that character according to a complex set of variables. Again, these health values are based on the Medium difficulty setting. Easy health values are 80 percent of the value shown here. Hard health values are 120 percent of the value.

Resistance

Some characters have a special resistance to certain types of damage. You can inflict five types of damage in Jedi Knight*:

▼ Impact (fists, falling, collision)
▼ Energy (lasers, bowcaster bolts, repeater gun)
▼ Fire (thermal detonators, mines, rail charges)
▼ Force (Grip, Destruction, Lightning, Deadly Sight)
▼ Saber (lightsaber only)

The resistance values shown in the character statistics depict the percentage of a certain type of attack that has no effect on that character. For

*NOTE: THE CONCUSSION RIFLE INFLICTS A COMBINATION OF IMPACT AND ENERGY DAMAGE.

example, the AT-ST Imperial walker has a 100 percent resistance to energy attacks; it's magnetically sealed (mag-sealed), causing all blaster fire to ricochet harmlessly off its durasteel hide. The AT-ST also has 50 percent resistance to saber attacks; that is, every lightsaber blow you land on a walker causes half the damage you'd normally score for a saber hit.

Special Instincts

These are specific reactions or movements triggered by combat or other situations. Following are some of the primary "instincts" assigned to certain characters in Jedi Knight.

- ▼ **Circle & Strafe:** The tendency in combat to try to flank the target, sliding sideways while facing and shooting at the target.
- ▼ **Jump:** The tendency in combat to, you guessed it, jump.
- ▼ **Dodge:** The tendency in combat to zigzag and dart when targeted.
- ▼ **Open Doors:** The ability to open doors that stand between the character and its target.
- ▼ **Hit & Run:** The tendency to fire a quick volley at a target, and then seek cover.
- ▼ **Special Attack:** This applies primarily to Dark Jedi. The two types of special attacks are jump attack (jump at target while swinging a saber) and charge attack (rush at target while swinging a saber).
- ▼ **Fly:** The ability to fly.
- ▼ **Swim:** The ability to swim.
- ▼ **Lead Fire:** The ability to lead moving targets.
- ▼ **Spread Fire:** Specific to the way Grave Tuskens fire their bowcasters in spreads of three to five bolts.
- ▼ **Sense Danger:** A flee response triggered by combat, by damage, or by the player's mere presence.

Initial Fire Time

This value is simply the amount of time after spotting you an enemy character delays before opening fire.

Drops

Anytime a character (human, alien, or droid) is destroyed, there is a random chance it will drop an item at the point of its demise. In some cases, a dropped item *always* appears; enemies carrying a weapon, for example, always drop that weapon when they die (except for Gamorrean guards, who go down holding their big axes in an unbreakable death grip).

Imperials

AT-ST

The All Terrain Scout Transport (AT-ST) is modeled after the larger AT-AT unit. Nicknamed "chicken," this combat and transport vehicle can deliver some wicked cannon fire, and looks awfully scary, to boot. But check out the AT-ST health stat—only 400! That's barely more trouble than, say, three Trandoshans would give you.

The secret to exploiting this surprisingly low health stat, however, is to use the correct weapon on the mechanoid monster. An AT-ST is mag-sealed, which means normal energy weapons are useless against it. Fire attack weapons, however, are quite effective—thermals, sequencers, and especially rail charges.

Your lightsaber inflicts damage, too, though at half its normal rate. So you can actually run up under an AT-ST, bash at its belly with your saber, and take the darn thing down! Really, what could be more fun than that?

Also of note—when an AT-ST goes down, it usually drops its driver, an officer or an Imperial commando.

Health: 400
Resistance: 100% Impact, 100% Energy (mag-sealed), 50% Saber
Weapon: Laser cannon
Initial Fire Time: 0.5 seconds
Fire Rate: 2 shots every 1.5 seconds
Special Instincts: None
Drops: Could drop a commando or officer
Levels: 6, 13, 19

Stormtrooper

Stormtroopers have several ranks, each with a different weapon and combat capability. You encounter the basic, rank-and-file trooper armed with an ST rifle in nearly every mission after your first Imperial confrontation outside Jerec's dark palace in Mission 6. Even these low-level troops are nimble and feature the deadly "circle & strafe" instinct; stormtroopers are relentless in their efforts to flank or get behind you.

Field stormtroopers wear distinctive shoulder patches to mark their particular weapons expertise. These soldiers can take a few more hits, but more importantly, they carry heavier weapons. Red-patch field troopers carry a repeater gun; yellow-patch field troopers carry a rail detonator, and frankly, we find them to be one of the worst mission-busters in Jedi Knight.

Stormtroopers tend to patrol in groups of two or more, and they're trained to react aggressively to any form of intrusion. So one good tactic

(mentioned in Chapter 1) is to create "awareness events" that attract groups of troopers. Stay out of sight and aim blaster fire into the far wall of a well-guarded room. Nearby Imperial soldiers immediately hurry to investigate. Once they congregate, train an explosive weapon—thermal detonator, concussion rifle, rail detonator—on the congregation.

Stormtrooper Regular

Health: 60
Resistance: None
Weapon: ST rifle
Initial Fire Time: 0.3 seconds
Fire Rate: 3 shots every 2 seconds
Special Instincts: Open Doors, Circle & Strafe
Drops: ST Rifle
Levels: 6, 8, 9, 10, 12, 13, 15, 18, 19

Field Stormtrooper with Orange Shoulder Patch

Health: 70
Resistance: None
Weapon: ST rifle
Initial Fire Time: 0.3 seconds
Fire Rate: 3 shots every 2 seconds
Special Instincts: Open Doors, Circle & Strafe
Drops: ST rifle
Levels: 8, 9, 10, 12, 13, 17, 18, 19

Field Stormtrooper with Red Shoulder Patch

Health: 70
Resistance: None
Weapon: Repeater gun
Initial Fire Time: 0.3 seconds
Fire Rate: 4 shots every 2 seconds
Special Instincts: Open Doors, Circle & Strafe
Drops: Repeater gun
Levels: 8, 9, 10, 12, 13, 17, 18, 19

Field Stormtrooper with Yellow Shoulder Patch

Health: 70
Resistance: None
Weapon: Rail detonator + Swing Attack
Initial Fire Time: .75 seconds
Fire Rate: 1 shot every 2 seconds
Special Instincts: Open Doors, Circle & Strafe
Drops: Rail detonator
Levels: 8, 9, 10, 12, 13, 17, 18, 19

Imperial Officer

They may be leaders, but they sure go down *fast*. Lacking body armor and carrying only a blaster pistol, officers are probably the least bothersome

Imperial opponent in Jedi Knight. Be aware that they are quite accurate shooters, however, rarely missing their target. And with their Dodge instinct, they're agile, too.

Health: 30
Resistance: None
Weapon: Blaster
Initial Fire Time: 0.4 seconds
Fire Rate: 2 shots every 2 seconds
Special Instincts: Open Doors, Circle & Strafe, Dodge
Drops: Blaster
Levels: 6, 8, 9, 10, 12, 13, 15, 18, 19

Imperial Commando

These crack troops, the Empire's finest, are basically very tough stormtroopers who can jump. They're quick, agile, and smart.

"I'd avoid hiding behind crates," warns Jedi tester Matthew Azeveda. "I've tried that with commandos. They just hop up on the crate." It's an unsettling experience: You look up and there they are, chiseled faces in helmets, leering down at you with guns blazing.

Azeveda claims commandos are smart about your sequencer charges, too. "Once, I laid a perimeter of mines in proximity mode and waited," he says. "The commandos just sat there. They wouldn't come after me. It scared me to death. They *knew!*"

Commando with ST Rifle

Health: 90
Resistance: None
Weapon: ST rifle
Initial Fire Time: 0.2 seconds
Fire Rate: 4 shots every 3 seconds
Special Instincts: Open Doors, Circle & Strafe, Dodge, Jump
Drops: ST rifle
Levels: 6, 8, 13, 15, 17, 18, 19

Commando with Repeater Gun

Health: 90
Resistance: None
Weapon: Repeater gun
Initial Fire Time: 0.2 seconds
Fire Rate: 5 shots every 2 seconds
Special Instincts: Open Doors, Circle & Strafe, Dodge, Jump
Drops: Repeater gun
Levels: 6, 8, 13, 18, 19

Probe Droid

Also called a probot, this hovering menace was originally built to gather intelligence and transmit information for Imperial purposes. However, a

few modifications in recent years have turned the probe droid into an effective patrol unit with deadly attack capability. One of the creepiest moments in Jedi Knight happens in Level 6, when you ride a lift up to a dark room full of "slumbering" probe droids.

Health: 90
Resistance: 50% Impact
Weapon: Turret Laser
Initial Fire Time: 0.3 seconds
Fire Rate: 1 shot every 2 seconds
Special Instincts: Fly
Drops: Could drop shield or energy cell
Levels: 6, 10, 12, 13, 16

Sentry Droid

The most salient (and exasperating) characteristic of the sentry droid is its Hit & Run special instinct. The sentry stings you with its blaster, and then zig-zags away. Fortunately, its loud, buzzing approach gives you plenty of warning. Target the unpredictable droid with an accurate energy gun like the Bryar pistol; two or three good hits will take the sentry off its watch for good.

Health: 60
Resistance: 50% Impact
Weapon: Blaster
Initial Fire Time: 1 second
Fire Rate: 2 shots every 1.5 seconds
Special Instincts: Fly, Hit & Run
Drops: Nothing
Levels: 5, 8, 12

Remote

Don't waste ammo on these buzzing little pests. A well-aimed swat with a lightsaber explodes them nicely.

"Most players I watch just ignore remotes and move on past," reports Azeveda. Their micro-blasters aren't much threat, except in the pipes below the fuel station in Mission 9. There, a stray laser sting can ignite an entire fuel pipe, serving up a helping of charbroiled Jedi.

Health: 15
Resistance: 50% Impact, 50% Energy
Weapon: Micro-blaster
Initial Fire Time: 0.4 seconds
Fire Rate: 1 shot every 1.5 seconds
Special Instincts: Fly, Circle & Strafe
Drops: Nothing
Levels: 4, 9

Sentry Gun Turrets

Robotic gun emplacements are one of the Empire's most lethal anti-intrusion devices. Placed in strategic locations, these "smart boxes" make life miserable for unauthorized visitors at Imperial military installations. Sentry gun turrets come in three varieties. The basic box turret and the smaller round turret usually hang from ceiling mounts. A larger, tougher version of the box turret is planted in the floor or ground.

Take these units out immediately; they not only track your movement, but can actually lead you with their shots. After taking a few hits, gun turrets go haywire, spinning wildly and spewing laser rounds. This is a death throe. One more hit can explode the turret, but it will explode anyway, so save the shot if you're low on ammo.

Box Gun Turret

Health: 80
Resistance: 95% Impact
Weapon: Turret laser
Initial Fire Time: .75 seconds
Fire Rate: 1 shot every 1.5 seconds
Special Instincts: Lead Fire
Drops: Could drop energy cell
Levels: 6, 8, 9, 12, 13, 17

Round Gun Turret

Health: 100
Resistance: 95% Impact
Weapon: Turret laser
Initial Fire Time: 0.5 seconds
Fire Rate: 1 shot every .75 seconds
Special Instincts: None
Drops: Could drop energy cell
Levels: 8, 10, 17

"Big Box" Gun Turret

Health: 150
Resistance: 95% Impact
Weapon: Turret laser
Initial Fire Time: 1 second
Fire Rate: 1 shot every 1.5 seconds
Special Instincts: Lead Fire
Drops: Could drop energy cell
Levels: 13, 17

Bounty Hunters

Despite its military might, the Empire isn't averse to hiring mercenary thugs to hunt down enemies and terrorize local populations. Here's a look at some of the rag-tag cutthroats you find in Jedi Knight.

Gran

Three-eyed Gran roam the corridors of Jedi Knight in a number of varieties. Some are unarmed brawlers. Drop them at a distance so they can't hurt you; use the Bryar pistol to save ammo. If you let one sneak a punch, however, you'll suffer major health damage.

Gran with stormtrooper rifles are tough and aggressive, but not particularly nimble. Engage them with standard tactics—shoot and strafe, duck, seek cover, use angles. Some LucasArts testers prefer to fire a few rounds to draw attention, and then duck through a door and let the Gran come to them.

They're big targets, easy to hit in doorways and bottleneck areas. Best, they die with gusto. The Gran death grunt is the punch line of many a galactic joke.

Thermal-armed Gran are by far the worst of the species. Sporting world-class arms and a seemingly endless supply of detonators, these guys are the bane of Nar Shaddaa. Target them first in any situation; the remarkable range and accuracy of their throws pose a significant threat to your health. Best bet—crouch and snipe them down before they see you.

Brown Gran (Fists)

Health: 50
Resistance: None
Weapon: Punch Attack
Initial Fire Time: 0.2 seconds
Fire Rate: 2 punches every 1.5 seconds
Special Instincts: Jump, Open Doors
Drops: Could drop health pack
Levels: 1, 2, 5

Black Gran (Fists)

Health: 60
Resistance: None
Weapon: Punch Attack
Initial Fire Time: 0.2 seconds
Fire Rate: 2 punches every 1.5 seconds
Special Instincts: Jump, Open Doors
Drops: Could drop health pack
Levels: 1, 2

Brown Gran with Thermals

Health: 50
Resistance: None
Weapon: Thermals + Punch Attack
Initial Fire Time: 0.5 seconds
Fire Rate: 1 throw every 2 seconds
Special Instincts: Jump, Open Doors
Drops: Could drop thermal belt, single thermal, health pack, or live thermal
Levels: 2, 5

Black Gran with Thermals

Health: 60
Resistance: None
Weapon: Thermals + Punch Attack
Initial Fire Time: 0.5 seconds
Fire Rate: 1 throw every 2 seconds
Special Instincts: Jump, Open Doors
Drops: Could drop thermal belt, single thermal, health pack, or live thermal
Levels: 2

Brown Gran with ST Rifle

Health: 50
Resistance: None
Weapon: ST rifle
Initial Fire Time: 0.5 seconds
Fire Rate: 1 shot every .75 seconds
Special Instincts: Jump, Open Doors
Drops: ST rifle
Levels: 1, 2, 5

Black Gran with ST Rifle

Health: 60
Resistance: None
Weapon: ST rifle
Initial Fire Time: 0.4 seconds
Fire Rate: 2 shots every 1.25 seconds
Special Instincts: Jump, Open Doors
Drops: ST rifle
Levels: 1, 2

Grave Tusken

LucasArts testers agree: Tuskens are very annoying. The Grave Tuskens who prowl the Sulon wasteland are close cousins of the violent Tusken

Raiders (also known as Sand People) of Tatooine. The opening sequence of Mission 3 in the perimeter area of the Katarn family compound features some of the most brutal, howling combat in Jedi Knight. Tuskens left, Tuskens right, some shooting bowcasters, some ST rifles, all yelling and jumping and hating you with visceral energy.

"Take these guys from a good distance," advises Matthew Azeveda. This is, of course, more easily said than done. But if you let Grave Tuskens get close, they can fire their charged bowcasters with a three- or five-bolt spread, and you'll die right quick. Strafe, keep moving, be aggressive with your blaster. And remember—honor isn't compromised if you run and seek cover when you face a Grave Tusken swarm attack.

Brown Tusken with Bowcaster

Health: 50
Resistance: None
Weapon: Bowcaster
Initial Fire Time: 0.5 seconds
Fire Rate: 1 shot every 1.5 seconds
Special Instincts: Jump, Open Doors, Spread Fire
Drops: Bowcaster
Levels: 3, 4

Black Tusken with Bowcaster

Health: 60
Resistance: None
Weapon: Bowcaster
Initial Fire Time: 0.5 seconds
Fire Rate: 1 shot every 1.5 seconds
Special Instincts: Jump, Open Doors
Drops: Bowcaster
Levels: 3, 4, 5

Brown Tusken with ST Rifle

Health: 50
Resistance: None
Weapon: ST rifle
Initial Fire Time: 0.4 Seconds
Fire Rate: 1 shot every .75 seconds
Special Instincts: Jump, Open Doors
Drops: ST rifle
Levels: 3, 4

Black Tusken with ST Rifle

Health: 60
Resistance: None
Weapon: ST rifle
Initial Fire Time: 0.4 seconds
Fire Rate: 2 shots every 1.5 seconds
Special Instincts: Jump, Open Doors
Drops: ST rifle
Levels: 3, 4, 5

Rodian

These scrawny, scaly cousins of Greedo aren't particularly tough, but they dodge and fire an accurate blaster. They're also pretty quick on the draw; note the initial fire time of just .2 seconds. So target Rodians quickly. Sometimes you can drop them with a single shot.

Health: 40
Resistance: None
Weapon: Blaster
Initial Fire Time: 0.2 seconds
Fire Rate: 1 shot every 1 seconds
Special Instincts: Open Doors, Dodge
Drops: Blaster
Levels: 1, 2

Gamorrean Guard

Get ready for a grunting, squealing surprise as you work your way through grimy Nar Shaddaa. Distinctly porcine in appearance, Gamorreans are a truly unpleasant species; huge, brutish, and powerful, they stand about 1.8 meters tall and weigh about 100 kilos. A Gamorrean guard can inflict *serious* impact damage with a single heinous swipe of his ax. Fortunately, Gamorreans are slow and lack range. In fact, if you can find a safe vantage point, they're ridiculously easy to snipe.

Health: 120
Resistance: 50% Impact
Weapon: Ax
Initial Fire Time: 0.2 seconds
Fire Rate: 1 swing every 2. seconds
Special Instincts: Open Doors
Drops: Could drop a health pack or bacta tank
Levels: 2

Trandoshan

A Trandoshan with a concussion rifle is a truly chilling sight. Key to survival: Get close, but not *too* close. Trandoshans won't unleash their compressed ionized air blast at close range; they may be ugly, but they're not stupid. Instead, they go into melee mode, trying to bludgeon you with the big gun. When you see a Trandoshan, make a zig-zag sprint toward him. Get into his melee range, and then strafe or back away, firing.

Note the health stat of 120; like Gamorreans, Trandoshans can take some good hits before going down. Matthew Azeveda suggests using Force Pull with particularly difficult Trandoshans. Just suck the weapon right out of their hands. "I don't use it much myself, because I'm kind of a purist about combat," he admits. In Mission 9, where Trandoshans roam the fuel station, he'd rather work to a high position and carefully snipe them from above. But he notes that Force Pull can prevent a lot of damage by neutralizing Trandoshan gunners.

Trandoshan With Concussion Rifle

Health: 120
Resistance: None
Weapon: Concussion Rifle + Swing Attack
Initial Fire Time: .75 seconds
Fire Rate: 1 shot every 2 seconds
Special Instincts: Open Doors, Circle & Strafe, Dodge, Jump
Drops: Concussion rifle
Levels: 9

Trandoshan with Rail Detonator

Health: 120
Resistance: None
Weapon: Rail detonator + Swing Attack
Initial Fire Time: .75 seconds
Fire Rate: 1 shot every 2 seconds
Special Instincts: Open Doors, Circle & Strafe, Dodge, Jump
Drops: Rail detonator
Levels: 9

Creatures

Mailoc

Meet the creepiest creature in Jedi Knight. This gruesome, overgrown wasp slams you with its "stinger"—a patch of tail spikes, really—that can penetrate your shields and hurt like hell. Mailocs often appear in swarms, and work hard to slip around behind you. Fortunately, they don't have much exoskeleton for protection. One good shot usually brings down this insectoid beast.

Health: 40
Resistance: None
Weapon: Sting Attack
Initial Fire Time: 0.3 seconds
Fire Rate: 1 sting every 1.6 seconds
Special Instincts: Fly, Hit & Run, Circle & Strafe
Drops: Nothing
Levels: 3, 4, 13

Kell Dragon

Have you wandered into the dragon pen in Jerec's palace yet? Holy cow. You won't meet many Kell dragons in Jedi Knight, but the few you encounter will trigger toothy nightmares. Energy weapons—pistols, ST rifles, bowcasters, repeater guns—are entirely useless against this mag-sealed monster. And its 80 percent resistance to fire damage means you'll need a *big* bucketful of thermal detonators or charges to bring the behemoth down.

So what kills a Kell? Your most effective weapon, as usual, is the lightsaber. But that means you must get close. Fortunately, this lizard is slow—well, slower than *you*, anyway. First, find a vantage point where the dragon can't reach you. (This is possible in all your Kell confrontations in Jedi Knight.) Weaken him with thermal detonators, your rail detonator, and/or sequencer charges. Then fire up your saber and start running. Hit and circle, avoiding head-to-head combat. A Kell is easy to outmaneuver, but don't get cocky, kid.

Health: 500
Resistance: 100% Energy (mag-sealed), 80% Fire
Weapon: Bite Attack
Initial Fire Time: 0.2 seconds
Fire Rate: 1 bite every 1.5 seconds
Special Instincts: None
Drops: Nothing
Levels: 8, 19

Water Cyc

Water cycs are beautiful killers. They drift gracefully; they take hits gracefully; they even die gracefully. But get too close to one and you'll get a lightning-fast tentacle slam upside the head. Water cycs don't move much, so most of them are entirely avoidable. But just to be safe, blast any you see.

Health: 100
Resistance: None
Weapon: Tentacle Attack
Special Instincts: None
Drops: Nothing
Levels: 4

Drugon

Drugons are mobile swimmers and tougher than water cycs. But five or six well-placed blaster shots are usually enough to hook these fish. Their bite hurts, but their biggest weapon is the element of surprise; often you won't see them in the water until they rear their ugly fins in your face. Don't let them sneak up under you in the Barons Hed canal or the river in the canyons outside the valley.

Health: 160
Resistance: None
Weapon: Bite Attack
Special Instincts: Swim
Drops: Nothing
Levels: 5, 13

Noncombatant Personnel

Pedestrian

Yes, people live in the galaxy. Innocent people. They just happen to be caught in the middle of your little war with the Empire. If you truly wish to honor the memory of your father and Jedi Master Qu Rahn, you won't harm the civilians who live and work in Nar Shaddaa or Barons Hed.

Nar Shaddaa Pedestrian

Health: 50
Resistance: None
Weapon: None
Special Instincts: Sense Danger (flee when damaged)
Drops: Could drop health pack, shield, or battery
Levels: 1, 2

Barons Hed Pedestrian

Health: 50
Resistance: None
Weapon: None
Special Instincts: Sense Danger (flee from combat)
Drops: Could drop health pack, shield, or battery
Levels: 5

Ugnaught

These handy little fellows work in the fuel station just outside Barons Hed. You'll also find a few poor souls trapped aboard the falling cargo ship in Mission 15. In either case, treat them with respect, or over to the dark side will you go.

Health: 30
Resistance: None
Weapon: None
Special Instincts: Sense Danger (flee from combat)
Drops: Could drop battery
Levels: 9, 15

Droids

Mouse Droid

These little droids scurry about, minding their own business. Destroying a mouse droid scores a battery for your inventory, but is it worth it? Only if you don't mind a nudge down the dark path.

Health: 10
Resistance: None
Weapon: None
Special Instincts: Sense Danger (flee from player)
Drops: Battery
Levels: 1, 10, 15, 17

R2/R5 Units

R2 and R5 units were designed as astromech droids, specializing in navigation, maintenance, and spaceship repair. Even the darkest Jedi would find it hard to destroy one of these.

Health: 50
Resistance: 95% Impact
Weapon: None
Special Instincts: Sense Danger (flee from combat)
Drops: Could drop power cell, battery, or shield
Levels: 1, 2, 10, 15

Power Droid (Gonk)

We like this droid. It's fun to run into a Gonk and listen to it say "Gonk."
This benign unit frequently holds power or energy cells, but you'll have to
kill it to get them. And that is not the way of the Force.

Health: 50
Resistance: 95% Impact
Weapon: None
Special Instincts: Sense Danger (flee from damage)
Drops: Could drop power cell or energy cell
Levels: 1, 2, 8, 15, 17, 18

Protocol Droid

Protocol droids can be fitted with a number of work modules, but are best
suited for general protocol and communications tasks. Capable of translat-
ing and speaking millions of languages, protocol droids have been known
to develop extensive personality traits—bordering on sentience, some sci-
entists believe. Thus, destroying such a droid is clearly an act with dark
consequences.

Health: 50
Resistance: 50% Impact
Weapon: None
Special Instincts: Sense Danger (flee from combat)
Drops: Nothing
Levels: 2, 10, 15

Medical Droid

These mechanoid medical centers are modeled after Too-Onebee (2-1B), the Echo Base droid who nursed Luke Skywalker back to health after his near-death on the ice planet Hoth. Medical droids appear only in Mission 6; you'll find two in the Imperial complex surrounding Jerec's Dark Palace. Each can inject a full dose of health into your veins, but you'll have to wait sixty seconds before you can use them again.

Note

Again, to find tips, information, and statistics on any of the seven Dark Jedi characters, consult the appropriate mission in Part 2, "Jedi Walkthrough."

Chapter 3
Weapons of a Jedi

JEDI KNIGHT IS ABOUT COMBAT, AND COMBAT REQUIRES DEADLY FORCE. Guns, bombs, mines—all these weapons are available, of course. But the game features a unique Jedi arsenal, as well. Wield the magnificent lightsaber, a fountain of pure energy and symbol of Jedi nobility for thousands of years. Or confound foes with your growing collection of Jedi Force Powers. (For more on Force Powers, see the next chapter.)

The Jedi Knight game manual provides a good basic rundown of the weapons in your armory; we reiterate some of that information here. But we also talked to the design and testing teams at LucasArts to garner additional tips and observations. Our primary tester spokesmen were Matthew Azeveda, who focused on the single-player game, and Tim Miller, a multiplayer expert.

Fists

Fists, frankly, are the last resort of desperate Jedi. There is never a compelling reason to punch rather than shoot, other than a need to conserve ammo.

"I never use my fists unless I'm playing the dark side and I'm taking out pedestrians," laughs LucasArts tester Matthew Azeveda.

He also notes that you take damage if you punch droids—which makes perfect sense, doesn't it?

Bryar Pistol

You'll best use this single-shot weapon for sniping. Its slow rate of fire can be maddening in melees, but because you acquire a stormtrooper rifle within the first minute of the game, you needn't face multiple foes with only a pistol.

"The Bryar is actually an excellent long-range weapon," reports Azeveda. It's also useful on the Hard setting, when ammo is more scarce.

Indeed, as long as your situation doesn't require rapid-fire capability, your trusty pistol is as good and accurate a weapon as you have in your arsenal.

Stormtrooper (ST) Rifle

Despite its standard-issue status, the ST rifle is a solid piece of armament.

"I usually start with the Bryar pistol at a distance," says Azeveda. "Then I switch to the ST rifle when I get closer and encounter more aggressive enemies."

In fact, this weapon is probably your best bet at close range; it's nearly as effective as the Imperial repeater gun, but expends far less ammo. It loses accuracy with distance, however. No surprise there. Anything Imperial tends to be powerful but imprecise.

Thermal Detonators

Thermals are fun. Use that secondary fire button to toss them—*clank! clank! clank!*—down metallic walkways. Watch them bounce. Watch them decimate squads of goons gathered to examine the blaster holes you just put in the far wall. Thermal detonators also serve as your best minesweepers. If sequencer charges lay ahead, roll a thermal up the hall. *Boom!* All clear.

Let's reiterate a tip from Chapter 1. Imperials know that elevators are often unavoidable means of passage from one level to the next. So if an elevator suddenly arrives on their floor, they all come running. *Who's there?* Imagine their surprise when nobody's on the elevator. Imagine their further surprise when a time-delay thermal detonator clanks down the shaft and rolls between their little white feet.

Bowcaster

Here's another good sniper weapon.

"When I finally get the bowcaster—one of my favorite weapons—I put up the crosshairs and assassinate people from long distances," says Azeveda.

Stormtroopers, for example, go down with two quick hits. Azeveda often uses his secondary fire (the Z key) because the bowcaster bolt is then mag-sealed; you get a nice ricochet off solid surfaces. It's great sport to nail people around corners with this bounce effect. Obvious tip: Don't mag-seal bolts if you're close to a target, or you might catch the rebound yourself.

Imperial Repeater Gun

This gun *rocks*. It has a major drawback, though: It burns a *lot* of ammo.

"It looks cool, but you need many burst hits to destroy an enemy," warns Azeveda.

On the upside, once you target an enemy with a stream of repeater fire, he has little chance to fire back. So if you're low on shields and/or health and can't afford to take a hit, single out solitary targets, sneak up as close as possible, and lay into them with the repeater gun.

Of course, if your supply of power cells is vast, the Imperial repeater gun is the perfect weapon for close-quarters combat with enemy swarms. Master the strafe-and-circle technique—sliding sideways while turning to keep your target in the crosshairs—with the repeater gun. It's a truly murderous maneuver and more fun than a barrel of Kian'tharian insectoids.

Rail Detonator

This weapon drives us nuts. In *our* hands, it's beautiful, man. Along with the lightsaber, this gun is your only truly effective weapon against Kell dragons and AT-ST Imperial walkers. (Seven or eight well-aimed rail charges take down a walker.) But when we run into a field stormtrooper wielding one *against* us—well, suffice it to say that anyone wearing a yellow shoulder patch provokes shrieking paranoiac reactions.

We asked Azeveda about that gut-wrenching moment after you hear the *whoosh* and suddenly find a time-delay rail charge stuck to your face. He laughed and shook his head. We pressed for more cogent advice. He said, "Well, you can run right at the guy who fired it and try to take him with you."

Sequencer Charges

Most Jedi players find that laying mines (using the Z key to plant sequencer charges) is only effective after you know where you're going and where your enemies will countermove—that is, after some basic exploration. Poke around and find each mission's natural bottleneck areas. Restart the mission, go to those areas, and draw attention from aggressive enemies. Then run through each bottleneck laying mines. Choose your spots carefully, though. If your enemies don't chase you, the mines seal off your route and you may have to waste thermal detonators clearing it again.

Sequencer charges can also make good bombs. Dropped on enemies using your primary fire button, they pack a very powerful punch. And mine-laying activities increase in value during multiplayer action. (More on this in Chapter 5, "Multiplayer Tips.")

Concussion Rifle

This is a powerful long-range weapon. If you've taken "conc" fire from a Trandoshan, you know just how much misery this gun can deal. Packing an eight-cell wallop, a primary-fire concussion shot kicks out explosive projectiles of compressed ionized air; the impact sends killer shock waves at anything close—including *you*, so don't hit nearby targets. As the game manual suggests, secondary fire mode offers a shotgun-like spray of four cells, better suited for close-range combat.

Jedi Lightsaber

Nothing is more elegant than a Jedi lightsaber. The hum of its swing, the crackle of a hit—all fruit of a focusing jewel formed in heat intense enough to melt durasteel. Your saber's pure-energy photoharmonics have been tuned by a thousand years of Jedi mastery. Can you imagine a more satisfying way to do battle with the minions of darkness? Neither can we.

Lightsaber moves are well-described in the game manual, but let us reiterate and add a few notes here.

▼ Use third-person view (push F1) when saber fighting. You get a much better perspective on the various swings. Plus, it's easier to track the movement of hyperactive opponents such as the bouncing Boc in Mission 20. In addition, you can adjust the setting in the set up screen to do this automatically (see page 10 of the manual: "Enable lightsaber auto-camera").

▼ Practice your strokes against the wall device in Morgan Katarn's workshop when you first obtain the lightsaber at the beginning of Mission 4.

The device lights up at the point of contact, so you can see where each type of saber swing connects with a target.

▼ In dark areas, wield your lightsaber as a substitute for your field light. It gives good illumination and saves battery power.

▼ Good tactic: Against Dark Jedi, hold the lightsaber in block position and wait for their strike. When the sabers clash, punch your primary fire button for a quick counter jab.

▼ Use the powerful swing triggered by your secondary fire button—a wide double-slash—to inflict maximum damage against slow or unwitting opponents. Example: If you have Force Persuasion active and are thus invisible to your opponent, inflict the double-slash with impunity.

▼ Against tough Dark Jedi, however, your secondary swing can be risky. It leaves you vulnerable for a moment, and a sabermaster such as Sariss or Jerec may be quick to exploit your weakness.

▼ Lightsabers inflict quick lethal damage on all non-Jedi enemies. But of course, you must be close enough to strike. Pick off as many enemies as possible from a distance with your guns; wield the saber in tight quarters.

▼ The saber's blocking ability is one of the coolest things in the game. It protects you, and man, it *looks* great. But the saber block is not infallible; some shots will slip past. Don't think you can just camp in front of an enemy like a batter in a batting cage, slapping shots back at him, without taking *some* damage.

▼ Against a single non-Jedi enemy, our favorite move is the block-and-rush. Hold the saber in block position as you sprint toward, say, an overmatched stormtrooper. The saber fends off his blaster fire. Then gore him with a quick slash. Note: Dark Jedi are less protected on their non-saber side. Use it to your advantage.

Chapter 4
Force Powers

IT'S ENTIRELY POSSIBLE TO PLAY JEDI KNIGHT AND WIN WITHOUT USING FORCE POWERS. But both combat (especially with Dark Jedi) and exploration become far easier, not to mention more interesting, when you employ the remarkable abilities conferred upon Kyle Katarn by his ever-growing unity with the Force.

Again, the Jedi Knight game manual describes the various Force Powers. But the Jedi Knight design team thoughtfully provided us with additional information and charts. Plus, we've added a few tips on Force Power usage based on our conversations with LucasArts testers.

Force Power Chart

Each Force Power has a specific Force Energy cost, duration, damage, and range. These values are often based on the number of Force Power stars (one to four) you've assigned to that power. (For more on Force Energy, see the section "Replenishing Force Energy" later in this chapter.)

NEUTRAL ABILITIES

FORCE POWERS	FORCE ENERGY COST	DURATION (SECONDS)
Speed	20	7.5/15/22.5/30
Jump	20	—
Pull	20	—
Seeing	30	10/15/20/25

LIGHT SIDE ABILITIES

FORCE POWERS	FORCE ENERGY COST	DURATION (SECONDS)
Healing	200	—
Persuasion	250	10/20/30/40
Blinding	100	—
Absorb	200	5/19/15/20
Protection	300	7.5/15/22.5/30

DARK SIDE ABILITIES

FORCE POWERS	FORCE ENERGY COST	DURATION (SECONDS)
Throw	30	—
Grip	50	1/2/3/4
Lightning	40/35/30/25	—
Destruction	200	—
Deadly Sight	300	3/6/9/12

DAMAGE	RANGE	SPECIAL NOTES
—	increases with rank	plus 10/15/20/25 mph
—	increases with rank	—
—	10/15/20/25	—
—	—	—

DAMAGE	RANGE	SPECIAL NOTES
20/40/60/80	—	—
—	—	—
—	20 30 40 50	—
—	—	—
—	—	75/150/225/300 added to shields

DAMAGE	RANGE	SPECIAL NOTES
physics of thrown objects	40	higher the rank the wider the cone of influence of objects
8/16/36/64	10	—
13 per second	—	—
20/40/60/80	—	—
24/48/72/96	30/40/50/60	—

Force Power Availability

Force Powers become available to you according to the following schedule. Remember, however, that to actually *use* a Force Power, first you must earn experience points in the form of Force Power stars, and then allocate those stars to available Force Powers. (For more on earning Force Power stars, see the next section.)

FORCE POWER	MISSION AVAILABLE
Speed	4
Jump	6
Pull	8
Seeing	10
Healing	12
Throwing	12
Persuasion	14
Grip	14
Protection	15
Deadly Sight	15
Blinding	15
Lightning	15
Absorb	16
Destruction	16

Earning Force Power Stars

There are 21 missions in Jedi Knight. Here's the schedule by which you earn Force Power stars:

▼ You earn two Force Power stars each time you increase your Jedi rank. Rank increases occur in missions 4, 6, 8, 10, 12, 14, and 18.

▼ In each of the 15 missions that have secret areas, you earn one bonus Force Power star for finding *all* the secret areas. (None of the six Dark Jedi missions—7, 11, 14, 16, 20, and 21—have secret areas.)

Thus, you can earn a total of 31 Force Power stars in the game.

Replenishing Force Energy

As the game manual notes, Force Power use depletes Force Energy; when your Force Energy is used up, you can't use your Force Powers. Force Energy units regenerate over time according to this simple formula:

half your Jedi rank (1 to 8) per second

For example, if you're a Jedi Lord (or Dark Lord), your rank is 8. Half of that is, let's see, I've got a scientific calculator, I'm hitting buttons, and the answer is, yes, carry the π, convert back to Base Ten—I've got it, it's 4. Thus, your Force Energy replenishes itself at the rate of 4 units per second.

Maximum Force Energy Per Rank

Listed below is the Maximum Force Energy available for each of the eight
Jedi Ranks:

RANK	FORCE ENERGY
1	50
2	100
3	150
4	200
5	250
6	300
7	350
8	400

Tips on Force Power Use

▼ In general, neutral and light side powers are defensive, while dark side
powers are offensive. But don't think of defensive powers as somehow
"passive;" they greatly enhance your standard attack capabilities.

▼ Assign at least one star to Force Jump early. Without Force Jump, you
can't gain access to certain high ledges. It also saves much time if you
can simply Force Jump back up onto platforms or walkways from
which you accidentally fall (or get blown off).

▼ The only way to break Force Grip is to cause damage to the gripper. If
you're taking Grip damage, quickly pull out a blaster and shoot your
opponent.

▼ Use Persuasion to slip undetected through heavily-guarded areas if your ammo or health meters are low.

▼ Counter Persuasion with Seeing. Two of your Dark Jedi opponents, Yun and Pic, use Persuasion to fade from your sight. If you don't have Seeing, watch for telltale blue sparkles that mark your invisible opponent's location.

▼ Blinding plus Persuasion is a powerful combination. Yun uses it on you to great effect. Try it on other Dark Jedi or powerful opponents such as Kell dragons.

▼ Protection adds significant strength to your shields. Known affectionately as "hamster ball" (because of its sparkling sphere effect) by LucasArts testers, Protection offers great advantages if you allocate several stars to it.

▼ Absorb is another favorite of the Jedi testing team. Let them throw the kitchen sink at you. Absorb sucks the Force Energy from enemy Force Power attacks and stores it as your own.

Chapter 5

Multiplayer Tips

JEDI KNIGHT'S MULTIPLAYER WORLD PROMISES TO BE ONE OF THE BIGGEST DRAWS ACROSS NETWORKS, MODEMS, AND THE INTERNET FOR YEARS TO COME. With team-oriented "Capture the Flag" levels and wild, free-fire "Jedi Training" levels, the game offers some truly innovative multiplayer experiences, all wrapped nicely in the *Star Wars* universe. Lightsaber battles, Force Powers, the Bespin mining station—come on, tell me you didn't wait your whole life for this.

As with other aspects of the game, we consulted LucasArts testers for insider tips on multiplayer Jedi Knight. Our primary contact was Tim Miller, assistant lead tester and one of the Jedi team's most accomplished multiplayer experts. According to Miller, no single omnipotent fighting style exists. You create your own style, and then tailor it to each unique situation.

"Each multiplayer arena offers specific challenges," he says. "But even when you really *know* an area, you can't get too comfortable with one approach. Human opponents figure out what you're doing eventually, and adjust."

Obviously, skill and practice make the Jedi Master. But another key to long-term success in multiplayer gaming is *unpredictability.*

Here are some more multiplayer tips passed along by Miller and his fellow testers.

Keep moving!

Multiplayer Jedi Knight is a *very* fast-paced game. Normal play is fast enough, but when you factor in Force Speed, you have a truly high-velocity experience. The games we watched at LucasArts were dizzying. And the number-one rule was pure shark: *Keep moving or die.*

Don't be afraid to take a big swing.

Miller prefers the secondary attack with his lightsaber. "It's a big, broad double-swing, and inflicts a lot of damage," he says.

One technique: Get face-to-face with an opponent and punch your secondary fire button to initiate the first half of the swing. Then, if you're quick enough, you can slide around to your opponent's *other* side to evade their block and catch them with the second half of the double-swing.

"A solid double-hit can knock 98 points off their health," says Miller. This puts a completely healthy opponent on the verge of death.

Hit fast off the block.

As mentioned in the "Weapons" chapter, one of the most effective saber moves is to hold a block while your opponent swings, and then quickly counterhit. You can strike a blow before they return fully to their block position.

Miller recommends trying an occasional strafing (moving sideways) swing or move backward to swing with an uppercut. "Both of those are low swings that can get underneath the defense and cause big damage," he says.

Keep your opponent in front of you at all times!

"Don't let anybody get behind you, or you're dead," says Miller. After all, your blocking cone is in front of you, not behind. So if you keep your opponents centered in your sight, you'll automatically block any blows they launch.

Try the slash-and-slide technique.

Corollary to the previous tip: Because opponents are most vulnerable from behind, work relentlessly to flank them. Slash and slide to one side, then the other. (In the single-player game, the Dark Jedi Sariss is particularly fond of this tactic. Learn from her.)

Jump over opponents.

If you leap completely over an enemy while executing a 180-degree turn in midair, often you can get a clean shot at their backside.

In larger group games, hit quick and run.

When lots of players run around swinging sabers, you should rely more on the quicker primary fire swing. If you go toe-to-toe with somebody for too long, somebody else inevitably will slip in behind and hack you to pieces.

Mine popular pathways, power-ups, and bottlenecks.

As you get to know each level, you learn where opponents want or need to go. Doorways, shafts, power-up items—all of these will see enemy use, sooner or later. So get there first and plant a nice row of sequencer charges in secondary (proximity) mode.

Find that rail det!

The rail detonator is a fun and effective multiplayer weapon. It inflicts a lot of damage, and its secondary fire mode sticks rail charges to opponents with a three-second delay before each explodes.

Make other rail gunners pay.

Conversely, if somebody sticks *you* with a delayed-action rail charge, sprint toward whoever shot you and make them pay for their impertinence by exploding yourself in their face.

Camp with a conc rifle.

As we said, movement is always good in multiplayer gaming: The more kinetic you are, the better. But sometimes it pays to stay put. Fortify yourself with health and ammo, grab a concussion rifle, and find a nice high perch overlooking a door or other critical passageway. Train the big gun on the door. Wait. Wait some more. When you hear the first sound of approaching life, open fire.

"I use that technique a lot myself," says Miller. "Particularly in the Nar Shaddaa loading terminal area, where a couple of nice high places let you camp safely and pick off people below." But don't stay too long; opponents soon realize what's happening and enter spewing gunfire at your position.

Another good place to camp is near any Dark Light Surge power-ups depending on your affiliation. They regenerate every minute, so you can keep your powers strong in 60-second intervals.

Try the old hop-"n"-drop tactic.

Another favorite multiplayer strategy is to activate Force Speed and rocket through the arena, hopping over opponents while using primary fire to drop sequencer charges on their heads.

PART II

JEDI WALKTHROUGH

(Hard Difficulty Mode)

Mission 1

The Double-Cross on Nar Shaddaa

THE GREAT JEDI MASTER OBI-WAN KENOBI once said of the Tatooine spaceport, Mos Eisley, "You will never find a more wretched hive of scum and villainy." Apparently, Obi-Wan never visited Nar Shaddaa. Jutting ominously into darkened skies, the infamous "vertical city" teems with galactic bog slime of the lowest variety.

Mission Objectives and Secrets

Stop 8t88 before he escapes with your father's data disk.

Secret Areas: 6

Enemies

Gran
Rodians

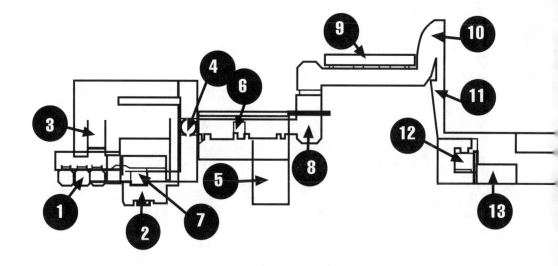

Legend for Maps

1. Start
2. Energy cells, stormtrooper rifle
3. Shield recharge
4. Ventilation fan (Rodian)
5. Hop to roof
6. SECRET AREA: Bacta tank, Health Pack, Shield recharge
7. Turbolift to energy cells, IR goggles
8. Door
9. Energy cells, shield recharge
10 Boxes for cover
11. Gran ambush
12. Turbolift
13. Shield recharge
14. Shield recharge
15. Gran
16. Jump point (to 17)
17. SECRET AREA: Shield recharges, energy cells, storm trooper rifle
18. Elevator button
19. Elevator button
20. SECRET AREA: Energy cells, health packs
21. Elevator track

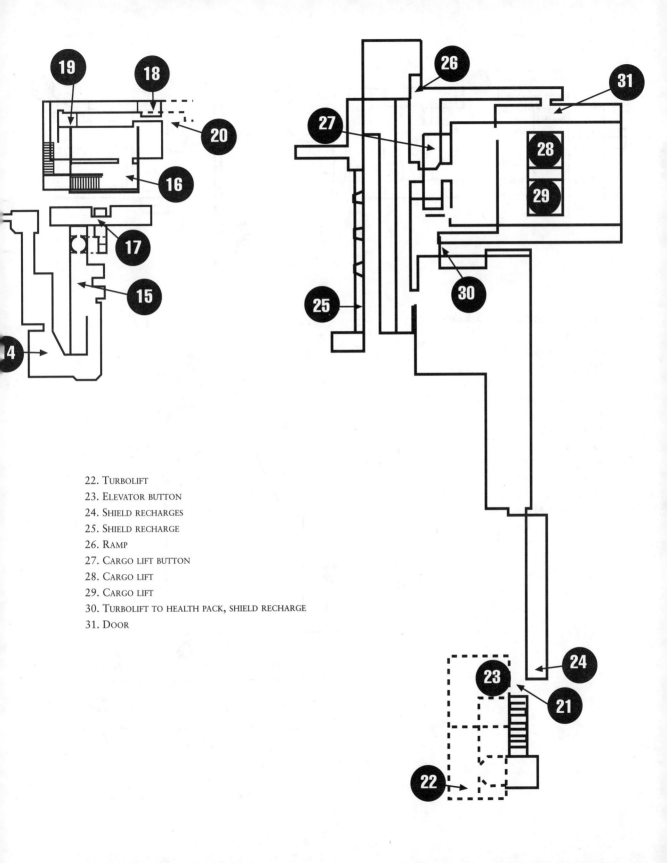

22. TURBOLIFT
23. ELEVATOR BUTTON
24. SHIELD RECHARGES
25. SHIELD RECHARGE
26. RAMP
27. CARGO LIFT BUTTON
28. CARGO LIFT
29. CARGO LIFT
30. TURBOLIFT TO HEALTH PACK, SHIELD RECHARGE
31. DOOR

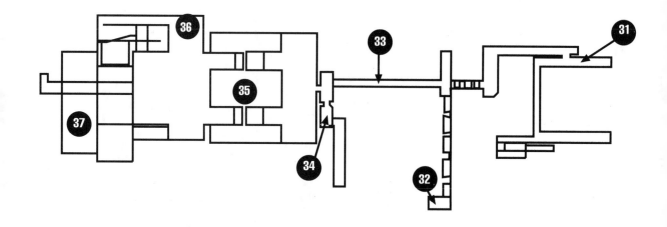

32. SECRET AREA: Smuggler backpack,
bacta tank
33. TIE bomber
34. Turbolift to shield recharge
35. Many Gran, shield recharges
36. Hatch control button
37. Jump point (to 38)
38. Box ledge
39. Turbolift
40. SECRET AREA: Thermal detonators, smuggler
backpack
41. Bacta tank
42. SECRET AREA: Energy cells, bacta tank
43. 8T88's shuttle

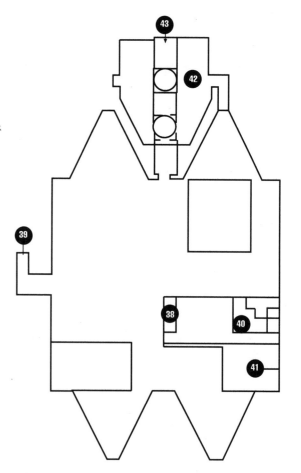

Walkthrough

You start in a secluded booth in the back room of Smuggler's Bar, the seediest joint this side of the Mos Eisley Cantina. The scar-faced bounty hunter you just slammed over your shoulder passes out on your table. His partner, a three-eyed Gran, quickly exits the room.

1. Start

Shoot that Gran now or shoot him later; he'll be waiting for you around the corner or in the bar. (Grab his stormtrooper rifle when he goes down.)

2. Bar Hop

Another ugly Gran wants you to get warped, loser. Leave a bloody mess for the surly barkeep, and don't forget to hop the counter and grab his stash of energy cells and a nice stormtrooper rifle. Exit and follow the ramp up to the open hall.

Note

This walkthrough applies to the Hard difficulty setting. In the Easy and Medium settings, you may find fewer enemies and more power-ups.

3. High Perch

More Gran. I hate these guys. They make dewbacks look cute. Watch for the sniper posted atop the tall grate. Shoot him down if you can. Or just grab the shield recharge at the grate's bottom and continue around the corner and down the ramp. (You'll see the sniper again soon enough.)

4. Ventilate the Rodian

Approach this ventilation fan carefully. A murderous green Rodian is posted there, licking his reptilian lips. Shoot him through the fan blades—he hops down if you get close—and then round the corner and gun down the three-eyed trio. Hop down to the graffiti-smeared lower platform for a shield recharge. Then step carefully to the far (southeast) corner of the platform.

5. Roof Climb

Hop onto the steeply slanted roof. Don't worry, you won't slip off. Climb to the top and jump to the upper platform where the air filtration units sit. Approach the floor opening.

6. Secret Area 1

Welcome to your first secret area. Before you drop through the opening, slide along its edge and pick off unsuspecting guards below. Now jump down. Polish off any remaining thugs and head east to nab the health pack, shield recharge, and bacta tank. Then go west, hop over the ventilation fan, and continue to the turbolift.

7. Your First Lift

Step onto the turbolift—this one activates automatically—and ride it up to the landing. There, a small stash of energy cells and a valuable pair of IR (infrared) goggles demand to be looted. (This is the same "high perch" from which the sniper tried to nail you back at 3. If you didn't shoot him then, shoot him now.) Slide down the grate, retrace your route past 4, and continue west to the blast door.

8. Your First Door

Action vets, bear with me. Rookies, this is a door. You'll find many in Jedi Knight. In some cases—including this one—you open it by pushing a glowing button near the door. Proceed warily through the open door.

9. Ledge Stash

Just around the next corner, another couple of Gran await you. Eviscerate them. Then hop down to the ledge and scoop up goodies—energy cells and a shield recharge. Proceed through the next passageway, where yet another Rodian wants to kill you.

"Eetaii!" to you too, lizard boy.

10. Box Cover

Advice: Hustle straight to the boxes in this corner. They provide cover from a trio of Gran snipers—one high, two low—across the way. Pick them off. Then move along the ledge, but stop before you reach the alcove marked at 11.

11. Alcove Ambush

A punch-drunk Gran may be hiding in this alcove. (See figure 1-1.) Fortunately, he's unarmed and only game for fisticuffs. Slug back with a couple of energy bolts and continue along the ledge to the open patio. Search it for dropped weapons and a shield recharge hidden in the far corner.

FIG. 1-1. SNEAK ATTACK. SEE THAT GUY HIDING JUST AROUND THE CORNER? HE HITS HARDER THAN A GUNDARK. DON'T LET HIM BUSHWHACK YOU.

Tip

Hit that quicksave button (F9) before you make the tricky jump back onto the narrow metal bridge at 13. It's easy to overshoot and take a screaming swan dive down a hundred stories or so.

12. Lift Up

Round the corner to the turbolift where a nice guard wants to hurt you bad. Hurt him first, and then ride the lift up. If you didn't nail the high sniper in 10, he waits at the top of the lift. Blast the hexagonal canister (and any others you find in Mission 1) to seek stored goods. Follow the passage to the metal bridge.

13. Leaping Ledge

Jump from the metal bridge onto this platform for a quick shield recharge. Then hop back.

14. Another Ambush

Another sly Gran lurks just inside the doorway (right side) to get the drop on you. A shield recharge sits in the corner, behind the boxes.

15. Jumping Guys

Hear that nasty comment? These Gran are hard to hit. Knock the spring out of their legs with some searing blaster rounds. Blast your way up the corridor and through the door, where an angry mob awaits you.

16. The Big Leap

See that guy down there? (See figure 1-2.) Shoot him dead. Then steel yourself for a breathtaking leap; you must reach his ledge. It'll hurt, but it's worth it (if it doesn't kill you). The drop causes 30 to 50 points of damage.

FIG. 1-2. THE BIG OUCH. BETTER HAVE PLENTY OF HEALTH POINTS—AT LEAST 50—BEFORE YOU TAKE THIS PLUNGE.

17. Secret Area 2

Here's your reward. This secret area harbors some shield recharges, a stormtrooper rifle, and a few energy cells. But that's not all. Ride the turbolift up to find a couple of health packs and a bacta tank to repair the damage you took in your big leap and add health to spare. Hop down through the ventilation fan and retrace your route past 16. Slide into the cargo elevator area with guns blazing.

18. Down the Track

The button here brings down a cargo elevator, but you don't want to ride up just yet. Instead, hop onto the elevator track and slide down to the lower level with weapon ready. Bad guys wait at the bottom.

Note

Before you push the button in 19, look ahead to 20 to see what you must do *after* you push the button as you ride the cargo elevator up.

19. Crane Room

After you clear the room—don't miss the bacta tank by the boxes—use this wall button to bring down the cargo elevator. Unfortunately, you can't get onto the elevator from your position at the button. So push it and sprint to the nearby black box, use the box to hop onto the upper ledge, and then hustle to the elevator. As you ride up, swivel to face the right (south) side of the track—and get ready to move.

20. Secret Area 3

As you near the top of the cargo elevator track, note the small rectangular opening on the right side. (See figure 1-3.) When you reach it, run in. You slide down another elevator track to a hidden room. Gather the useful items and battle down the corridor to a hole in the floor. When you jump down, you're right back at 18.

FIG. 1-3. ELEVATOR SURPRISE. AFTER YOU HOP ON THE FIRST CARGO ELEVATOR, SWIVEL RIGHT AND WATCH FOR THAT HIDDEN PASSAGE NEAR THE TOP.

Now you can press the button at 18 to lower the cargo elevator. Hop aboard and ride to the top. Turn left, slide around the corner, and nail any guards across the metal bridge. Cross the bridge and continue forward to yet another cargo elevator track.

21. Lower Red Room

When you reach the track, turn around and back onto it. Why? Because when you slide down, you're positioned to blast a pair of nasty guards posted on the ledge below. Open the door to an eerie, red-lit room with three more three-eyed Gran waiting inside.

22. Lift to Elevator Control Room

Push the glowing button to bring down the turbo-lift. Then ride it up to the elevator control room.

23. Elevator Call

Get ready to hustle. Push the glowing button— it activates the cargo elevator just outside— and then sprint out to the cargo elevator track. Trouble rides down to meet you; gun down the Gran on the elevator. Then hop aboard and quickly face right.

24. Shield Boost

Halfway up the track, a small ledge on the right bears a vicious little Rodian with a pistol. Spill his lizard guts while hopping to the ledge to score a pair of shield recharges. After you do this, you must slide back down the elevator track to the lower red room. Go back to the lift at 22 and repeat steps 22 and 23 to catch the cargo elevator again. This time, ride to the top.

25. Alcove Corridor

Cross the plaza and go through the far door. A long corridor runs north, with a series of alcoves on the left. A shield recharge sits in the first alcove; if you leap to it, a squadron of goons opens fire from below. Pick them off, using the alcove as a sniper post. Hop back to the corridor and continue north. (Watch out for the Rodian waiting in the fourth alcove.) Go past the open doorway on the right; we'll come back to it in a moment.

26. Goon Squad

When you reach the landing pad, take the ramp down into the metallic cavern below. If you were a good marksman from the alcove back in 25, you'll find little here but some goon leftovers. Otherwise, get ready for a tough firefight. After you finish, climb back up the ramp and go to the doorway.

27. Lift Button

Cautiously enter this small control room. Armed guards are posted just around the corner. Skewer them, search the room for weapons, then push the button at 27. This lowers a cargo lift in the bay beyond. Enter the cargo bay and pick off the sentry on the ledge above. Then move around the edge of the hole left by the lowered lift and pick off any visible guards in the room below.

28. Cargo Lift 1

Hop down onto the lowered lift. Beware of lurking guards. Search the lower bay for items and dropped weapons, then press the wall button to lower the other lift.

29. Cargo Lift 2

Step onto the edge of the second lift and press the button again to ride up. At the top, leap across to the ledge, turn right, and fight your way up the passage to the turbolift.

30. Lift to Supplies

Ride the lift up to a platform loaded with goodies. Then come back to the turbolift shaft and jump down. (It's not as painful as leaping from the open platform.) Follow the ledge around to the door.

31. Door

Enter carefully; a guard unit is posted on the other side. Move up the hallway, where two more guards wait just around the corner. Continue across the metal bridge. Then turn left to the slanted ledge.

32. Secret Area 4

Move along the ledge, hopping carefully over the alcoves cut out of the ledge. (You can slip off if you're not careful.) At the far end of the ledge a secret area holds a bacta tank and a smuggler backpack. Return along the slanted ledge to the platform and go down the enclosed passage leading west.

33. TIE Bomber Area

Here's a cruel surprise. The passage leads to a long, open catwalk. A nasty Rodian sniper sits on a ledge far above. Worse, as soon as you step onto the catwalk, a massive TIE bomber pops up and flies by you on its way out of a dock below. Best move: Take a step out to activate the bomber; then back up quickly wary of the Rodian. Cross the catwalk.

34. Lift to Rodian Ledge

Ride this turbolift up to the ledge where the Rodian sniper waits. (If you nailed him from the catwalk, all the better.) Grab the shield recharge, push the button to summon the lift, and ride it back down. Open the door on the left side of the short passage to enter another large cargo bay.

35. Red River Valley

A metal valley, patrolled by numerous armed Gran guards, halves this cargo bay. Move down one side and up the other to the other half of the bay. More guards sit above you in a control room; pick them off, if you can. Several shield recharges and other items lay scattered about the bay. Then find the ramp that leads up to the control room.

36. Hatch Controls

Here's your first truly challenging maneuver in Jedi Knight. Push the button and move to the window. See those hatch doors slide open? They reveal a large cargo storage area far below. But you can't get to the opening with the hatch doors open; they block your way into the cargo bay! So hit the button again to close the hatch doors. Then do the following very, very quickly:

1. Push the button to open the hatch doors.
2. Sprint around the corner and hop down the ledge. (Don't go all the way back to the ramp; you don't have time!)
3. Keep sprinting to the sliding hatch door!
4. Hop up through the gap before the hatch slides shut to get into the cargo bay.

37. Long Way Down

Look down at the cargo storage area—lots of boxes and Gran guards. Pick off as many thugs as possible from up here. Then, from the west side of the opening, note the stack of boxes with the three-box "ledge" recessed in its upper edge. (See figure 1-4.) Yes, that's your next destination.

38. Secret Leap

Feel springy? Gosh, I hope so. To reach the this secret area, you must take a running leap from 37 down to the ledge marked at 38. It's not an easy jump. Fortunately, if you miss, you can try again. Check out the next step.

FIG. 1-4. BOX LEDGE. BACK UP TO THE WALL AND MAKE A RUNNING LEAP TO THAT THREE-BOX LEDGE IN THE STACK ACROSS THE OPENING.

39. Try, Try Again

If you miss your leap onto the box ledge (as described in 38), use this turbolift to get back up to the cargo bay. But be warned: Many Gran guards prowl the floor of the bay, seeking violent amusement.

40. Secret Area 5

Once you make the leap to the ledge, move across the top of the box stack to the secret passage—a hole at the back. Follow the passage to a Rodian guard and your reward—a strand of thermal detonators and a smuggler's backpack. But don't hop down to the floor yet! Another hidden item awaits you.

41. Bacta Relief

Crawl back up the secret passage to the top of the stack. Go to the south edge of the stack and drop straight down to the boxes below. You'll find a bacta tank stashed in a hole. Now you can jump down to the floor. But be careful. Punchy Gran brawlers await your arrival below.

At this point, you can roam the floor of the storage area, rooting through its nooks and crannies. Guards are posted here and there, but by now you should be adept at handling the fellows. The next major point of interest lies up the ramp in the northeast corner of the area.

42. Secret Area 6

At the top is a small passage into a large area above a pair of ventilation fans. Two armed guards try to keep you from their supply of energy cells and a valuable bacta tank, but their task is futile. (Don't you feel bad for doomed subsidiary characters sometimes?) Before you hop down through one of the fans, try to shoot the guards below through the rotating blades. Then hop down and go through the north door.

43. Mission Objective: 8t88's Shuttle

And there he is, 8t88, trying to make his escape. Move down the ramp to trigger the mission-ending scene.

Mission 2

The Hunt for the Lost Disk

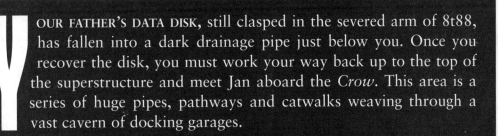

YOUR FATHER'S DATA DISK, still clasped in the severed arm of 8t88, has fallen into a dark drainage pipe just below you. Once you recover the disk, you must work your way back up to the top of the superstructure and meet Jan aboard the *Crow*. This area is a series of huge pipes, pathways and catwalks weaving through a vast cavern of docking garages.

Mission Objectives & Secret Areas

Find 8t88's severed arm to retrieve Morgan Katarn's data disk.

Work your way back to the top of Nar Shaddaa to meet the *Crow* for escape.

Secret Areas: 8

Enemies

Gran
Rodians
Gamorreans

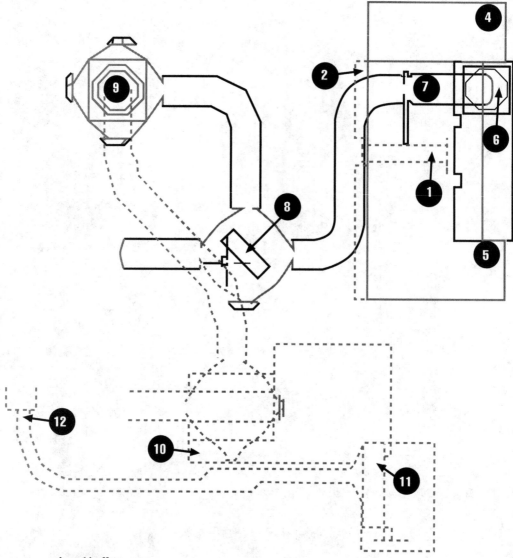

Legend for Maps

1. Energy cells
2. Thermal detonators
3. Shield recharge
4. Shield recharges, energy cells
5. Gran
6. Ventilation pipe
7. Data disk (Gran ambush)
8. Gran
9. Ventilation pipe (Gran below)
10. Health pack, shield recharge, thermal detonators
11. Rodian
12. Ledge (Gran below)

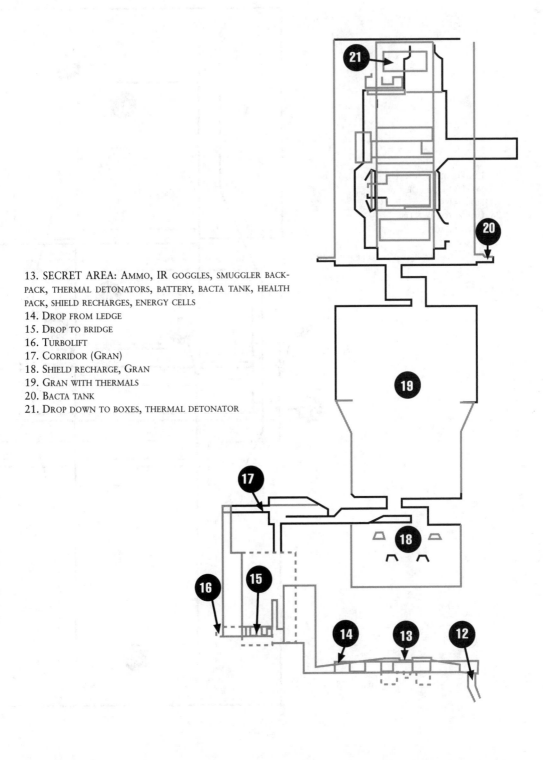

13. SECRET AREA: AMMO, IR GOGGLES, SMUGGLER BACK-
PACK, THERMAL DETONATORS, BATTERY, BACTA TANK, HEALTH
PACK, SHIELD RECHARGES, ENERGY CELLS
14. DROP FROM LEDGE
15. DROP TO BRIDGE
16. TURBOLIFT
17. CORRIDOR (GRAN)
18. SHIELD RECHARGE, GRAN
19. GRAN WITH THERMALS
20. BACTA TANK
21. DROP DOWN TO BOXES, THERMAL DETONATOR

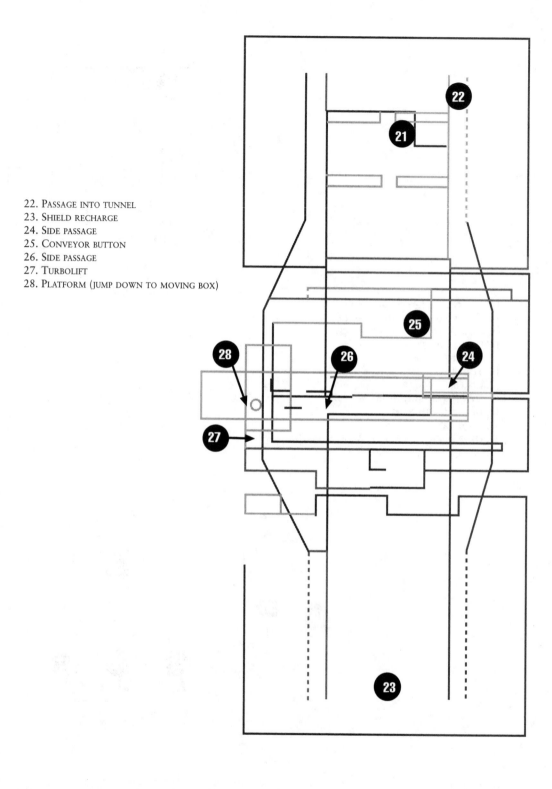

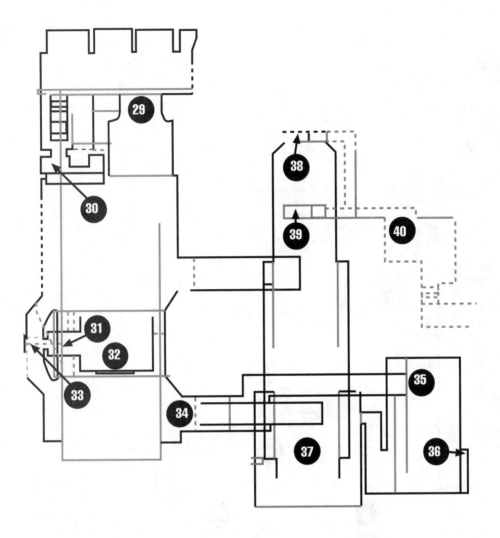

29. DOOR BUTTON
30. RED KEY (OPENS 31)
31. RED KEY DOOR
32. DOOR BUTTON (OPENS 34)
33. RAIL ACTIVATION BUTTON
34. UPPER CARGO DOOR
35. GRAN WITH THERMALS
36. SECRET AREA: ARMOR VEST
37. DOUBLE CONVEYOR BELT
38. LEDGE (HOP ONTO BOX)
39. RAMPS
40. HEALTH PACK (GAMORREANS)

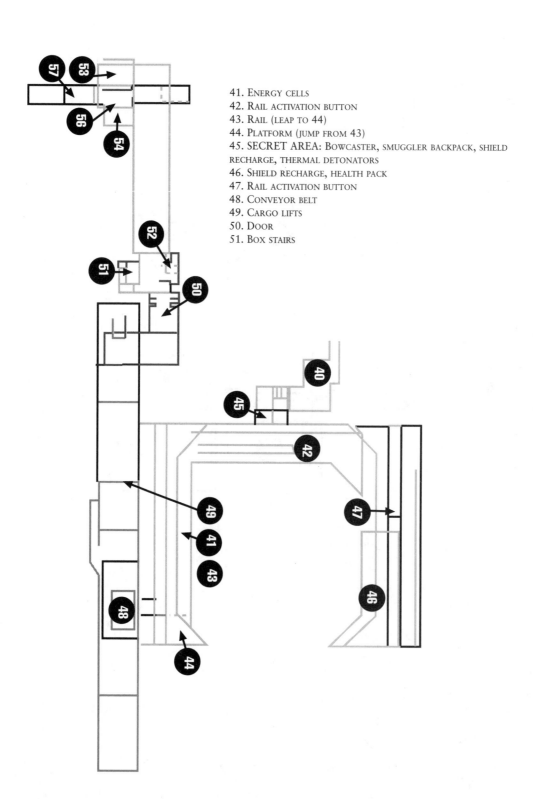

41. ENERGY CELLS
42. RAIL ACTIVATION BUTTON
43. RAIL (LEAP TO 44)
44. PLATFORM (JUMP FROM 43)
45. SECRET AREA: BOWCASTER, SMUGGLER BACKPACK, SHIELD RECHARGE, THERMAL DETONATORS
46. SHIELD RECHARGE, HEALTH PACK
47. RAIL ACTIVATION BUTTON
48. CONVEYOR BELT
49. CARGO LIFTS
50. DOOR
51. BOX STAIRS

52. SECRET AREA: Shield recharge, thermal detonators, armor vest (on ledge to the east)
53. Cargo lift
54. Cargo lift
55. SECRET AREA: Bacta tank, armor vest
56. SECRET AREA: Shield recharge
57. SECRET AREA: Energy cells, battery
58. SECRET AREA: Super shield, smuggler backpack
59. Wild Gran melee!

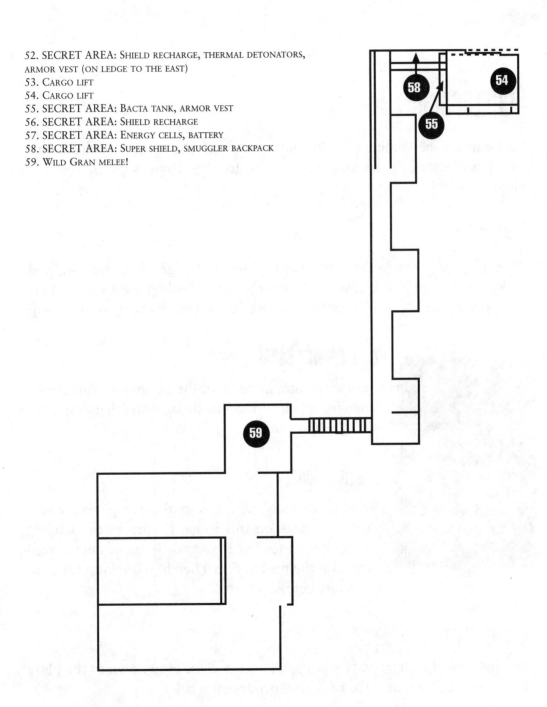

Walkthrough

You start on the landing pad, watching Jan bank the *Crow* into the incoming TIE fighters. Then...silence, except for the toxic sigh of the Nar Shaddaa wind.

1. Start

After the *Crow* disappears, move along the west edge of the landing pad, picking off any Gran below. Drop off the ramp leading west onto a platform just underneath to score some energy cells. Hop back up to the ramp.

Note

The next two steps involve slightly risky jumps that could send you plummeting to the platform below. You'll probably survive but you'll miss out on the power-up items at 4.

2. Firepower Boost

Take a running jump from the ramp onto this sloped ledge for a belt of thermal detonators; then hop back down to the ramp.

3. Shield Boost

Another running jump from the ramp nets you a shield recharge on this ledge. Return to the landing pad and head for the Bryar pistol full of energy cells sitting on the north edge. Then hop down to the platform just below.

4. Quick Boost

Ah, two shield recharges, two packs of energy cells. Hop down to the plaza below and relieve the dead of their stormtrooper rifles.

5. Fun With Detonators

Creep carefully to the edge of this platform. Below, a pair of Gran brutes look for excuses to get violent. One lugs a standard rifle, but the other has a seemingly limitless supply of thermal detonators and a world-class arm. Best bet: Roll a couple of detonators (using the Z secondary fire key for a three-second delay) over the edge. Follow them up with blaster fire, if necessary.

6. Down the Pipe

Looks like the only way to go is down. Hop into the huge ventilation pipe. Once you jump, there's no climbing back up. But that's OK. We'll find a more fun way back up.

7. Mission Objective: The Data Disk

And there it is: 8t88's severed arm, still clutching the data disk. Get ready. A moment after you pick it up, the metal door in front of you slides open to reveal two samples of the local scum and villainy. Slide and shoot fast; you've got no place to hide. After the slaughter, continue down the tunnel-like ventilation pipe.

FIGURE 2-1. ARM YOURSELF. HOP DOWN THE VENTILATION PIPE TO FIND 8T88'S APPENDAGE, STILL CLUTCHING MORGAN'S DATA DISK. SCOOP IT UP TO FULFILL YOUR FIRST MISSION OBJECTIVE.

8. Deadly Hail

A Gran shooter waits at this first intersection. Worse, another Gran from the bullpen lobs a steady hail of thermal detonators from a ramp up above. (How'd he get up there, anyway?) Good tactic: Pick off the shooter from a distance, and then inch slowly forward until you can just see the tosser above. Squeeze off a few shots before he knows you've sighted him.

Note

Cheaters can fly up to check out this perch. Jedi Knight object placer Christopher Ross put a backpack there for your viewing pleasure, but you can't take it.

9. Down Again

Only the north passage leads anywhere. Follow it to a drop down another pipe. Before you hop in, pick off the squad of Gran bad guys below. (Roll a few thermals down the pipe, if you have any.) Then slide down and follow the pipe to the next intersection.

10. And Again, Down

After you fight through the intersection, you reach still another drop, the last one in the pipes. This one's a doozy, though. The slide down can hurt; Gran goons open fire at the bottom; and you have no cover nearby. One tactic: Roll thermal detonators down first. If you have none, slide down, sprint out of the pipe, turn right, and hustle around the corner. The corner provides cover, and the alley holds a stash of good stuff for health and shield repair.

11. Lizard Meat

After the battle, go through the door; an R2 unit and a harmless citizen wait on the other side. But around the corner below lurks an amoral Rodian bounty hunter; a female Rebel sympathizer warns you, "Look out!" Waste the lizard and continue to the next opening.

12. Long Passage

Hustle down the long passage and pause at this ledge. Two Gran wait below. Snipe away or toss a couple of detonators. Then hop down and continue along the corridor.

13. Secret Area

At the opening halfway down the corridor, look down. See the rim of a ledge below? That's a secret area. To get down, turn away from the ledge, and then back very slowly off. It's a painful drop, and a brutal surprise waits below—a pair of Gamorreans, one in each wing of the area. These grunters are bloody infighters with their big axes. If your health is low, one swing of the blade can kill you. Avoid hand-to-hand combat with them at all costs.

After you gut the guards, scoop up a veritable treasure trove of supplies—ammo, IR goggles, smuggler backpack, thermal detonators, battery, bacta tank, health pack, energy cells, and several shield recharges. Not a bad haul, eh? Then take the turbolift up to another hidden ledge.

14. Ledge Hopper

Another pair of guards—a Gran and a Rodian—wait to greet you. When their silence is complete, move to the western end of the ledge, hop down, and follow the passage west.

15. Take the Back Way

The passage leads to a set of ramps leading up. (See figure 2-2.) You can climb them—a squad of deadly Gamorrean guards line the route to the top—but we prefer a back-door route here. Go past the ramps to the ledge and look down. See the metal bridge below? It leads to a door in the far wall. Be aware that a killer squad—two Gamorreans and two deadly bomb-tossing Gran—is encamped directly below.

Hop down to the bridge, sprint to that door, and then quickly hit the (Spacebar) to open it and hustle through. If you have strong shields and good firepower, spin to face the door and blast baddies as they come through, one by one. But if your shields are low, keep running onto that lift dead ahead at 16.

FIGURE 2-2. GOING
UP OR DOWN? HERE,
DOWN IS BETTER.
IT GIVES YOU EASIER
ACCESS TO
THE LEDGE ACROSS
THE WAY.

16. Turbolift

Take this lift up to the ledge. If you haven't killed the goon squad below yet, use the ledge as a long-distance firing post. (You can also jump back down the turbolift shaft without taking damage, if you so desire.) Then proceed across the ledge to the next turbolift.

17. Stealth Target

Step onto the lift and turn right, facing east. At the top of the shaft, take one quiet step forward off the lift. A Gran bomb-thrower faces away from you at the end of a short corridor. Shoot quick, because you have no escape route (other than a very long and painful fall down the shaft).

Note

Note the amazing power and accuracy of alien arms; those Gran can toss thermal detonators to your ledge with great frequency. So nail the throwers first, or they'll kill you quick. Then you can pick off the Gamorreans at your leisure.

Once the Gran is eliminated, you can pick off any Gamorrean guards in the next room from a safe perch, either here or from the balcony on the left. It's really fun, like shooting fish in a barrel. Don't fall, though, or the Gamorreans will hack you into twitching gobbets of meat. And Light Jedi candidates, watch out for the little R2 unit scurrying around.

Head up the ramp and follow the hall through the next door. Fight your way straight ahead; then turn right through the entryway into an open plaza.

18. Plaza Combat

Two Gran brawlers loiter in the plaza. Gun them down and score the shield recharge. Then go back through the entryway, turn right at the door, and step forward into another plaza.

19. Bombs Away

Another squad of Gran bomb-tossers prowls this plaza. Give them a taste of their own medicine by tossing any thermal detonators you have ahead of you. Then head north through another entryway into a huge cargo transport area.

Tip

Remember, a good tactic against Gran bomb-tossers is to keep moving and run at them, blasting away. When you get close, they won't throw their ordnance at you, but try to punch you out, instead.

20. Take a Bacta Break

Look high when you enter this area. A pair of sure-shot aliens are posted on platforms above, one on each side. Hug the wall and follow it to this tiny ledge, where somebody stored a much-needed bacta tank. A pair of thermal detonators sits due west on a matching ledge on the opposite side of the area.

21. Box Jump

Three large openings lead down to lower cargo loading areas. The farthest (northernmost) opening offers a damage-free way down. First, leap across to the small ledge halfway down, and then hop down onto the stack of boxes. Once you land, work your way along the edge of the boxes, blasting Gran criminals on the floor around the stack. (Thermal detonators work well here; don't miss the ones tucked into a small ledge in the southeast corner of the boxes.)

22. Left Tunnel

After you clear the immediate area, hop down and prepare for more combat. Turn to face the stacks. Then enter the left (eastern) tunnel. Several more Gran killers line the tunnel. Fight your way through to the far end.

23. Southern End

Yet more Gran thugs lurk in the south end of the cargo loading area. Be sure to grab a well-deserved shield recharge; then reenter the tunnel you took to get here. (Remember, you're facing north now, so it's on the right-hand side as you face the stacks.)

24. Side Ramp 1

Turn into this side passage halfway down the tunnel. Climb the ramp all the way up to the Conveyor Control Room.

25. Conveyor Control Room

Fight your way to this button and give it a push. Note that you've activated the conveyor belt; boxes ride the belt to a cargo lift, which hauls each box to the top level of the cargo loading area. Your next goal: Get aboard a box and ride it up. But how?

Try this: Go back down the ramp and follow the tunnel back out to 22. Then enter the other tunnel (the western one).

26. Side Ramp 2

Fight your way to this side passage halfway down the tunnel. At the top of the first ramp, veer to the right into the opening that leads to the box stacks.

27. Box Battle

Fight and hop your way up through the boxes until you reach this turbo-lift. Ride it up to the platform above the conveyor belt.

28. Ride the Big Box

Jump down onto any of the boxes passing under you on the conveyor belt. Ride the box all the way to the top of the lift. Then hop off to the north and follow the ledge.

FIGURE 2-3. BOX TOP PRIZE. AFTER YOU GET THE CONVEYOR BELT GOING, HOP DOWN ONTO ONE OF THE CARGO BOXES AND RIDE IT UP TO THE NEXT LEVEL.

29. Door Button

Push the button here to open the huge blast door—but be ready for action. Four cutthroat Gran wait on the other side. After you win, hop the boxes to reach the stairs. Climb the stairs and enter the red key room.

30. Red Key Room

One more guard waits just around the corner. Once he's down, loot the room for energy cells, a shield recharge, and, most importantly, the red key. (See figure 2-4.)

Now that you have the key, retrace your route back to the lift where the cargo boxes ride up. Walk across one of the twin rails that spans the opening; then go left down the hall to the door.

FIGURE 2-4. RED KEY.
WHAT ARE YOU WAITING FOR,
KYLE? GRAB THAT KEY!
YOU NEED IT TO UNLOCK
THE CONTROL ROOM
ON THIS LEVEL.

31. Red Key Door (Need Red Key)

If you have the red key, open the door and face a wild melee with a pair of
Gamorreans. (If you don't have the red key yet, see 30.) Enter the room and
grab the shield recharge.

32. Upper Cargo Door Button

Push this button to open the upper cargo door (34) outside the window.
Exit the room and go to the button just outside the door on the opposite
wall.

33. Rail Activation Button

Push this button on the wall to activate the movable rails, sliding them
south. Then use the rails to cross to the upper cargo door.

34. Upper Cargo Door

If you pushed the button in the control room (see 32), this door is now open. Don't try to penetrate the red force field! You can't; it only causes damage. Instead, follow the upper conveyor belt to the cavernous room.

35. Cavernous Room

Aside from bomb-tossing Gran defenders and a few cargo boxes, this room seems empty. But after you eliminate the defenders, check out the far (southeast) corner of the room.

36. Secret Area

To reach the armor vest tucked into this high alcove, get on the ramp or the smaller box, and then leap onto the tall multicolored box. From there, hop to the alcove, grab the vest, and then follow the ramps up to the double conveyor-belt tunnel. (Don't miss the energy cells behind the hexagonal canisters at the top of the ramp.)

37. Double Conveyor Tunnel

This double-sized conveyor belt transports huge cargo boxes. You must move up the belt to 38, avoiding boxes along the way. Fortunately, narrow alcoves line the walls; duck into them when a box rides down the belt.

38. Ramp Up

When you reach here, watch for snipers high on the ramp to the south. Climb to the top of this sloped ledge. When the next box drops to the bottom of the shaft, hop aboard and run across to the sloped ramp across the way at 39. (For a nice health boost, run first to the bacta tank in the tiny alcove under the sloped ramp, to the left.)

39. Moving Bridges

Climb the ramp, battling bad guys on the way. When you come to what seems a dead end, look across the shaft. See the sloped ramp on the far side? Getting there is tricky. Climb as high up your ramp as you can. When the next box drops down the shaft, sprint across its top to the other side. Climb some more until you reach another dead end. Then repeat the foregoing procedure to cross the shaft to the next ramp.

40. Goring Gamorreans

When you finally reach the top of the ramps, you enter a room with a contingent of four Gamorrean guards. Continue through the room; don't miss the health pack in the corner, though. You emerge into a gigantic, well-guarded docking/unloading bay.

41. Quick Stash

Pick off as many enemies as you can around the vast bay. (Remember, your Bryar pistol is a surprisingly good sniper weapon.) Then, before the tricky stuff starts, grab the pack of energy cells amidst the boxes in this platform.

42. Railroad Split

You face two choices here. First, drop into the trench. See the button? It activates the big set of striped rails just above you. If you use this mechanism to reach 46 and score some items, you can't get back, and you miss the secret area at 44. But reaching 44 is a perilous endeavor.

To reach 46: Push the button in the trench. Hop up onto the now-moving rail platform, run down the left (northern) rail, and hop over to 46. Skip ahead to step 46 in this walkthrough.

To reach 44: Don't push the button. Hop out of the trench and climb up onto the right (southern) rail. Go to the next step.

43. Death-Defying Leap

Save your game here! Go to the very end of the rail to sight your jump target—that little diagonal slice of ledge at lower right, next level down. (See figure 2-5.) Then go back down the rail, turn, and take a long running leap to the ledge at 44.

Tip

Some obvious advice: Your rail ride over to 46 is much more pleasant if you sharpshoot the pair of guards stationed there before you make the move.

FIGURE 2-5. I'M GOING WHERE?
THERE, THAT SLIVER OF LEDGE WAY,
WAY ACROSS THE BAY. SAVE YOUR
GAME AND TAKE A SCREAMING LEAP
ACROSS THE ABYSS.

44. Jump Target

Leap here from the rail at 43. Then head west along the trench to another pair of rails. Walk out on the left rail to the alcove; watch out for the Rodian sniper posted there.

45. Secret Area

This isolated alcove holds a smuggler backpack, shield recharge, some thermal detonators, and a powerful bowcaster. For fun, nudge the Gonk unit a few times, save your game, and carefully hop back up onto the rail. Skip ahead to 48.

46. Diving Platform (Upper Level)

Jump here from the moving rail you activated in 42. (This eliminates steps 43 to 45.) After claiming the power-up items—shield recharge, health pack—from this platform, jump off the northern edge down to the next level.

47. Trench Button

Here's another rail mechanism. Press the button in the trench to activate the set of rails clear across the bay; they begin to slide back and forth. Walk out to the edge of the stationary rail on your side of the bay; wait for the moving rails to slide past. Then leap onto them.

48. Obstacle Course

An opening in this room's floor reveals a large conveyor belt moving lots of cargo. Hop down and run up the belt, dodging boxes, until you reach the ramp that leads down on the left side. Two Gran thugs wait at the bottom; blast them senseless and grab the belt of thermal detonators in the corner. Go back up the ramp. Now comes a tricky maneuver.

49. Ride or Slide

See the three cargo lifts? Ride one up to the next level. It isn't easy, though; you have to avoid boxes and time your leap perfectly. If you miss, you slide down the belt to the room below and must reclimb the ramp for another try.

FIGURE 2-6. DO THE BOX HOP. RUN UP THE CONVEYOR BELT TO THE LIFTS, WAIT FOR A SMALL OR MEDIUM BOX TO LOWER ON ONE OF THE THREE LIFTS, AND THEN HOP OVER IT TO GET ABOARD THE LIFT.

> **Tip**
>
> Try running up the far edge on either side of the conveyer belt, hopping over the lift as it lowers.

50. Door to Hell

Continue past the conveyor belt and down a passage to this button-activated door. Some Nar Shaddaa criminal element waits on the other side, so we recommend you open the door and immediately hustle down the narrow space to the right. This keeps you covered, so you can pop out and pick off the guys below one by one (or, better, toss down a few thermal detonators).

51. Jump Point

Once you've cleared the floor, hop down and turn left. Boxes form a stairway up. At the top, take a running leap to the alcove in the stack directly across the room. (Careful: A Gran bomb-tosser hides in the alcove.)

52. Secret Area

Here, you'll find a small stash of goods—a shield recharge and a detonator belt. If you wish, explode yourself atop the two crates to the east to grab an armor vest. Now hop down to the floor and head west along the inactive conveyor belt.

53. Staggered Lifts

Two surly Gran guard this lift area. Gun them down, scoop up the wealth of items near the lift, and hop aboard. At the top, you'll see another lift across a moving conveyor belt. Warning: Don't just hop onto the belt! If a box traps you against the force field, you're doomed. Instead, time your leap. When you arrive at the top, wait until the next box moves past, and then immediately run across the belt and hop onto the lift at 54.

54. Second Lift

Here's a nifty little move. As the lift ascends, watch for a ledge under the next floor level (it's about halfway up). When you get there, leap onto it.

55. Secret Area

Follow the first ledge to a second running perpendicular to it and hop over. Secret area! A nice bacta tank and a rugged armor vest reward your peerless exploration. Move back to the first ledge and hop back onto the moving lift.

56. Secret Area

Ride the lift down, wait until the box passes, and step quickly onto the moving conveyor belt. Now step off the east edge of the conveyor belt and drop to the thin strip of a platform jutting out from just below the belt. Secret! Not much reward, though. Grab the shield recharge and step carefully through the opening onto a narrow ledge. Hop onto the first lift at 53, then run back across the belt to 54.

57. Secret Area

Guess what? A third secret area lies just above the conveyor belt. Hop from the lift at 54 to one of the moving boxes on the belt, then quickly up to the alcove where two energy cell packs and a battery wait for you.

Hop back over to the lift at 54, ride to the top, and hop off. Follow the corridor.

58. Secret Area

And the secrets keep on coming, folks! When you reach the bottom of the ramp leading up to the open area, look up behind you. A Gran thug hunkers in an alcove. How do you get up there? First, save your game. Climb the ramp; a Rodian opens fire in the distance, joined by a bomb-tossing Gran. Gun them down, carefully walk the narrow ledge, and hop into the alcove.

Wow! A smuggler backpack—and, yes, a super shield!

Hop out of the alcove and cross the ledge. Then cross the metal bridge to the landing pad area.

59. Mission Objective: Meet the *Crow* for Escape from Nar Shaddaa

Six Gran killers ambush you here. It's an ugly firefight, and you can't avoid it. Of course, if you nab the super shield back at 58, sprint here posthaste, and shoot fast and true, it's no contest. Nail all six goons; Jan won't land the *Crow* until you've eliminated every one of them.

Note

Remember, super shields make you invulnerable, but only for about 30 seconds. For best results, don't take the super shield until you're ready to sprint to the final, enemy-infested area at 59.

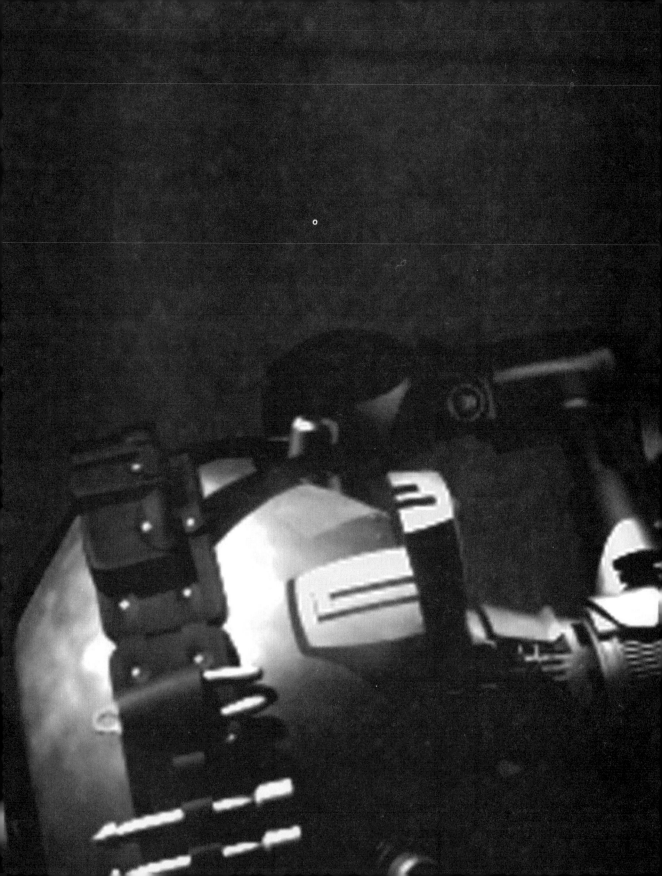

Mission 3

The Return Home to Sulon

K yle is patched up and ready to pursue his destiny back at the Katarn family compound on Sulon, his home planet. Jerec's minions have come and gone. A cruel contingent of Grave Tuskens, the most barbarous scavengers in the galaxy, have claimed the place as their personal property. In the compound's inner sanctum—Morgan Katarn's workshop—an ungainly homemade droid named WeeGee is Kyle's key to decoding the data disk.

And one other note: After you complete this level, Jedi Knight offers you your first Force Power.

Mission Objectives & Secret Areas

Get inside the Katarn family home.
Get past the live battery trench that powers the house.
Locate WeeGee, the old family droid, in Morgan Katarn's workshop.

Secret Areas: 8

Enemies

Grave Tuskens
Mailocs

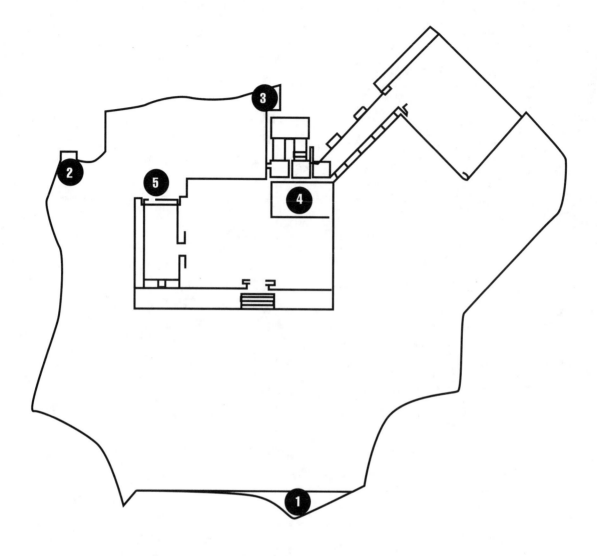

Legend for Maps

1. SECRET AREA: Bacta tanks, armor vest

2. SECRET AREA: Bowcaster

3. Shield recharge

4. Shield recharges

5. Window entrance

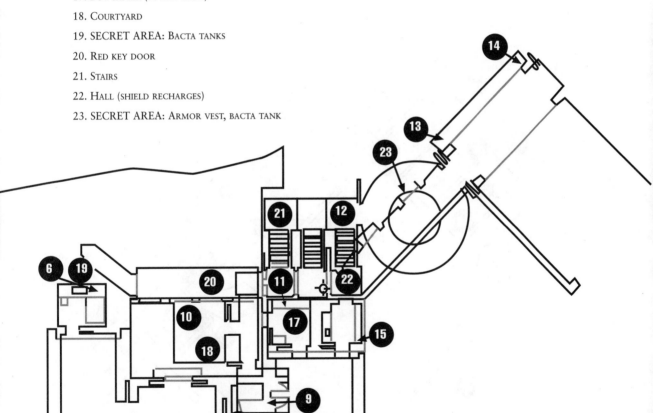

24. Shield recharge

25. Hall

26. Shield recharge

27. Yellow wrench (use at 34), shield recharge

28. Passage to lower level

29. Health pack

30. Blue wrench (use at 34), thermal detonators, smuggler backpack, shield recharge, power cells

31. Opening

32. SECRET AREA: Shield recharge, thermal detonators

33. Underwater passage

34. Wrench slots, shield recharges

35. Passage

36. Passage to battery trench

37. SECRET AREA: Smuggler backpack, thermal detonators

38. Platform

39. Bacta tank

40. Platform

41. Batteries, health pack

42. Platform

43. Passage (Mailocs!)

44. SECRET AREA: Smuggler backpack

45. Workshop

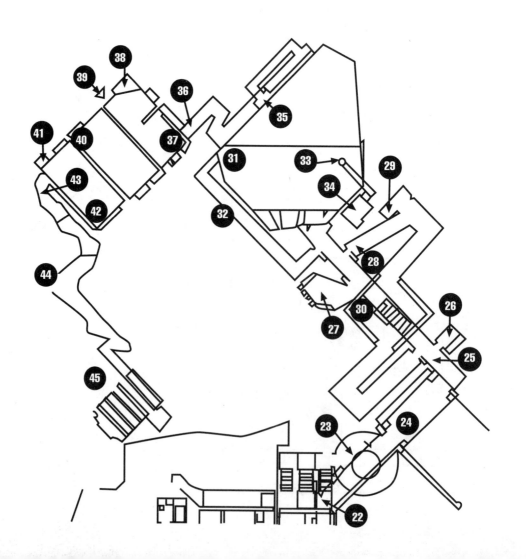

Walkthrough

You start at the perimeter of the Katarn family compound on Sulon. The place has been overrun by Grave Tuskens armed with bowcasters and other fierce weaponry. Use cover, move fast, and good luck.

1. Secret Area

Welcome to some real combat. Just surviving this opening sequence is an accomplishment. Many savage Tuskens patrol the front area of the house; many more roam the west side and back area. From the start position, turn right and hustle up the hill. A Tusken waits by the wall; shoot him. Then shoot the wall. It shatters, revealing a couple of bacta tanks and an armor vest. Trust me. You'll need them.

2. Secret Area

Shoot the perimeter wall here to blast open another small secret area. Inside lies a bowcaster with a full load of power cells.

3. Shield Recharge

Don't miss the spare shield recharge tucked into this alcove.

4. Hex Stash

Another Grave Tusken is posted here. Hustle him off to his Maker, grab the two shield recharges, and start blasting canisters for enclosed goods. Watch out for Tusken snipers posted in the windows just around the corner.

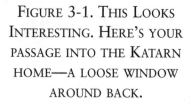

Tip

These canisters may be your only source of health power-ups for a while, so don't neglect to blow them open.

5. Mission Objective: House Entrance

Nudge open the middle window on this wall. (See figure 3-1.) Voila! Entrance.

FIGURE 3-1. THIS LOOKS INTERESTING. HERE'S YOUR PASSAGE INTO THE KATARN HOME—A LOOSE WINDOW AROUND BACK.

6. Another Shield

Check out this dark room. The basin water looks refreshing, but far more so is that shield recharge on the shelf. Return to the main room and exit through the only door.

7. Grave Situation

The only thing of interest in this room is a Grave Tusken armed with a crossbow. The door that leads north is locked from this side, so approach the east door. Hear that sound? Some Tuskens have pushed open the previously jammed front entry.

8. Tusken Trio

Three Grave Tuskens camp in the front entry to the right. Two are immediately visible, but a third is nearby outside.

9. Ride the Board Down

A wooden beam spans a hole in the floor. Seems like the perfect bridge, doesn't it? Wrong. When you step on it, it falls to the room below. Nothing can prevent it, so enjoy the ride. Exit through the only door. Then veer into the first room on the left.

10. Can Room (Lower Level)

Nothing here but a strand of thermal detonators and a canister to blast. Exit the room, turn left, and follow the passage to the next corner, around which another Grave Tusken waits for unsuspecting fools.

11. Secret Area

Fortunately, you're a suspecting fool. Gun him down and swivel right to locate another exploding wall. Move to the end of the hall for safety. Then blow open the wall to reveal a pair of shield recharges and a bacta tank. Acquire them and continue toward the stairway.

Climb one flight of stairs to the first landing. Another Tusken is posted at the top of the second flight of stairs. Eliminate him and go to the door on the first landing.

12. Circular Hall

A pair of Grave Tuskens patrols the circular hall just beyond the door, so open the door firing. Follow the curve of the hallway to the next set of doors.

13. Killer Garage

Need anything fixed? These seven Grave Tuskens will be happy to oblige you. That's how Tuskens are. Five of them roam the floor of the garage, and two more shoot from a connecting walkway above. To battle so many Tuskens, of course, you need ammo. So grab the smuggler backpack in this corner.

14. Red Key

After you clear out the Tuskens, grab the red key in this corner of the garage. Then wander around, blasting hexagonal canisters for supplies. Don't miss the shield recharge atop a box near the garage door. And if you really want some fun, put a blaster bolt into the light racks on the ceiling. Then retrace your path back to the stairs at 11 and climb the second flight to the door at the top.

15. Bacta Tank

As you move through this small connecting room, grab some much-needed health—the bacta tank on the bench. Beyond the next door is another bad guy, so let a few blaster bolts precede you into the room.

16. Battery

This ransacked room looks pretty empty, but don't miss the battery hidden behind a fallen chair. Exit through the north door (next to the door through which you entered).

17. Storage Room

This connecting room is full of cabinets and little else but a bowcaster full of power cells. Continue through the far door, ready for grave combat.

18. Courtyard (Upper Level)

Three Grave Tuskens catch rays in this sunny, open courtyard. Help them catch bolts of death, too. The south door leads back to the room at 7; this is the door that was jammed shut before. Instead, head up the dead-end passage leading northwest.

19. Secret Area

"Looks like someone doesn't like to have company." And when it looks like that, your job is to intrude. See that patched piece of wall on the left side next to the beam? Back down the corridor a few steps and fire a few shots at the patch. A booby trap explodes, ripping open the wall to reveal a pair of bacta tanks.

FIGURE 3-2. BOOBY PRIZE. BLOW OPEN THIS BOOBY-TRAPPED WALL NEAR THE BARRICADE AND WIN A PRIZE—TWO HEALING BACTA TANKS.

20. Red Key Slot (Need Red Key)

Approach the circular key slot by the door and press the [Spacebar]. If you found the red key in the garage (see 14), the door unlocks. Open the door and slide in carefully; a Grave Tusken guard opens fire from the stairs to your left.

21. Stairs to Third Level

Kill the Tusken and climb the two flights of stairs to the next floor of the house.

22. Connecting Hall

Some Grave Tuskens patrol in the hallway beyond this door. (This is the shooting post you dodged back at 4.) Destroy them. A couple of shield recharges have been stored in the hall's twin alcoves. But watch it. Another Tusken crouches near the second alcove.

23. Secret Area

Shoot the wall behind the second alcove to trigger open a secret door. Inside, grab the armor vest and bacta tank. Continue down the hallway and through the door. You emerge onto the connecting walkway above the garage.

24. Alcove

Somebody put a shield recharge in this alcove next to the walkway. It's a fairly easy jump to get there, but for some reason, the hop back is hard. (If you fall to the garage, retrace your route back up here.) Continue across the connecting walkway to the next set of doors.

25. Back Hall

This large hall is lined with doors. Four Grave Tuskens are pretty adamant that you leave, or, alternatively, die shrieking. Change their philosophical perspective with some well-placed blaster bolts. Then head for the first door on the right side of the hall.

26. Shield Room

This small storage room holds a shield recharge. Grab it and exit. The door across the hall is locked from this side, so continue up the hall to the next door on the left.

27. Yellow Wrench

A guard lurks in this room. Put him down and grab the shield recharge and, more importantly, the yellow wrench. Exit and go to the next door on the right.

28. Passage Down

Kill the Grave Tusken and follow this passage down to the first landing.

29. Health Pack

Grab the health pack stashed in this alcove just off the first landing, then continue down the passage to the large storage room at the bottom.

30. Blue Wrench, Et Cetera

Three Tusken guards seek your removal. Blast them and loot the room of its many wonders—blue wrench, thermal detonators, smuggler backpack, shield recharge, power cells, and a couple of canisters to blow up for random supplies. Follow the corridor up the other side. It leads to the door that was locked.

FIGURE 3-3. BLUE WRENCH. THE OTHER STUFF IN STORAGE ROOM 30 IS GOOD, BUT THIS DEVICE IS ESSENTIAL. ADD ANOTHER NOTCH TO YOUR TOOL BELT.

31. Time for a Little Swim

The Katarn Reservoir. How nice. Hop into the water and swim to the opening just right of the waterfall. Climb the rock ramp and watch for a trio of Grave Tuskens with mayhem on their minds. Then turn into the alcove on the right.

32. Secret Area

Congratulations. Another secret area. This one holds a shield recharge and a thermal detonator belt. Return to the ramp and climb to the previously locked door.

33. Breathe Deep

How long can you hold your breath? Let's find out. Hop back in the reservoir and swim to 33. Press Ⓒ to submerge, pitch yourself down to face the hole, and swim into it. Move quickly along the underwater cave.

34. Blue/Yellow Wrench Slots (Need Blue/Yellow Wrenches)

Pop up in this hidden control room, manned by a pair of Grave Tuskens. Scoop up the shield recharges; then activate the two dam control mechanisms—one yellow and one blue. Of course, this works only if you have the appropriate wrenches—the yellow wrench from 27, the blue wrench from 30. Turn both controls to align the two sections of the dam outside; you can see them move through the window.

Now go back through the water tunnel. When you surface in the reservoir, go to the right (east) end of the dam and hop over. (A single Grave Tusken blocks your way.) Proceed to the now-open passageway.

FIGURE 3-4. THOSE
DAM CONTROLS. IF YOU
FOUND BOTH WRENCHES
(BLUE AND YELLOW),
YOU CAN TURN THESE
MECHANISMS TO FORM A
DAM OUTSIDE.

35. Passage Opening

Climb the ramp and follow the passage to the wall sign with the lightning
bolt. Just around that corner lies an unpleasant surprise.

36. Mailocs for Indigestion

Meet the Fabulous Flying Mailocs. Ugly, aren't they? And painful, too, if
you get stung. They go down fast—one or two hits kills them—but don't
let these huge insectoids get close. Once you've ended the threat, move to
the edge of the pit. My God, that's a live battery trench!

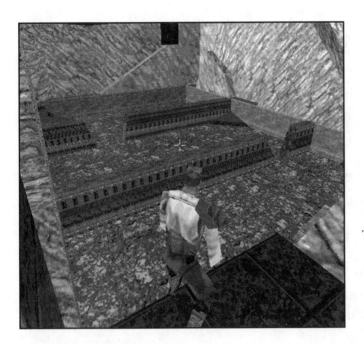

FIGURE 3-5. ACID TRENCH. THIS LIVE BATTERY TRENCH IS AN INGENIOUS WAY TO POWER A HOME, BUT MAKES FOR PAINFUL SWIMMING. DROP STRAIGHT DOWN TO FIND A SECRET AREA; THEN WORK FROM PLATFORM TO PLATFORM TO THE OPENING ON THE FAR SIDE.

37. Secret Area

Sorry, but just as in real life, you have to take some damage to get the good stuff. (See, computer games do teach valuable lessons.) Drop straight down to the ledge below, then hop into the trench and swim down to this alcove. Move quickly now! Scoop up the stormtrooper backpack and thermal detonators; then stroke hard around the wall to the platform at 38.

Note

Any swim in the Katarn battery trench will slowly but surely sap your health, so move quickly through the electrical sludge.

Caution

Ignore that slope just left of the secret alcove. You'll just keep slipping back into the battery trench, causing lots of unnecessary damage.

38. Safe Platform 1

Take a breather here, and then turn to the narrow ledge that slopes up from the top corner of the platform.

39. Hidden Health

Take a running hop up the ledge while veering right. This takes you into a tiny alcove where a beautiful bacta tank sits unattended. Drink up if you need it. Then slide back down to the platform. Hop into the trench, swim through the gap in the wall—jump to get through—and then make a beeline for the platform at 40.

40. Safe Platform 2

From this platform, hop up onto the sloped ledge and follow it to the southwest. When the ledge ends, look down. Aha! Stuff!

41. Light and Health

Good stuff, in fact. Two batteries and a nice health pack are tucked into an alcove below. Hop down to gather them. Ready for more pain? Hop back into the sludge and swim directly for the platform at 42.

42. Final Platform

Climb up onto the platform and follow it northwest to the opening at 43.

43. Mission Objective: Passage to Morgan's Workshop

Time to use those batteries you just grabbed. Hit F2 to activate your field light and move on down this passage. Watch for pesky Mailocs—seven of them, in fact, infest this tunnel. Keep a sharp eye out for a small alcove on the right-hand side.

44. Secret Area

Somebody tucked a fully loaded smuggler backpack into this little alcove. Watch out, though. A Mailoc may lurk here, thinking the backpack belongs to him. (They're stupid that way.)

45. Mission Objective: Morgan Katarn's Workshop

Here it is. Your father's workshop. And WeeGee's down there, somewhere. Time for some answers.

Mission 4

The Jedi's Lightsaber

KYLE KATARN FINALLY GETS A LIGHTSABER. Good timing, because things are heating up now. The Empire may be reeling since the death of Emperor Palpatine and the destruction of his second Death Star, but Imperial forces are still powerful, deadly, and ubiquitous. Of course, you've got a few Grave Tuskens to face first. These guys are living proof that biological life evolved from primordial slime.

By the way, this level of Jedi Knight would make a great water theme park. Irrigation channels, aqueducts, spillways, huge cisterns, reservoirs—get ready for one wet and wild ride.

Mission Objectives & Secret Areas

Make your way to the water purification plant.
Raise the water level inside the purification plant.
Find the passage to the river dam.
Rendezvous with Jan just past the dam.

Secret Areas: 6

Enemies

Remotes
Grave Tuskens
Mailocs
Water Cycs

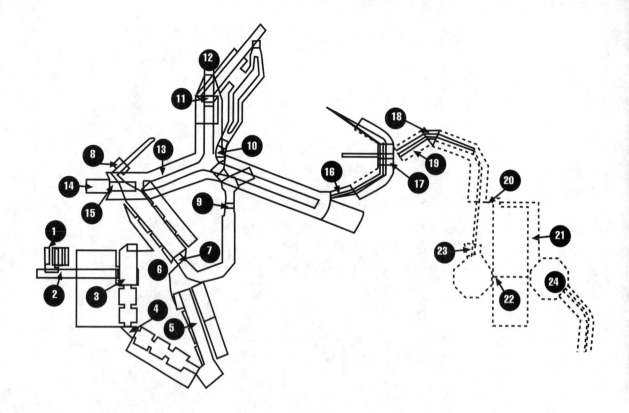

Legend for Maps

1. Wall button (remotes)

2. Floor grate

3. Irrigation channel (Grave Tuskens)

4. Grave Tuskens

5. Channel door button

6. Shield recharge

7. Bacta tank (under culvert)

8. SECRET AREA: Shield recharge, thermal detonators

9. Ambush!

10. Shield recharge, health pack

11. Water chute

12. Underwater grate

13. Irrigation channel

14. Ledge

15. SECRET AREA: Power cells, energy cells, shield recharges, battery, bacta tank, thermal detonators

16. Upper tributary

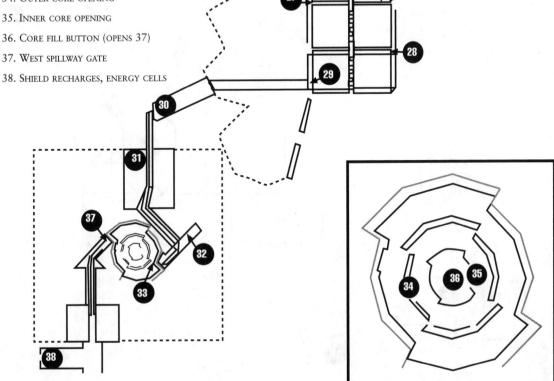

39. Passage to dam area

40. Elevator

41. Elevator (shield recharge)

42. Guard post

43. Underwater passage (Water Cycs!)

44. SECRET AREA: Power cells, energy cells, thermal detonators, health pack, armor vest

45. Trench opening

46. Trench

47. Health pack, smuggler backpack

48. Sequencer alert!

49. Shield recharges

50. Door

51. Elevator

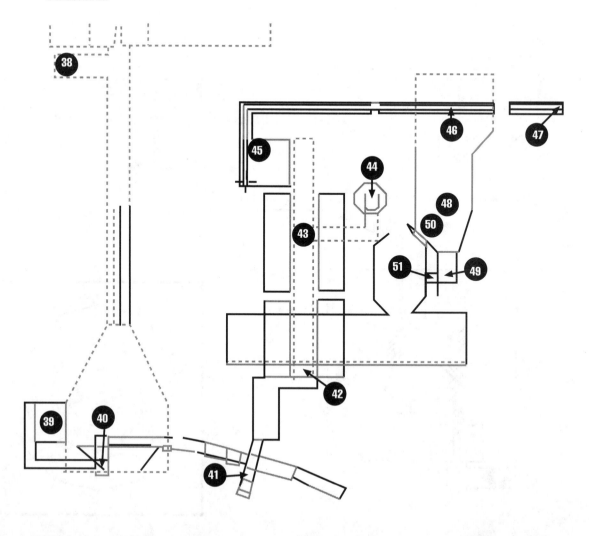

Walkthrough

You start in Morgan Katarn's workshop, wielding the Jedi lightsaber. As Kyle says, "Let's see what this saber can do." Go ahead, swing it around a bit. Didn't you spend your childhood waiting for this moment? WeeGee, the family droid, hovers nearby. If you're feeling morose, take a few whacks at him; it propels you toward the dark side.

Remember, you have Force Speed at your disposal now, too—that is, if you earned any stars in previous missions and used them to acquire Force Speed ability. For more on this, see the "Force Powers" section of Part 1, "General Strategies."

Tip

I prefer lightsaber combat in third-person view, and so does most of the LucasArts team. Press F1 to watch Kyle. You get a much better idea of how each type of saber swing works.

1. Start

Want a Jedi workout? Push the button in this small back room. A remote—a small floating droid—drops through the ceiling of the main room and attacks you. Remotes aren't particularly vicious, but they're not harmless either; their mild laser blast stings enough to degrade your shields. As the Jedi Knight manual points out, remotes provide excellent lightsaber training for the aspiring Jedi.

2. The Grate Escape

Use the lightsaber to slice open this floor grate and hop in. Kyle says, "The irrigation channels are my way out of here." Trust him on this. Proceed to the next grate. Fortunately, a hot lightsaber cuts through metal grating with ridiculous ease. Continue forward to the end of the channel.

FIGURE 4-1. HOT KNIFE, BUTTER. YES, THIN METAL MELTS QUITE NICELY WHEN STRUCK BY A PURE GLOWING ENERGY BLADE. THIS METHOD WORKS ON MANY GRATES AS YOU PROCEED THROUGH JEDI KNIGHT.

3. Tusken Fodder

A Grave Tusken trio loiters in the large channel below. Ambush them and head south down the channel.

4. More Resources

Two more Tuskens wait here for you to plunder their corpses for guns and ammo. Keep following the channel around to 5, where another trio of Tuskens waits.

5. Channel Door

Push the wall button to slide open the channel door. Continue down the channel and climb the ramp at the end. Watch out for roving guards.

6. Shield Boost

Grab the shield recharge here. You probably need it by now. Move along the edge overlooking the moving water below, picking off any guards in sight. Then hop into the canal for a refreshing swim.

7. Health Boost

If your health is hurting, swim upstream to the bacta tank tucked under the cement culvert where the water flows out of the enclosed tunnel. To get beneath the culvert, swim under the platform on the left side, move across to the bacta tank, and then retrace your route out—quickly, or you'll drown. Now you can lazily ride the current downstream to the grate.

8. Secret Area

Jedi time again. Cut through the grate with your lightsaber. Isn't it a nifty little weapon? You wash into a secret area where you'll find a shield recharge on the left bank and a thermal detonator belt on the right bank. Swim back upstream to the culvert at 7 and enter the tunnel. Continue moving upstream until just before the tunnel opens up to the sky again.

9. Watch Your Back

A Grave Tusken waits in ambush atop the culvert opening here, above your head. More guards lie just around the corner. Our advice: Stick close to the left wall and back up the channel. Pick off the guy above you first; then swivel quickly to nail the fellows around the corner. Climb the dry ramp to the left.

10. Crouching Death

Careful. A guard may be hiding behind a small, box-like pillar here. Get him before he gets you. Then help yourself to the spoils of war—a shield recharge and a health pack on a ledge. Metal bars obstruct the opening in the culvert, but you can crouch or jump to get through.

Continue up the dry channel. Five more Tuskens patrol the plateau at the top. Gun them down. Continue north to the grate and grab the shield recharge. Then get ready for the water slide from Hell.

11. Wild Ride

No choice but to hop in here. But before you do, arm yourself with the lightsaber. Then take the plunge. Water pulls you through a chute, and away you go!

12. Slice of Hell

The current slams you up against a metal grate here. Slice through with the lightsaber and ride on.

13. Emerge Here

You wash out into another irrigation channel, but you're under a walkway bearing three ugly Tuskens. Best bet: Hold your breath (if you can) and ride the current around the bend until you see the end of the walkway above you. Then quickly veer to the right and climb onto the concrete bank of the channel. This way you bypass the Tuskens and won't get ambushed when you emerge from the water.

Work your way back up the channel, gunning down the guards as they come at you. Then head downstream to the lip of the roaring waterfall. See the ledge across the chasm? Guess where the next secret area is hidden.

FIGURE 4-2. CHASMIC COINCIDENCE. THIS WATERFALL SEEMS TO FALL INTO ETERNITY. BUT THAT LEDGE ACROSS THE CHASM LOOKS LIKE AN INTERESTING DESTINATION.

14. Chasm Hopping

Advice: Save your game here! This presents a true test of leaping skill. Step off the end of the metal walkway and take a running leap from the lip of the waterfall across the chasm to the metal ledge. (If you make it on the first try, you get a Lifetime Achievement Award from the game gods.) Once you make it, climb up the ledge to the passage above.

15. Secret Area

Scoop up this cornucopia of delights—power cells, energy cells, shield recharges, battery, bacta tank, and thermal detonators. Continue east to the floor opening, hop down into the water, and swim to the channel bank. Hop over to the walkway and follow it upstream, veering left at the fork to head up the east channel.

16. Upper Tributary

A Grave Tusken opens fire from this platform. Take him out and work upstream until you reach an opening that reveals another irrigation channel below.

17. Change Channels

Looks far, but it's not bad. Jump down. After you land, walk down the slope. See those Tusken guards down the spillway? Pick them off from here.

18. Down Again

Hop in the water, ride down to the first platform (where the spillway bends right), and hop out. Creep to the upstream (west) edge of the platform and look down. More guards. And just look at all that stuff. Toss down a few thermal detonators, and sharpshoot the survivors.

19. Secret Area

When the coast is clear, drop down and gather the spoils. Go downhill to the small trench, turn left, and follow it to an opening. (Oddly, the secret area "tag" doesn't sound until you leave.)

20. Plaza Entrance

Look down. A very deep elevator shaft opens just below you. Hop over it to the ledge—don't fall in!—and proceed to the next opening.

21. Secret Area

Four brutal Tuskens guard a bowcaster full of power cells and a shield recharge. Exit through the small passage at the back and walk the narrow ledge overlooking a vast but empty octagonal reservoir. Hop down to the dry spillway.

22. Spillway Up

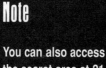

Note

You can also access the secret area at 21 if you survive a fall into the empty holding area between the two octagonal reservoirs. A small lift runs up a shaft to the ledge just under the opening at 20.

Move up the spillway to another octagonal reservoir. This one's full of water and ugly Tuskens. After you shoot them, hop in the water and swim (or walk precariously along the reservoir ledge) to the spillway platform.

23. Shield Boost

This is the bottom of the spillway that begins back at 17. Grab the pair of shield recharges here.

Return to the dry spillway at 22, cross it to where it "empties" into the dry octagonal reservoir, and hop down to that reservoir's floor.

24. Spillway Down

This opening leads to another dry trough that runs downhill. A swarm of creepy, shrieking Mailocs roams the spillway. Gun them down one by one—watch your back!—and follow the trough to a huge superstructure of girders spanning an acid pit.

25. Kill Bugs Dead

Another swarm of Mailocs hovers around the girders of the superstructure. Swat them down and step onto the nearest girder. Turn left and hop up onto the sloped ledge at 26.

26. Ledge Walking

Follow the sloped ledge as far as possible. In the middle of the structure, you must step onto the center girder, and then back onto the sloped ledge on the other side. Continue west along the ledge to the opening.

Caution

The pool looks blue and inviting, but don't take the plunge. Even if you survive the fall, the water is deadly acidic and kills instantly. Nothing of interest is down there, anyway.

27. Opening One

Step carefully through the opening; more bloodthirsty Mailocs flit around on the other side. Turn left and follow the sloped ledge to the center girder. This time, use the girder to cross to the other side. Turn left and follow the ledge to the next opening.

28. Opening Two

Again, step carefully through, watching for Mailocs just around the corner. Go to the center girder, cross to the other side, and continue east to the girder just over the trough.

29. Channeling

From here, slide right and pick off those Mailocs hanging out in the entrance of the tunnel across the way, if you can. Then hop in the channel and ride the current across to the tunnel mouth.

30. Quick Shield

Before you reach the spillway, hop out here and grab the shield recharge stashed on the platform. Then slip into the water and take another wild water ride. Be aware that Grave Tuskens are posted at regular intervals along the channel.

31. Platform Pick-Me-Up

Hop out of the aqueduct onto this platform, right after you emerge from the tunnel spillway. A shield recharge and a health pack sit near the wall. Hop across to the opposite bank, move down to the end of the platform, then walk along the narrow edge of the aqueduct to the next platform at 32.

32. Secret Area

Go down this slope to a small room that holds a pair of precious bacta tanks. Look out at the massive water purification core; it's your next destination. Climb back up and return to the channel. Hop in and get ready for the Big Plunge!

33. Water Purification Core

Yes, this water's pure, and there's a lot of it. Your objective: Fill this core to raise the water level up to the opening on the west side.

34. Outer Core Opening

Swim around to the far (west) side of the core structure. Take a very deep breath; you won't resurface for quite a while. Dive straight down and find the large opening—it's about halfway down the core structure—that leads into the mid-core area.

35. Inner Core Opening

Enter the mid-core area and swim around to the far (east) side of the inner core structure. Pitch down again and swim to the inner core opening near the bottom. Enter the inner core area.

36. Core Fill Button

Dark depths below look interesting, but nothing's there, and your lungs are probably seizing up by now. So kick straight up toward that hole at the top of the core. You emerge in a small room with a ledge and a wall button. Approach the button. When you push it, the hatch below closes and the water level rises. Don't panic, though. The hatch opens right up again, and you get a small air pocket at the top to breathe in while you wait.

By the way, you've just opened the west side spillway to fill the water purification core. Dive straight down through the hole. Retrace your swimming route out, but exit the inner core opening at 35 carefully. A deadly Water Cyc dangles gracefully just above your head, ready to slam you senseless with its powerful tentacles.

37. Mission Objective: Dam Access

Once you swim through the outer core opening at 34, swim directly up to the now-open west-side spillway. Continue upstream along the spillway until you reach the platforms. Then hop out.

FIGURE 4-3. SWIM TO THE HOLE. HERE'S THE CORE OF THE MATTER. WHEN YOU FILL THE WATER PURIFICATION CORE, THE WATER LEVEL RISES TO LET YOU SWIM OUT OF THE CORE THROUGH THE WEST-SIDE SPILLWAY.

38. Good Stuff

Tuskens are here, but you can handle them. Grab the pair of shield recharges on the spillway bank. Then turn into this room and score some much-needed energy cells. Return to the spillway bank and follow it down to the dam reservoir at the bottom, blasting Tuskens en route.

39. Mission Objective: River Dam Detour

Swim directly to the opening at the right. Of course, more Grave Tuskens block your path. Kindly direct them to oblivion, battling down the passage to the elevator.

WARNING

Don't get swept over the spillway! You can't get back up.

40. Elevator Up

Step onto this elevator and ride up to the next level of the dam structure. (Ignore the wall button. It brings the elevator back down.) By the way, after you step aboard, turn completely around. Many Tuskens await your arrival above.

41. Elevator Down

Fight your way past seven grisly Grave Tuskens to reach this next elevator. (One more goon waits at the dead end of the passage.) One shield recharge boosts you before you step aboard. And of course, another Tusken greeting party awaits your arrival below. Dispatch them and proceed.

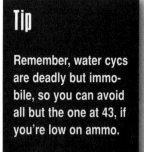

Tip

Remember, water cycs are deadly but immobile, so you can avoid all but the one at 43, if you're low on ammo.

42. Tusken Shooting Post

Two Tusken guards occupy this post overlooking the water cyc–infested trough below. Kill both species of pest from the sloped banks of the trough. Then slip into the water.

43. Secret Passage

Blast the water cyc in front of this underwater passage. (You can't get past him without provoking an attack.) Then swim up the passage.

44. Secret Area

Wow, jackpot! Power cells, energy cells, thermal detonators, health pack, armor vest. Stock up, then swim back out. Head to the far end of the water trough.

45. Up the Bank

A pair of Tuskens opens fire when you appear. Climb the sloped bank and follow the tunnel.

46. Open Trench

Another Tusken camps where the tunnel becomes an open trench. Continue down the trench to the slope leading up into another dark tunnel.

47. Dark Stash

Two more Tuskens hide in the darkness above. Draw them out, gun them down, and then take a running leap up into the tunnel. (It's a tough jump, but you can do it.) There, you find a health pack, a canister, and a smuggler backpack tucked behind the box. Go back out to the open part of the trench at 46.

See the two-level guard post across the water? It's a long-range shot, but try picking off the guards from the trench. Then kill the two water cycs in the water below, and dive in.

FIGURE 4-4. TENTACLE TERROR.
STAY AWAY FROM WATER CYCS!

48. Sequencer Alert!

Swim to the post, shooting at any remaining guards high or low. Careful! Three deadly sequencer charges line the edge of the water here. If you're taking fire from the guard post, pop out of the water and sprint past the mines. (This is a good place to use Force Speed, if you have it.) If the guards are dead, you can swim close to the mines, and then backstroke furiously when you hear the beeping. (Either way, you'll probably take some damage.)

49. Double Shield Boost

Fight your way beyond the box barricade to grab a pair of shield recharges. Then go around to the door.

50. Door to Transport Bay

Here's a hornet's nest for you. Three tough guards lick their chops, just waiting for you to open the door. Clean out the room. Tip: Shoot those dark fuel canisters by the boxes. You'll get a real bang out of it, taking out a Tusken or two. A long, sleek troop transport sits in the bay, but Jan's waiting, so you must find a way out of those big bay doors. Go to the elevator.

51. Elevator

Press the button in the elevator to ride up. More guards wait at the top, of course. But after you gun them down, press the button on the far (east) wall. This opens the bay doors downstairs. Now ride the elevator back down. Step out through the bay doors and wave to Jan as the *Moldy Crow* descends.

Mission 5

The Barons Hed: The Fallen City

Welcome to Barons Hed. As Kyle says, "The Empire sure knows how to ruin a perfectly good city." Once a thriving commercial center, the town now decays in the shadow of Imperial power. Dominated by Jerec's towering dark palace, Barons Hed's low-slung dwellings and markets have been overrun by Gran and Grave Tusken mercenaries operating with Jerec's tacit consent. Terrorized citizens keep to themselves, but fortunately, back alley sentiment for the Rebellion runs strong.

A zone of scorched ruins and barricades surrounds the Imperial compound in the center of Barons Hed. If you can get into the city and survive its mean streets, your next challenge is to penetrate the shattered, droid-patrolled no-man's-land and find 8t88.

Note: This mission also features the enigmatic House of Max, the wildest Easter egg in Jedi Knight.

Mission Objectives & Secret Areas

Work your way up the canal into Baron's Hed.
Find a passage to the no-man's-land that surrounds Jerec's palace.
Secret Areas: 6

Enemies

Gran
Grave Tusken
Sentry Droid
Possibly Max (that's right, I said Max)

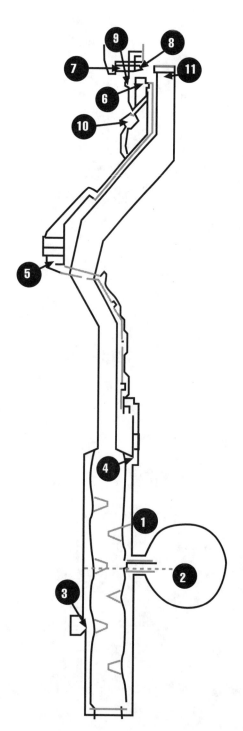

Legend for Maps

1. Canal

2. SECRET AREA: Armor vest

3. Shield recharge

4. Thermal detonators

5. Dark rooms (power cells)

6. Shield recharges

7. Alley to Barons Hed

8. Floor grate

9. Thermal detonators

10. Cistern (underwater passages)

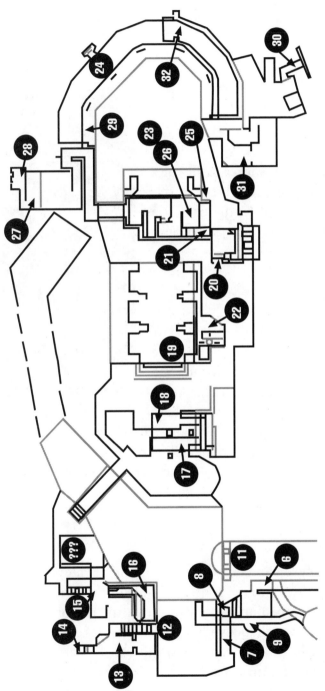

11. PLATFORM

12. DOOR

13. SHIELD RECHARGES

14. SECRET AREA: REPEATER GUN

15. MAIN HALLWAY

16. BALCONY (UPPER), TAVERN (LOWER)

17. PASSAGE TO ROOF

18. SHIELD RECHARGE

19. BAZAAR (GRAN WITH THERMALS)

20. POWER CELLS, SHIELD RECHARGES, BATTERIES

21. SECRET AREA: AMMO, SHIELD RECHARGES, THERMAL DETONATORS, WEAPONS, IR GOGGLES

22. SHIELD RECHARGE

23. PLAZA (HEALTH ITEMS)

24. SECRET AREA: POWER CELLS

25. JUMP TO UPPER LEVEL

26. UPPER LEVEL

27. CLUB ROOM

28. SECRET AREA: HEALTH PACK, BACTA TANK

29. JUMP TO ROOF

30. SECRET AREA: SMUGGLER BACKPACK, BACTA TANK, THERMAL DETONATORS

31. PASSAGE TO BALCONY

32. HOP DOWN TO END MISSION

??? MYSTERY HOUSE

Walkthrough

You begin this mission at one of the source pools of a canal that flows south from Barons Hed. Here, water is pumped up from the subterranean depths of Sulon and channeled into the canal. Your first objective is to work your way north upstream into the city.

Tip

If your shields are still strong, skip step 2 and return when you need a big armor boost.

Note

Remember, you have Force Speed at your disposal now—that is, if you earned stars in previous missions and used them to acquire Force Speed ability. For more on this, see the "Force Powers" section of Part 1, "General Strategies."

1. Take Some Damage

From your starting point, follow the ledge around the right side of the source pool to the canal. A Gran bomb-tosser is posted downstream to the left (south); a Grave Tusken patrols to the right. If thermal detonators sap your shield strength, don't worry too much. Just head back to the source pool and dive in.

2. Secret Area

The odd structure submerged in the middle of the pool is a water pump. Swim to the southwest side of the structure; then dive to the opening and swim down the center hole. Kick hard to the small alcove halfway down, where a glistening armor vest sits. Surface and return to 1.

Turn left and fight your way downstream to the end of the canal. Some fool left a strand of thermal detonators on the ramp there;

go ahead, take them, he won't mind. (He's probably dead.) Now cross to the opposite (west) bank and proceed to the first passage opening.

3. Double Room

Not much here but a shield recharge. Better than nothing, though. Cross back to the east bank and continue upstream.

Note

Enjoy your first encounter with pesky sentry droids. These nimble little robots pack a mean little punch, and they're difficult to hit from long range.

4. Quick Strand

Enter this passage. Blast the Gran in the tunnel and grab the strand of thermal detonators in the room at the end. Just outside the room is a pair of health packs and more vermin. Battle your way down the right bank of the channel to the bridge, cross over to the left bank, and follow the passage into a tunnel.

5. Dark Forces

Bad guys lurk in the darkness just inside the first room. This could be a good place to roll in some detonators, but a dazed civilian wanders nearby. Blast canisters in the second room and grab the pack of power cells stuffed behind the box. Then battle north up the passage and along the channel ledge to the closed door.

6. Tight Quarters

Test your weapons skills in this room. Two Grave Tuskens share space with an innocent civilian. One shield recharge sits behind the boxes. See that floor grate at the bottom of the stairs? We'll check it out in a moment.

7. Mission Objective: Barons Hed

Slip into this covered alley and fry the Tuskens. Congratulations, you've accomplished your first mission objective; Barons Hed lies just around the corner. But before we infiltrate the fallen city, let's grab one more stash of ordnance.

8. Grate Access

Use the lightsaber to slash through the floor grate here, and then hop down.

9. Detonators

Follow the dark passage south to some thermal detonator belts tucked in a small alcove. From here, you can continue exploring south—see 10 below—but to be perfectly honest, you won't find anything of value. In fact, just skip ahead to 12 to continue this walkthrough.

10. Cistern

Two underwater passages connect this cistern to the
main irrigation channel. You'll find a bacta tank on the
floor of the cistern. (In the Hard difficulty setting, you
won't find items in either passage.)

11. Drugons Ahoy

By the way, an alternate route into Baron's Hed is to hop
from 6 onto this platform. But to reach the city from
here, you must swim across drugon-infested waters in a
heavy enemy crossfire.

Note

You could access the
room at 6 by swim-
ming in from the
channel, hopping up
here out of the cis-
tern, and then slash-
ing upward through
the grate at 8.
However, the combat
is much tougher when
you hop up through
the grate, so we rec-
ommend the
sequence of steps in
this walkthrough.

FIGURE 5-1. THE TROUBLE
WITH DRUGONS. WELL,
BASICALLY, THEY BITE. SO WE
SUGGEST YOU STAY OUT OF THE
BARONS HED LAGOON.

12. House Entry

Hop up out of the grate at 8 and head west down the alley. Peek around the corner and try to pick off Grave Tuskens in the upper window of the house across the open plaza. (Don't waste too much ammo, if you're low; it's a tough shot.) Sprint around the corner and make a beeline for the house door. Climb the stairs and pause at the top.

13. Charge and Recharge

First, slide around the doorway on the right. Look before you shoot! One civilian and one Tusken thug hang out in the east room. Then turn and enter the left (west) room. Quickly grab those two shield recharges on the shelf. Then swivel and blast the pair of Grave Tuskens in the next room. (Your job is easier, of course, if you nailed one or both of them back at 12.)

14. Secret Area

Note how the wall in this corner is discolored? Whack at the wood with your lightsaber. Aha! A secret closet. But it's empty! Don't give up. Tilt up and whack at the ceiling. Another passage! Hop up and find a powerful reward—the deadly, three-barreled Imperial repeater gun.

15. House Hallway

Exit the rooms to the main hallway, where an armed Gran learns what "repeater" means when you unleash a vicious burst of cell-fire into his goatish gut. Continue down the hall to a room with a male civilian and a health pack. Then proceed south onto the balcony. (On the map, it's directly above the bar marked at 16.) You find a shield recharge, and the open deck provides a nice vantage point for sniping bad guys across the waterway.

Go back inside. Before you exit via the stairway just across the hall, read the "House of Max" sidebar on this page. Careful, another Grave Tusken lurks on the landing below.

Jedi Easter Egg
The House of Max

The house marked by three question marks (???) on the map holds a deep, dark secret. To uncover it, take the following steps:

1. Go down the stairs from the hallway marked 15 on the map.
2. The first time you reach the bottom stair, listen. The door of the mystery house opens.
3. Hurry around the corner. A woman walks over the bridge to the marketplace.
4. You can follow her. But according to level designer Reed Derleth, your best bet is to wait for her return. Hang out at the nearby lamppost and keep your eye on the bridge.
5. Soon the woman returns. Follow her into the mystery house.
6. Approach the odd creature sitting on the chair.

FIGURE 5-2. "HE'S A BUNNY. I'M A DOG.
WE'RE DANGEROUS, BUT WE WORK
CHEAP."

Does this fellow look familiar? If you're a LucasArts or Steve Purcell fan, you recognize Max, the psychotic bunny with a penchant for wanton violence. If you've never read Purcell's *Sam & Max: Freelance Police* comics or played the LucasArts classic, Sam & Max Hit the Road, I feel sorry for you. Life offers so few pleasures these days. They must be savored. As Sam says, "Max, crack open the Tang and those little cereal boxes with the perforated backs! I love that crap!"

But wait. Finding the House of Max is only the beginning of your Jedi Max adventure:

- ▼ Approach Max and activate him (that is, push the *z*). He starts wandering around, lost in his own psycho-bunny world.
- ▼ Open the door for Max. Set the bunny free.
- ▼ Once Max is active, activate him again to get the MaxCam view. See the world through bunny eyes.
- ▼ Max has trouble hopping over the bridge. You may need to give him a gentle nudge or two in the right direction.
- ▼ Try to guide Max toward bad guys. See what happens.
- ▼ Whatever you do, don't attack Max! He'll go psycho stalker on you, and that's bad: His gun hurts, and he's practically invulnerable.
- ▼ Remember my favorite Sam & Max Science Tip: "Kids, try imagining how far the universe extends! Keep thinking about it until you go insane."

16. Bar Brawl (Lower Level)

From the bottom of the stairs at 15, continue down the alley to the right (heading south) until you hear the sounds of a bar brawl. Wait and listen for awhile. The Gran will thin their own ranks. After you hear two of them drop— "Aaauugh!"—the fight's over. Enter and complete the thinning process. One Gran drops a thermal detonator belt; grab the shield recharge behind the bar, too. And ignore what the sour bartender has to say about shooting his paying customers.

FIGURE 5-2. "NO, SHMORG, I'VE GOT IT." MY THEORY: THEY'RE FIGHTING OVER THE BAR TAB. IN ANY CASE, IF GRAN ARE STUPID ENOUGH TO KILL EACH OTHER, BE SMART ENOUGH TO LET THEM.

Double back through the alley; then turn right and follow the path to the bridge. The door on the building to the right is locked. (See the "House of Max" sidebar to learn how to gain entrance.) Continue across the bridge to the big flagstone plaza.

17. Passage to Roof

Head south across the plaza to this doorway. Enter and blast the Grave Tuskens just around the corner to the left. Turn around and follow the ramp up to the roof. Watch for a bomb-throwing Gran on the way.

18. Rooftop Bar

Seems to be a sort of coffee bar up here, with a counter, a game table, and a few peaceful patrons. Grab the shield recharge in this corner and go back down the ramp. At the bottom, go right and follow the passage out to the east plaza. Cross the plaza walkway to the big bazaar-like marketplace.

19. How Bazaar

Watch out here. An armed Gran occupies the first booth on either side of the market; if you rush one, the other snipes at your back. Advice: Post up near the right-side wall and pick off the far Gran first; he has thermal detonators, so he's potentially more dangerous. Then swing around the corner and nail the second Gran, who merely totes a rifle.

Continue through the bazaar. The third booth on the left side holds three batteries. When you reach the other (east) end of the market, turn right.

20. Store Spree

Listen at this door for a moment. Two Gran hassle a sales clerk, who proclaims: "I know nothing. Leave me alone. Leave us in peace!" Open the door brandishing your lightsaber (if you blast harassers with a gun, you risk hitting the woman). Slash the Gran and stock up on sale items—power cells, shield recharges, and batteries. Jump to get the stuff on the top shelves. (It's OK, man, she wants you to have them.)

Now the fun part. Slash the cracked wall behind the counter. (Be sure to herd the woman away from you first, so you don't accidentally slash her, too.) When it explodes, it rips a gaping hole in the wall, revealing a secret Rebel storeroom!

21. Secret Area

Nice stash. Energy and power cells, shield recharges, thermal detonator belts, a bunch of weapons full of more ammo, and some IR goggles. Best of all, when you exit the storeroom, the clerk hails you with, "Long live the Rebellion!" Exit the store and head across the plaza to the open door under the awning.

22. Another Store

Work your way behind the male clerk and blast the canisters for goods. Then hop from the counter onto the top shelf and grab the shield recharge. Exit and go back across the plaza through the passage to the right of the Rebel lady's store at 20.

23. Harass the Harassers

Round the corner is a truly sordid sight—Gran bullies beating up the harmless citizens of Barons Hed. Halt the brutality with brutal precision; citizens are everywhere. (You also find a few Grave Tuskens and some health packs scattered about in booths.) Then head toward that cockeyed door across the big plaza.

FIGURE 5-3. SHAKE DOWN. THESE GRAN HOODLUMS HAVE THE BARONS HED POPULACE UNDER THEIR BRUTAL THUMB. SHOOT IT OFF.

24. Secret Area

Push the door; it falls down. Enter the small passage, grab the power cells, and say, "Look's like someone doesn't like to have company." Apparently, an entire section of Barons Hed has been sealed off! How do we get in there? Note that there seems to be a second level to many of the buildings around this plaza.

25. Route to Upper Level, Barons Hed

Climb this ramp to the door, open it, and enter. No bad guys in this establishment, just a bunch of shoppers. Grab the shield recharge in the corner. Suddenly, a Tusken appears. Aim carefully!

Open the door and exit. Don't go far, though. Turn left and hop up onto the rail. (It's directly above the secret area marked 21 on the map.) Turn and make a big leap to the roof. Now you're on the second level of Barons Hed.

FIGURE 5-4. HOP TO LEVEL 2. JUMP UP ON THE RAIL OUTSIDE THE SHOP. TURN AROUND. SEE THAT ROOF? GO FOR IT. BARONS HED LOOKS SO MUCH BETTER FROM ABOVE.

26. Citizen Savior (Upper Level)

Move down the roof. Again, you hear Gran bad guys terrorizing citizens. Hop over to the sloped roof and swivel quickly. Cut down the riffraff in the room. Fight north through the rooms, cross the ramp, and follow the walkway to the colored awning.

27. Club Hed

Take the passage under the awning to the door. Enter and squeeze through all the citizens in the club. Go to the northwest corner of the room, where the lower part of the wall is badly cracked (left of the female entertainer on the stage.) Saber time! Hack through the wall, crouch, and enter.

28. Secret Room

Another secret stash. This one's good for your health. Grab the health pack and bacta tank; then retrace your route back down to the awning.

29. And Up Again

Jump carefully onto the ledge next to the awning. Then use that to jump up to the marketplace roof. Run the length of the roof to the far (south) end. Ignore the door for now and go down the ramp into the small plaza.

30. Secret Area

Take a running leap up this fallen balcony. (Keep trying. You'll make it eventually—Force Speed can help as well.) At the top is a small passage with a smuggler backpack, bacta tank, and a couple of thermal detonator belts. Now go back up the ramp to the door.

31. Private Quarters

Somebody ransacked this nice apartment. Move through to the first room to the balcony. Then hop across to the roof.

32. Passage to Palace

Incredible. Somebody literally filled in entire streets and passages to keep intruders out. But that tunnel below looks promising. Hop down and get to work.

Hey. Is that an Imperial probe droid I hear?

Mission 6

Into the Dark Palace

THIS KILLER MISSION IS ACTUALLY A CONTINUATION of the previous one. (In the original Jedi Knight game design, Missions 5 and 6 were a single mission. Imagine that!) In Mission 5, you survived the mean streets of Barons Hed; you bypassed the obstructions blocking the route to the towering spires of the Dark Palace. Now you must find passage into and through the sprawling, well-guarded palace complex, where you face your first Imperial troops.

Be warned: This mission features some of the fiercest melee combat in all of Jedi Knight.

Mission Objectives & Secret Areas

Find a route through the ruins to the palace tower plaza.
Gain entry into the tower via the upper plaza deck.
Locate the primary bulkhead doors protecting the main entrance.
Find a way into the control room above the inner door.
Fight through the main anteroom to find passage to the top of the palace.

Secret Areas: 1

Enemies

Probe Droids
Stormtroopers
Officers
AT-ST Walkers

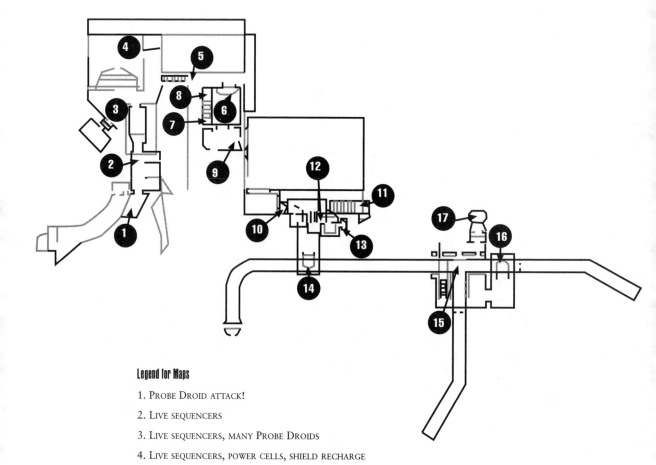

Legend for Maps

1. PROBE DROID ATTACK!

2. LIVE SEQUENCERS

3. LIVE SEQUENCERS, MANY PROBE DROIDS

4. LIVE SEQUENCERS, POWER CELLS, SHIELD RECHARGE

5. LIVE SEQUENCER

6. LIVE SEQUENCER, SHIELD RECHARGE

7. THERMAL DETONATORS

8. JAMMED DOOR (USE SABER)

9. LIVE SEQUENCERS

10. DROP DOWN HOLE

11. SEQUENCER CHARGES

12. LIVE SEQUENCER (UNDERWATER)

13. SECRET AREA: RAIL DETONATOR, ARMOR VEST

14. CULVERT PASSAGE (LIVE SEQUENCER)

15. REPEATER GUN, LIVE SEQUENCER

16. LIVE SEQUENCER, POWER CELLS

17. TURBOLIFT

18. STORMTROOPERS! (ENERGY CELLS, SHIELD RECHARGES)

19. ENTRANCE TO PALACE PERIMETER

20. STORAGE AREA ENTRANCE

21. ARMOR VEST, SEQUENCER CHARGES

22. SENTRY GUN TURRET

23. STORAGE AREA ENTRANCE

24. RAMP TO SECOND LEVEL

25. ARMORY (ARMOR VEST, STORMTROOPER BACKPACK, BACTA TANK, IR GOGGLES)

26. ATRIUM

27. STORMTROOPER BACKPACKS, IR GOGGLES

28. MEDICAL DROID

29. STORAGE AREA ENTRANCE

30. BRIDGE CONTROL SWITCH

31. BRIDGE CONTROL SWITCH

32. RAMP TO CONTROL ROOM

33. CONTROL ROOM

34. STORMTROOPER MELEE! (BACTA TANK, STORMTROOPER BACKPACK)

35. STORMTROOPER MELEE! (HEALTH PACK, STORMTROOPER BACKPACK)

36. EXTENSION BRIDGE (UPPER LEVEL)

37. AT-ST

38. (A, B) SENTRY GUN TURRETS

39. ARMOR VEST, SHIELD RECHARGES

40. GUARD ALCOVE

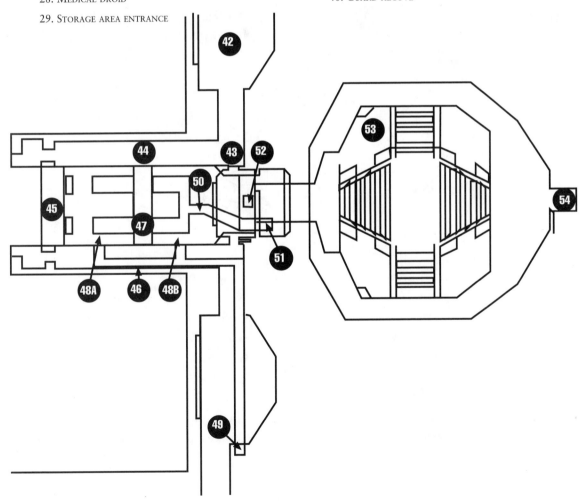

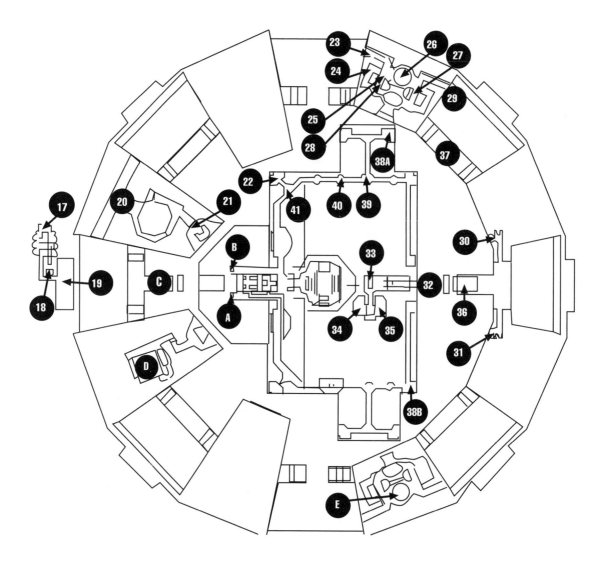

41. HEALTH PACK, STORMTROOPER BACKPACK

42. GUARD ALCOVE

43. DOOR TO DOOR CONTROL ROOM (LOCKED)

44. BULKHEAD DOOR SWITCH

45. BULKHEAD DOOR SWITCH

46. BULKHEAD DOOR

47. BULKHEAD DOOR

48. (A, B) SENTRY GUN TURRETS (PASSAGE TO 49)

49. WALL GRATE

50. WALL GRATE

51. AMMO, ARMOR VEST, STORMTROOPER BACKPACK

52. DOOR BUTTON, FLOOR GRATE (ABOVE ENTRY DOOR)

53. ANTEROOM

54. ELEVATOR

A, B. BRIDGE CONTROL BUTTONS (TO C)

C. BRIDGE (AT-ST)

D. AT-ST LIFT AREA

E. STORAGE AREA (MANY TROOPERS AND POWER-UPS)

Walkthrough

Time for some Imperial entanglements. As you work your way to the Dark Palace, watch out for sequencer charges, proximity devices that explode when you get near them. (Look carefully and listen for their telltale beeping.) Once you reach the massive palace complex, watch for robotic sentry gun emplacements. These are "smart" sentries that track unauthorized intruders and fire powerful laser blasts.

1. Probe This

Your presence in this restricted area has alerted a fleet of Imperial probe droids. One opens fire immediately. Shoot it down; five or six blaster hits destroy it. Or, more fun—and less costly, ammo-wise—simply wield your lightsaber and keep the crosshairs on your attacker. Your saber not only blocks blasts, it deflects shots back. (You may take a little shield damage, but not much.) Before long, deflected hits destroy the floating menace.

> ### Note
>
> This walkthrough focuses on what level designers call the "critical path"—the most direct route to completing a mission while still discovering all the secrets. Some areas in Mission 6 aren't on that critical path. Notes about these areas (labeled A to E) are included at the end of the section.

2. Sequencer Alert

Here's the first pair of many sequencer charges planted along the route to the palace. Best tactic: Toss a thermal detonator at them. If you're low on detonators, run toward the nearest mine and veer quickly into the second stall on the right. (Grab the battery and thermal detonators.) The stall's wall conveniently protects you from the blast. This sequencer charge also sets off a second charge just outside the far door.

FIGURE 6-1.
SEQUENCER
CHARGES. YES,
YOU'LL GET A
CHARGE OUT OF
THESE TWO DEVICES.
TRIGGER THEM FROM
A SAFE DISTANCE BY
ROLLING A THERMAL
DETONATOR AHEAD
OF YOU, OR TRY A
FORCE SPEED SPRINT
PAST THEM.

Now step through the far door. A whole squadron of probe droids hangs around outside. One hovers just above your head over the building. Others prowl the courtyard just ahead.

3. Sequencer Alert

Two sequencer charges are planted on the barrier blocking this passage to Barons Hed. Toss a detonator or just steer clear.

4. Triple Sequencer Alert

Two packs of power cells and a shield recharge sit out in the open here. Careful, though. It's a booby trap. Two sequencer charges lie next to the items. Toss a thermal detonator ahead of you. But wait: Another charge is set behind the boxes in the corner. Shoot the canister there to detonate it before you explore for items. Then exit the room, turn left, and proceed down the stairs to the east.

5. Sequencer Alert

Yes, that's another sequencer charge on the bottom stair. Toss a detonator or sprint full speed past it.

6. Sequencer Alert

And another one here. You can't sneak past this one, so try the full sprint technique again. Then blast open the two canisters and sweep the room of any power-ups, including the shield recharge in the corner.

Note

If you're lucky, one or two probe droids will hover near the sequencer charges planted at 3 and 4, triggering explosions.

Tip

To save thermal detonators, use Force Speed to sprint past sequencer charges placed out in the open.

7. Stairs to Upper Level

Tired of booby traps yet? More to come. Here, though, you get a thermal detonator belt. Climb the stairs to the door at the top.

8. Jammed Door

Try to open this door. It's jammed, Kyle tells you. Fortunately, you have a lightsaber. Hack open the door and attack the probe droid waiting on the other side. Or wait until the droid appears in the crack and gun it to scrap.

9. Ledge Crawl (Sequencer Alert)

Two sequencer charges—one inside, one outside—infest this passage. And another probe droid dangles its ugly tentacles, too. Eliminate threats and follow the passage to the collapsed room, watching for hovering droids above you.

10. Hole New Passage

Enter this room carefully. No sequencer charges here, but avoid the hole behind the fallen beams until you're ready to use it. Walk the beams to grab the health pack in the back of the room. Then drop through the hole.

11. Nice Respite

Climb the stairs ahead to find a blocked passage and a pack of five sequencer charges for your very own. (Now you can inflict some pain on the bad guys.) Go back down the stairs and go to the flooded stairway.

12. Swim Time (Sequencer Alert)

Ready for an extended underwater swim? There's a lot of submerged stuff below, so keep track of your location and return here for air if necessary. But wait: A sequencer charge sits underwater just below. Do you hate these things, or what? Toss down a detonator, take a deep breath, and swim down both flights of stairs.

13. Secret Area

A pair of health packs and a shield recharge sit on a shelf in this room. Grab them, pitch up, and swim through the opening in the ceiling. This leads to an awesome rail detonator gun, an armor vest—and, mercifully, an air pocket! Now you can kick back up one flight of stairs to the big room off the first landing.

14. Culvert Passage (Sequencer Alert)

Yes, another sequencer charge is planted near the opening in the floor. Swim into the opening and turn left, not right. (Right leads to a dead end with nothing but a repeater gun.) Surface and proceed warily up the tunnel-like pipe.

15. Probing Pair (Sequencer Alert)

The pipe opens at an intersection where two probe droids float like malevolent jellyfish. Destroy them and explore the area. Note: A repeater gun full of power cells sits on a nearby ledge, but somebody set a sequencer charge right behind it.

16. Goods

Detonate the sequencer charge and grab the power cells in this room; then exit and head up the stairs to the control room where a broken door leans against the wall. Go through the open passage.

17. Turbolift

Ride this lift up to a creepy roomful of probe droids. One or more may attack immediately. Nail the active ones, then move around the room, blasting droids as they float peacefully in their storage pods. Shoot fast; the first hit activates each droid. Then exit down the corridor at the far (south) end of the room.

18. Palace Guard

No more bounty hunters or mercenary riffraff. Time to face the Empire's finest. An entire battalion of stormtroopers and officers is deployed around the central spires of the Dark Palace. The first two are posted in this side room along the corridor. Inside, you'll find energy cells and a couple of shield recharges. Exit and continue to the door at the end of the corridor.

19. Entrance to Palace Compound

Yes, that's an Imperial AT-ST walker directly across the huge open plaza. Some serious firepower is arrayed before you in the palace perimeter defense. Hop down off the ledge and sprint directly to the opening to the left. More troopers attack.

FIGURE 6-2. THE DARK PALACE. SO 8T88 IS UP THERE. YOU'RE DOWN HERE. SHALL THE TWAIN EVER MEET? MANY DOZENS OF STORMTROOPERS THINK NOT. PROVE THEM WRONG.

20. Trooper Hive Number 1

Continue to the first opening on the right and get ready for some fierce extended combat. This perimeter storage area is heavily guarded. Don't rush wildly into the central courtyard. Post yourself here and nail the big gold canisters on both sides of the courtyard; this sets off a chain reaction explosion and wipes out Imperial obstacles. After you clear the courtyard, climb the stairs up to the surrounding ledge, scoop up all the dropped ammo, and proceed to 21.

21. Goodie Store

Run to this storage alcove, grab the pack of sequencer charges, and don the armor vest. Move around the corridor to one side and take out the stormtroopers; repeat on the other side. Then hop down and go left a few steps to where the passage opens into a large plaza.

22. Robotic Sentry

Here's the first of many annoying sentry gun emplacements. To avoid it, move along the tower walls, passing directly underneath it. Continue hugging the walls and sprint to the passage opening at 23.

23. Trooper Hive Number 2 (Lower Level)

> ### Note
>
> Sentry guns are installed in almost every second-level corner alcove of the towers. They track you and fire powerful turbolaser blasts. Stick close to tower walls, keeping out of their line of fire. When you get closer, shoot them out.

This equipment storage area swarms with stormtroopers. Best approach: Stick to the left wall and sprint down the entry passage from 23. When you reach the first corner, spot the opening in the wall on the right—it's a ramp that leads up to the second level. Sprint up that ramp.

24. Ramp to Second Level

Take this ramp up to the second level before you engage the swarm of troopers on the first floor.

25. Trooper Armory (Upper Level)

Here's where you stock up on powerful power-ups—armor vest on one shelf, a stormtrooper backpack, bacta tank, and IR goggles (with a battery) in the storage alcoves. Around the corner is an overlook posted with guards (at 23 on the map, upper level). Gun them down and move to the atrium areas.

26. Atriums

Troopers patrol the upper level of both atriums. Take them out, and then work around the edges, tossing down thermal detonators and/or picking off troopers below. Stay on the upper level, though! You have quick access to goods at both 25 and 27.

27. More Armor and Ammo (Upper Level)

Three stormtrooper backpacks and IR goggles (with battery) sit in the storage alcoves on this side.

Tip

Avoid engaging the enemy in the lower atrium areas. On the ground floor, each atrium is a double-deadly killing ground with a full squad of troopers on the lower level plus more shooting down at you from above. If you take the upper level first, you fight only those troops; then you can roll thermal detonators down onto the lower-level troops. Plus, the second level features plenty of ammo and armor power-ups to keep you going.

However, if your health gets dangerously low, you may need to hustle down to the medical droid at 28 on the lower level; it's the only health item in this sector.

28. Medical Droid (Lower Level)

Feeling droopy? Roll up your sleeve and take a shot of full health from the medical droid in this alcove. Don't use him unless you're seriously depleted, though. His ministrations restore your health meter to a full 100, so the lower your health, the more health he delivers. If you wait, the medical droid will recharge and can be used again.

FIGURE 6-3. MEDICAL DROID. WANT A SHOT OF SOMETHING GOOD? BARE YOUR ARM AND LET THIS GUY JAB A NEEDLEFUL OF HEALTH INTO YOUR JEDI VEINS.

29. Storage Area Exit

After you've cleared out the equipment storage area in steps 23–28, exit the lower level here. Watch for guards, of course. Then sprint hard along the left wall; stay against the wall around corners all the way to the passage at 30.

30. Bridge Control Room Number 1

Battle the guard unit—four stormtroopers and an officer—and grab the shield recharge in the storage alcove; then move to the observation room. Pull the switch, go to the window, and watch the ramp slide slowly out from the near side of the bridge at 36 (it stays out for 10 seconds or so, and then retracts). Store that critical information for now. Exit the control room and head for the doorway dead ahead.

31. Bridge Control Room Number 2

Same as 30 here—battle four guards (plus one officer in the observation room), grab power cells and a shield recharge, pull the switch. This one activates the ramp on the far side at 32.

Eventually, you need to get up to the second level where all those AT-STs are stomping around. But for now, let's clear our path for that maneuver. Pull the switch here at 31, leap out the window, and sprint (using Force Speed, if available) to the doorway at 32.

32. Passage Up to Ramp

As the ramp extends from 32, it clears the passage that leads up to another control room for the same ramp.

33. Control Room

Kill the officer manning the controls to keep him from pestering you later. Exit the room. Now make a choice:

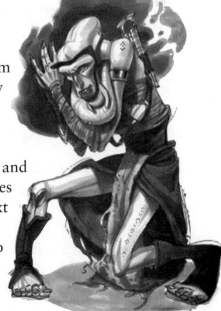

▼ If you like maniacal combat against steep odds and enjoy the spectacle of stormtrooper corpses piled in festering mounds, proceed to the next step.

▼ If you seek a more efficient, less violent path to victory, skip ahead to 36.

34, 35. Swarm Combat!

Continue up the ramp. Sixteen stormtroopers—eight in 34, eight in 35—stand at inspection, ready to march out. The moment one spots you, all hell breaks loose. This is a bloody melee of the first magnitude. If you survive, loot Imperial supplies from the two rooms—bacta tank and stormtrooper backpack in 34, and a health pack and another stormtrooper backpack in 35.

36. How to Reach Level Two

Here's where your Force Speed really comes in handy. (You can still complete this step without it, but it's far more difficult.) Take the following steps:

▼ Return to the ramp switch at 30.
▼ Pull the switch at 30 and sprint (using Force Speed, if available) to the other ramp switch at 31.
▼ Pull the switch at 31, hop out the window, and continue your sprint up the ramp at 32.
▼ At the first landing, turn and speed across the two extended ramps, which are momentarily connected in the middle.

Do this if you lack Force Speed:

▼ Hit the switch at 31, then run over and hit the switch at 30.
▼ Now run up the ramp (32). The inner half of the drawbridge retracts.
▼ Hit the switch in the control room (33) to send the inner bridge back out.
▼ If your timing is perfect, you'll be able to cross the bridge just as the outer half begins to retract.

FIGURE 6-4. FORCE SPEED AHEAD. THROW THE SWITCH AT 30, RUN TO 31 AND THROW THAT SWITCH, AND THEN HOP OUT THIS WINDOW AND SPRINT (USING FORCE SPEED, IF AVAILABLE) TO THAT TOWER ENTRANCE BEFORE THE BRIDGE RAMPS RETRACT AGAIN.

You may have to jump if the first ramp has begun to retract. But if your timing is good, it should be easy to get across, even in Hard mode. And congratulations, you're on the second level of the complex.

37. Stalking Walkers

Head north by northwest. A thundering AT-ST walker prowls the overpass up ahead. Lay into it with the rail detonator gun, if you have rail charges. Otherwise, get under and slightly behind the walker and bash at its belly with your lightsaber. It's great fun. The big thing can't sight you, and your lightsaber inflicts surprisingly quick damage. (Don't forget that a driver hops out after the AT-ST falls.)

FIGURE 6-5. BELIEVE IT OR NOT, THIS IMPERIAL AT-ST AND ITS DRIVER CAN BE TAKEN OUT WITH JUST A LIGHTSABER. STAY UNDER AND SLIGHTLY BEHIND THE BEHEMOTH AND WHACK AWAY.

38A, 38B. Mission Objective: Tower Entry

Now you must get across to the central tower area. Proceed northwest to 38A, take out the sentry gun there, and jump across to the alcove. (You can also do this at 38B, down at the southeast corner of the towers.)

39. Armor Boost

On these corner shelves you find an armor vest and two shield recharges. Turn right and head west down the long narrow corridor.

40. Hall Monitors

Guards line the hallway, tucked in each alcove. It's quite a battle; fight forward, but watch your back as other troopers join the action from eastern positions.

41. More Stuff

These shelves hold a health pack and a stormtrooper backpack.

42. Officer Corps

Continue up the ramp to this alcove, where two officers and two stormtroopers stand guard. Disobey their orders and continue south to the palace entry area, a deep trench barricaded by heavy bulkhead doors.

43. Mission Objective: Primary Bulkhead Doors

Here's the door to the entry control room. Unfortunately, it's locked. Even more unfortunate, you can't unlock it from outside. But you can bypass it with a little ingenuity. Pick off all the guards in the trench area.

44. Bulkhead Door Switch Number 1

Pull the switch here to activate the heavy bulkhead door at 45.

45. Bulkhead Door Number 1

As the door lowers into the entry trench, use it as a ramp to sprint across to the far side. (If you don't make it, just wait for the door to rise again.) Hustle to the button at 46.

Note

If you miss your leap and fall into the trench, don't despair. Just skip ahead to step 48.

46. Bulkhead Door Switch Number 2

Quickly pull this switch as the bulkhead door activated by switch number 1 is still moving. Turn to see the other bulkhead door at 47 start to lower, too. Hop aboard!

47. Bulkhead Door Number 2

See the two big concrete slots atop this door? Crouch and duck into either one. Then calmly ride the door back up. At the top, a huge locking mechanism slides through the slot, pushing you out into a small crawl space. If you get trapped the locking mechanisms will crush you. Don't worry. Skip ahead to step 50.

48A, 48B. Entry Sentries

If you fall into either half of the trench, a robotic sentry gun opens fire on your sorry hide. Whoever built this palace is pretty paranoid, wouldn't you say? Shoot out the gun and hop into its bay. See how the back wall is blown out? Step through into a gun maintenance tunnel and follow it east, and then south. About halfway down, you must hop up to another level to continue down the tunnel.

49. Hop, Slash, Exit

When you reach the end here at 49, turn around and look up to see another grate. Wield your lightsaber. Then jump and slash to cut open the grate. (Watch out for a snoopy Imperial officer who may suddenly appear and fire at you through the new opening.) Now you can hop out and battle your way back north to the entry trench.

50. Grate Entrance

When we left you back at step 47, you were crammed into a tiny locking slot above the entry trench. Hack that grate with your lightsaber. Follow the passage to the end.

51. Mission Objective: Palace Entry Control Room

Hack through the floor grate and drop into this well-stocked supply room—power and energy cells, armor vest, and stormtrooper backpack. Drop the officer at the controls.

> **Note**
>
> Or you can continue to explore the outer passages that run around the south half of the palace. It's entirely optional: They're nearly identical to the ones you just reconnoitered.

52. Entry Door Button/Secret Grate

Your reward for getting this far is a choice of entry into the palace from this very spot:

▼ **Hard way:** Pull the switch to open the inner entry door below. Quickly hit either exit door button, hustle out, hop into the trench, and rush through the inner door.

▼ **Easy way:** Slash the floor grate; you actually drop on top of the inner entry door. Pull the switch to lower the inner door ... and yourself.

53. Main Anteroom

Of course, once you get through the inner door, you may wish you hadn't. It's another hornet's nest of troopers, with a pair of ceiling gun turrets adding to the cacophony. Not only that, but the elevator at 54 takes a painfully long time dropping to the anteroom level. And just when you think you've cleared the room, you discover that there's an endless supply of stormtroopers. However, you can find some respite under the stairs.

54. Mission Objective: Elevator to Top of Palace

This elevator arrives after a couple of weeks. When it does, dive in. Mission accomplished.

Additional Areas

A, B. Bridge Control Buttons

Push either one of these buttons to extend the bridge to the AT-ST walker at C. Why go down there and tangle with an Imperial walker? Clearly, you savor a good challenge and want to take on a powerful opponent. But if you hop down and go for the AT-ST, you'll have to go all the way back around to the east side of the complex and repeat step 36 to get back up to the second level.

C. AT-ST Walker

Push the button at A or B to extend this bridge. Now you can run over to face the AT-ST walker, if you're so inclined.

D. False Hope

As you enter this area, you see an AT-ST walker raised on a turbolift to the second level. (It's a teaser; you can't reach the lift, even with Force Speed.) Another AT-ST is on the ground. Pick off troopers and officers first. Lure the lower AT-ST to either cluster of fuel canisters, run away, and then shoot the canisters. The explosion often deals the walker a fatal blow.

E. Equipment Storage

This storage bunker is identical to the area you battled through in steps 23 to 29—swarming with troopers on two levels, open alcoves in the middle, plenty of power-ups on the upper level, and a medical droid for a shot of total health.

Mission 7

Yun: The Dark Youth

QU RAHN'S ASSESSMENT OF YUN: "YUN, A YOUNG AND WILLING DARK JEDI, THE NEWEST ADDITION TO THE CAUSE. BRASH AND EAGER, HE IS READY TO PROVE HIMSELF TO HIS MASTER AT ANY COST. THESE ELEMENTS MAKE HIM A DANGEROUS AND UNPREDICTABLE FOE."

Yun Statistics

Health: 500
Resistance: 50% Impact, 50% Energy, 90% Fire
Special Instincts: Jump, Open Doors, Special Attack (jump attack), Circle & Strafe
Force Powers: Blinding, Persuasion

Combat Tips

Yun uses Force Blinding and Force Persuasion; at this point, you may counter him with Force Speed and/or Force Jump, depending on how you allocated your Force ability stars in previous missions. Yun is young, brash, agile, and has more health hit points than an AT-ST walker. Good luck.

- ▼ As you move around the room, destroy the furniture to get it out of the way.
- ▼ Force Jump up to the high window. Yun will soon follow, but before he does you can get in some free shots with standard energy weapons—pistol, ST rifle, and so on—while he's still below, weakening him a bit. Caution: When Yun finally leaps up to you, quickly wield your lightsaber, or you're doomed.
- ▼ When Yun uses Force Persuasion, look for the blue, sparkly particle aura around him. Careful, though—the flickering isn't constant, and you can lose him.
- ▼ When Yun uses Force Blindness, you can still see the vague outline of his figure. Approach carefully!
- ▼ When Yun combines Blinding and Persuasion, you should simply avoid him, using Force Speed to run from one end of the room to the other until the blindness wears off.
- ▼ LucasArts testers suggest that, in general, you hold your lightsaber until Yun swings; let your saber block his blow, and then launch a quick counterstrike. Tester Matthew Azeveda's approach is to keep sliding from side to side, then make sudden runs at Yun, striking blows and then hopping over him.

Hidden Areas

Two hidden areas hold bonus power-ups for your first struggle with the dark side. If you face the east wall, push either of the two rightmost wall panels. One holds four shield recharges, the other holds four health packs. These rooms give you a brief respite from combat, but don't think you can camp here. Yun will open the doors and hop in for a visit.

Mission 8

Palace Escape

O K, you got in. You survived your first Dark encounter. Now you need to get out. Let's escape the Dark Palace and find 8t88 again, shall we? Morgan Katarn's map is destroyed, but you know its impression is logged somewhere inside 8t88's thick titanium skull.

Mission Objectives & Secret Areas

Escape the ballroom to the palace roof.
Work your way back into the tower via the air ducts.
Use the palace ventilation system to cross to the far tower where 8t88's shuttle is docked.

Secret Areas: 5

Enemies

TIE Bomber (on roof)
Stormtrooper
Field Stormtrooper
Imperial Officer
Imperial Commando
Kell Dragon

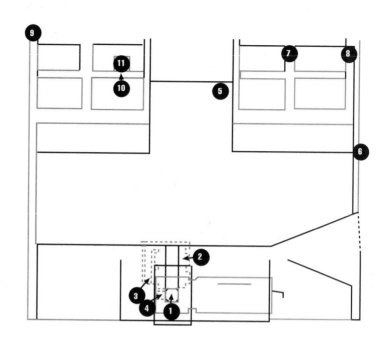

Legend for Maps

1. TURBOLIFT

2. STORMTROOPERS

3. SECRET AREA: SHIELD RECHARGES, THERMAL DETONATORS

4. ELEVATOR CIRCUIT (BEHIND GRATE IN SHAFT)

5. THERMAL DETONATORS (ROOF LEVEL)

6. NARROW LEDGE

7. CLIMB STRUT

8. SENTRY GUN TURRET

9. SENTRY GUN TURRET

10. JUMP DOWN TO 11

11. AIR DUCT OPENING

12. SECRET AREA: HEALTH PACK, SHIELD RECHARGES

13. SECRET AREA: THERMAL DETONATORS, ENERGY CELLS, BACTA TANK

14. AIR DUCT OPENING

15. RAMPS

16. ELEVATOR

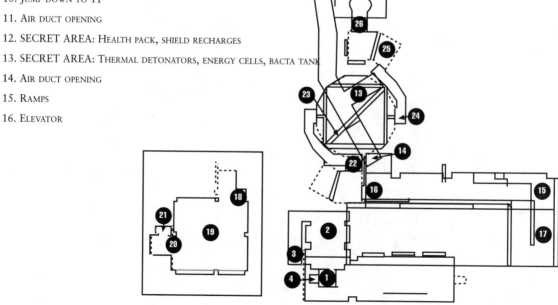

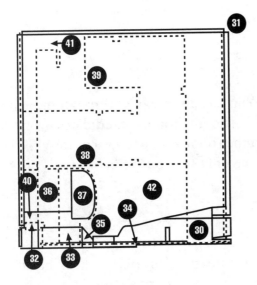

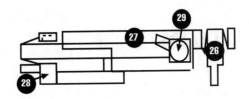

17. SHIELD RECHARGE, THERMAL DETONATORS, BACTA TANK

18. TURBOLIFT

19. DRAGON ROOM

20. LEDGE: ENERGY CELLS, SMUGGLER BACKPACK, BACTA TANK, BATTERY

21. DRAGON PEN (BUTTON FOR 18)

22. SHAFT ALCOVE

23. STEEL BEAM

24. PASSAGE OFF SHAFT

25. ELEVATOR (RIDE ON TOP)

26. AIR SHAFT

27. LEDGE MELEE! (TOUGH TROOPERS)

28. JUMP INTO AIR SHAFT

29. SECRET AREA: ARMOR VEST, BACTA TANKS

30. AIR SHAFT

31. NARROW LEDGE (TO 32)

32. SECRET AREA: AMMO, BACTA TANKS

33. TOUGH TROOPERS, GUN TURRET

34. NARROW LEDGE (BACTA TANKS)

35. NARROW LEDGES

36. TROOPERS

37. ARMOR VEST (UP SHAFT LEDGES)

38. SHIELD RECHARGES

39. SHIELD RECHARGE

40. ELEVATOR

41. ROOF: DOOR TO LANDING PAD

42. ROOF: MEET THE CROW

Walkthrough

You begin in the palace ballroom. Yun has just escaped through the ceiling via some sort of Jedi levitation. A trio of honors candidates from the Imperial Military Academy light up the room with energy, courtesy of their rifles. Looks like Yun's turbolift is the only way out of here.

1. Ballroom Dancing

Rid yourself of troopers, then step onto this turbolift, which begins to lower. Immediately turn right when you step aboard so you face the attack at the bottom.

2. Reload

Eliminate the trio of stormtroopers in this basement storage area; then proceed around the corner into the back storeroom.

3. Secret Area

This storeroom holds two thermal detonator belts and two shield recharges. These detonators will be very useful later. Return to the lift at 1, wield your lightsaber, hop aboard and turn right. Watch the grating carefully as you rise.

4. Lift Circuit

As the turbolift rises, watch for a small compartment behind a grate. Use the lightsaber to cut through the grate and hop in. (If you miss, don't worry; the elevator keeps going up and down.) Once inside, slash the circuit board on the wall. Then hop back onto the turbolift on its next pass and ride it to the roof.

Note

If you don't slash the circuit, the elevator will never rise above the ballroom level.

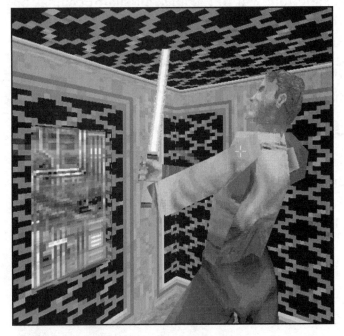

FIGURE 8-1. CIRCUIT BREAKER. SLASH YOUR WAY THROUGH A GRATE INTO A HIDDEN CIRCUIT ROOM IN THE ELEVATOR SHAFT. THEN HACK UP THE CIRCUIT SO YOU CAN RIDE THE LIFT TO THE ROOF.

5. Mission Objective: Palace Roof

OK, so the first secret area and mission objective came easy. This is no rooftop picnic, though. The minute you step off the lift, one of those damned robotic sentry guns opens fire, a TIE bomber begins lethal bombing runs across the roof, and a pair of stormtroopers tries to pick you apart.

Best move: Sprint directly for this corner, where a thermal detonator belt sits on a box. Gun down the troopers and keep an eye out for the howling TIE bomber. Then head around the corner to the left.

6. Ledge Walk

Step onto this narrow ledge and follow it to the huge air shaft openings on the roof. Careful. The TIE bomber's ordnance is unsettling, and a field stormtrooper wielding a rail detonator begins to launch missiles at you from the rooftop of the tower across the way. (Don't waste ammo on him; you can't hit him.)

7. Shaft Climb

Hop carefully onto the rim of the shaft (it's slippery). Walk to the center strut and quickly climb it to the top.

8. Sentry Gun Number 1

When you reach the top of the shaft structure, an annoying sentry gun opens fire. Kill it with relish. Then move west across the rooftop to another air shaft opening.

9. Sentry Gun Number 2

Another sentry gun. Blast it, or it will harass you while you set up the next delicate maneuver.

10. Jumpoff Point

Move along the struts at the top of the air shaft to this position. Look down. See the air duct opening into the shaft across the way? Guess where you're going next. Advice: Save your game here.

11. Air Duct Target

Take a running leap off the strut and land in this air duct opening. (Be brave. It's easier than it looks.) The moment you land, a small sentry droid opens fire. Knock it out and proceed down the air duct.

12. Secret Area

See the rusty patch on the floor of the duct? Look closely; you can see stuff through the holes. Slash it apart and hop down to grab the health pack, squencer charges, and three shield recharges. Continue down the duct and consider Kyle's complaint: "There's gotta be a better way to make a living."

13. Secret Area

Look at the air duct wall here. Looks pretty rusty, too. Imagine what a swipe of the lightsaber might do. Act on the mental picture and scoop up thermal detonators, energy cells, and a bacta tank. Continue to the end of the duct.

14. Thermal Surprise (Upper Level)

Creep quietly up to the end of the duct. Just below, an officer and two troopers look bored. Spice up their lives with a couple of thermal detonators; then follow the bombs down.

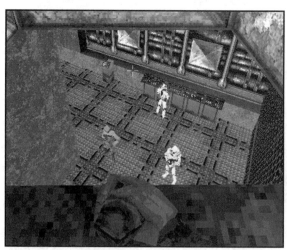

FIGURE 8-2. BOMBS AWAY. HERE'S WHERE YOU GET PAYBACK FOR THAT DAMNED TIE BOMBER ON THE ROOF. DROP A FEW THERMALS INTO IMPERIAL LAPS.

When you hit the ground, you hear: "Call for reinforcements!" Just around the corner is another stormtrooper. Killing him prevents a new wave of troops from surging through the doorway. A well-aimed thermal detonator can thin their ranks. Pick off the survivors and proceed down the corridor.

15. Ramps to All Levels

Go down the ramps to the next level.

16. Elevator Entrance (Middle Level)

An Imperial officer and a stormtrooper guard this elevator, so you know it must lead to something important. Don't take it yet, though. (We'll be back in a minute.) Continue down the ramp, instead.

17. Small Depot (Lower Level)

A small squad of troopers led by an officer roam this basement area. After the battle, steal their stores from the back room—shield recharge, thermal detonators, and a bacta tank.

Return to the elevator on the second level (at 16) and press the call button. When the elevator arrives, enter and press the button inside to ride down.

18. Turbolift Down . . . to What?

When the elevator reaches bottom, exit, terminate the officer, and step onto this turbolift. Ride down and step off at the bottom. The turbolift ascends, with no call button in sight.

Hmmm. Before you step out into the large room, go around the corner to the right and grab the shield recharge.

Boy, are you gonna need it.

19. Kell Killer

Welcome to the Palace Dragon Room. When you step into the light, a monstrous Kell dragon escapes from its pen and attacks. Only explosive devices or your lightsaber have any effect on this killer. One tactic: Run around the pen for awhile, dropping sequencer charges as you go. Then make a Force Jump up to the ledge at 20.

FIGURE 8-3. KELL FROM HELL. DON'T WASTE CELL-FIRE ON A KELL DRAGON. USE THERMAL DETONATORS AND SEQUENCER CHARGES, AND THEN FINISH HIM OFF WITH YOUR LIGHTSABER. KEEP YOUR DISTANCE UNTIL THEN!

20. Pitiful Store

A well-timed Force Jump can get you up to this safe ledge lined with energy cells, smuggler backpack, bacta tank, and a battery—none of which really help you do battle against the beast. But here you can safely toss all your thermal detonators at the toothy fellow.

When all your explosives are gone, hop down and finish off Kell with the lightsaber. Keep moving! Don't let him corner you! A Kell dragon's massive jaws will grind you into Jedi gristle in a few bites. Fortunately, he's easy to outmaneuver. Run in wide circles, strike quickly, and then run like hell again.

21. Turbolift Call Button

Enter the Kell dragon's pen and push the wall button. This opens the door to a back room with a health pack. The button inside the back room brings down the turbolift at 18. Press it and walk to the lift. (Take your time; it's a slow lift.) Ride up, and then take the elevator back up to the second level.

22. Shaft Passage Number 1

Gee, it's great to be alive, isn't it? Use the boxes in the elevator to hop up through the opening in the elevator ceiling. (Again, it helps to use Force Jump here.) From

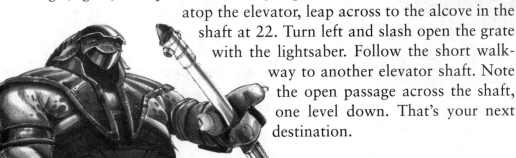

atop the elevator, leap across to the alcove in the shaft at 22. Turn left and slash open the grate with the lightsaber. Follow the short walkway to another elevator shaft. Note the open passage across the shaft, one level down. That's your next destination.

> **Note**
>
> You probably want to defeat the Kell dragon. You're a Jedi, right? But escape is possible. Tricky, but possible. Jump ahead to step 21; push the buttons while continuing your evasive action. When the turbolift at 18 comes down, wait until it starts rising again before you sprint to it and leap aboard. Otherwise, you'll be trapped in a corner, facing big dragon teeth for an eternity of painful seconds.

23. Beam Walker

Hop down onto the steel beam, turn right, and walk to the end. Once there, hop down onto the big center beam just below. Cross this beam to the far side, then turn right and follow the smaller beam to the open passage at 24.

24. Shaft Passage Number 2

Follow this passage to yet another elevator shaft, running two elevator cars. Your goal: Reach that big hole down low on the far left side of the shaft. First, hop onto the top of the nearest elevator car.

25. Stepping Stone

From the top of this elevator car, step onto either of the top two horizontal beams in the center of the shaft. Hop over onto the top of the other elevator.

26. Fall Guy

From the elevator, hop across to the round opening. Your jump will probably carry you over a floor grate that opens under you like a trap door. Don't worry, the fall won't hurt you, and it's a necessary plunge. You end up at the bottom of a huge ventilation pipe.

27. Firefight

Yes, here's a fight. When you hop out of the pipe, a squad of very tough soldiers, including an Imperial commando, two field stormtroopers—one with rail charges, one with a repeater gun—and some regular troopers, trains a deadly fire on you. Continue along the passage to the small ledge overlooking an air shaft.

FIGURE 8-4. ELITE CORPSE. IMPERIAL COMMANDOS ARE THE EMPIRE'S FIERCEST SOLDIERS. THEY LOOK TOUGH EVEN WHEN DEAD, DON'T THEY?

28. Ear Timing

Hear that howling wind? It's blowing hard out of the air shaft below. Note how the wind ebbs and flows. Wait until it's quietest, and then hop into the air shaft, turn right, and sprint up the shaft. Hop down the hole at the end of the shaft—you land on a metal grate—and look up. That small alcove near the top of the shaft is your next destination.

Tip

The following sequence can be difficult, so we recommend you save your game here.

29. Secret Area

Listen to the airflow again. As it builds in intensity, start jumping. Soon the wind pushes you high enough to step into the alcove, where you find a glowing armor vest and two bacta tanks.

When the wind builds again, step out of the alcove and aim upward. As the wind lifts you, start running. In a few seconds, you'll be propelled right out of the air duct.

FIGURE 8-5. AIR SHOT. YOUR TASK HERE IS TO RIDE THE WIND FROM ONE AIR DUCT OVER THE GAP TO THE DUCT ACROSS THE WAY. BUT FIRST, HOP DOWN WHEN THE WIND DIES AND FIND THE SECRET AREA IN THE DUCT BELOW.

Tip

If you're quick, you can jump right back out and let the wind push you to your next destination. But the alcove also cuts off the wind, so you can take a breather, save your game, and wait for the next cycle of wind.

30. Ride the Wind

As you shoot out of the air duct, aim for this duct directly across the gap between the palace towers. Once you arrive here, immediately hop out of the duct on the right side, or its own airflow will blow you over the edge into oblivion. Then step down onto the very narrow ledge.

31. Walk the Line

Follow the narrow ledge completely around the outside of the tower. Careful when you reach each of the two corners; the wind tries to push you off. Turn in toward the building as you walk to keep from getting blown off.

32. Secret Area

Slash through the grate at the end of the ledge near the southwest corner of the tower. Hop in to grab a well-deserved reward—energy cells, power cells, and three bacta tanks. Before you leave, peek through the far grate. See that armor vest in the open shaft? We'll get to it soon.

Return to the air duct at 30. (Again, be careful at each corner.) Climb atop the duct and follow the passage west.

33. Tough Troopers

Four field stormtroopers, one with a rail detonator, ambush you here with the help of a sentry gun turret on the ceiling. If you survive this melee, you deserve the next discovery.

34. Bacta Break

Don't miss the pair of bacta tanks stashed precariously on this tiny ledge. Stick close to the wall as you move toward them. Then continue west. Jump across the small gap to the platform at 33, and look down.

35. Ledge Hopping

See the small ledge just below? Step carefully off the platform and drop down to it. A flashing light reveals another ledge below. Drop down to that ledge. Using this pair of ledges eliminates impact damage from falling. Now drop down to the floor. Proceed through the low opening into the room with the flashing light.

> **Tip**
>
> If you face out when you step off ledges, you may miss the next ledge below. Best technique: Back very slowly off each ledge, and then move forward while dropping.

36. Guys in the Dark

Some dangerous field stormtroopers confer with an officer here. An Imperial commando mans the elevator at 40. What's going on? Maybe you don't want to know. In any case, blast them, then head over into the semicircular shaft to score three shield recharges.

37. Impossible Armor

By the way, remember that armor vest you saw through the grate in the secret area at 32? Look up the semicircular shaft. See the rows of thin ledges? The vest sits on the third ledge up. Holy cow, even Force Jump couldn't get you that high in one hop. To reach it, you'd have to Force Jump up the shaft from ledge to ledge. (I couldn't do it. I didn't meet anyone at LucasArts who had, either. But you're most welcome to try.)

Now head north into the next room.

38. Hangar Crew

Another officer and two field stormtroopers patrol this huge, hangar-like room. And a whole mess more troops are stationed just around the corner.

Lay them all to waste. It's a thick, hellish fight. Wade in singing. Don't miss the pair of shield recharges.

39. Scant Reward

So much bloody work and all you get for it is a lousy shield recharge. Just remember that process is everything.

40. Elevator to Landing Platform

Enter and push the button inside to activate the elevator. Ride to the top with your eyes peeled. About halfway up, note 8t88's shuttle tucked into a launch bay.

41. Mission Objective: Landing Pad (Roof Level)

As you move down this corridor, Kyle contacts Jan on the *Crow*. One last field stormtrooper stands guard at the end of the hall. Poor, sad little man. End his vigil, but don't cross the threshold of the doorway. First, prepare to sprint.

42. Moving Finale (Roof Level)

Stepping onto the metallic roof triggers the final event. The roof slides open in sections so 8t88's shuttle can escape. Hit the roof running and sprint directly south along the wall to the platform at the other end.

Watch the Imperial shuttle depart. Then Jan and the *Moldy Crow* arrive. Time to change CDs!

Mission 9

Fuel Station Launch

THAT 8T88 HAS ESCAPED TO JEREC'S MASSIVE CARGO SHIP, which is about to debark from a fuel station for the Valley of the Jedi. Jan drops you on the station roof. Work your way into the station and get past the huge primary fuel tank. Shut down the fuel pipes so you can use them as a route to the refueling gantry where the cargo ship is docked.

Mission Objectives & Secret Areas

Get from the rooftop into the fuel station.
Drain the primary fuel tank and pass through it.
Shut down the fuel pipes.
Use the fuel pipes to reach the reservoir under the cargo ship.
Find a way up the fueling gantry and sneak onto the cargo ship.

Secret Areas: 10

Enemies

Trandoshan
Remote
Stormtrooper
Field Stormtrooper
Imperial Officer

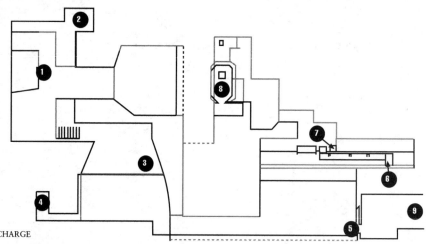

Legend for Maps

1. Ugnaught

2. Rail detonator, shield recharge

3. Generator

4. SECRET AREA: Armor vest, rail charges

5. Door (need yellow key from 8)

6. Small passage

7. Battery

8. Observation post (yellow key, bacta tank, batteries, shield recharges)

9. Trandoshan attack!

10. L1: Fuel switch

11. L1: Fuel canisters (jump to 12)

12. SECRET AREA (L1): Sequencer charges

13. L1: Back room

14. L2: Fuel canisters

15. L2: Fuel canisters

16. L2: Fuel switch

17. L2, L3, L4: Turbolift

18. L3: Fuel switch

19. L3: Vantage point

20. L4: Control room (Super shield!)

21. L4: Lookout post

22. L4: Door to crawl space

23. SECRET AREA (L4): Health packs

24. L4: Drop

25. L4: Fuel switch

26. L4: Turbolift to wrench (use at 30)

26A. SECRET AREA (L4): Power cells

27. L5: Fuel switch

28. L5, L6: Turbolift

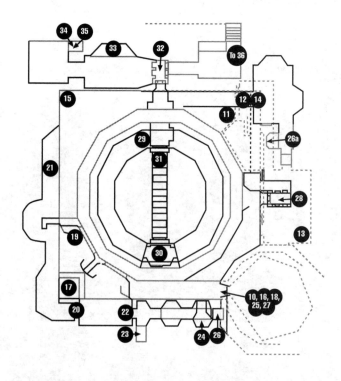

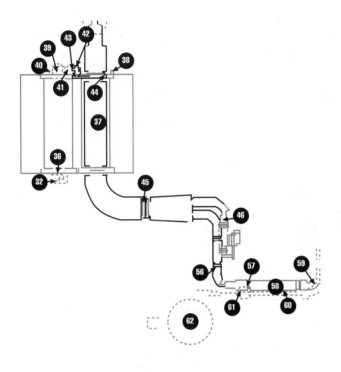

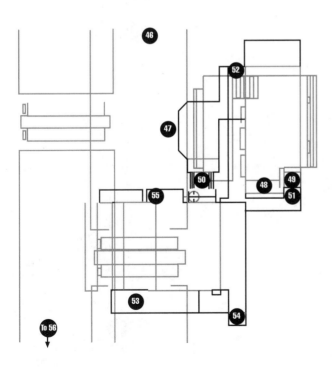

29. L6: Shield recharges

30. L6: Tank hatch controls (need wrench)

31. Fuel tank catwalk

32. Turbolift

33. SECRET AREA: Shield recharges

34. SECRET AREA: Armor vest (upper alcove)

35. SECRET AREA: Concussion rifle (lower alcove)

36. Ramp button

37. Fuel pipe

38. SECRET AREA: Power boost!

39. Sentry turret guns, thermal detonators, health pack, bacta tank, shield recharges

40. SECRET AREA: Power cells, bacta tank

41. Fuel pipe switches

42. Turbolift

43. SECRET AREA (behind grate): Bacta tank

44. Entry into fuel pipes

45. Pipe door (remotes!)

46. Pipe door

47. Guard station entry (upper level)

48. Stormtrooper backpack, bacta tank

49. Turbolift

50. Healing station! (lower level)

51. Midlevel crawl space

52. Health pack

53. Shield recharges

54. Fuel canisters

55. Hatch control switch

56. Pipe door (remotes)

57. Remote

58. Engine fuel pool

59. Fall down pipe

60. Pipe fork (upper/lower)

61. Armor vest, revive pack, thermal detonators, bacta tank

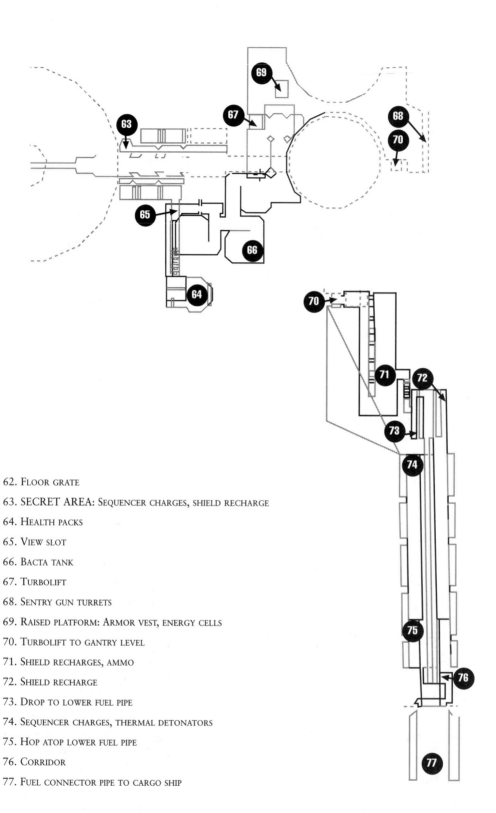

Walkthrough

Kyle hops out of the *Crow* onto the roof of the fuel station. The first thing you see up ahead is an Ugnaught using a wrench on some sort of power unit.

1. Start

Give the Ugnaught a nudge just to hear him grumble. Gosh, he's cute. Should we kill him? I'll let you think about it for a moment. OK, the answer is no, not unless you crave the Force Powers of the dark side.

Go left, climb the stairs, and double back to the platform above the left side of the stairway.

2. Items for Later

Take a big running leap across to this platform. Just around the corner sits a couple of items— a shield recharge and a rail detonator full of rail charges. Return to the stairs and follow the corridor to the humming power generator.

> ### Note
>
> You have Force Speed, Force Jump, and Force Pull at your disposal now—that is, if you earned stars in previous missions and used them to acquire these abilities. For more on this, see the "Force Powers" section of Part 1, "General Strategies."

3. Trandoshan Territory

Be wary here. You may meet your first Trandoshan. These savage reptiles roam this fuel station, and most (including this one) carry powerful concussion rifles. Gun him down from the generator platform, but don't jump down yet! First, head to the right (west) and hop to the narrow ledge.

FIGURE 9-1. LIZARDS OF WAR. MOST OF THESE WEB-HANDED POND MUTATIONS CARRY CONCUSSION RIFLES. TRANDOSHANS AREN'T STUPID. IF YOU GET IN CLOSE, THEY WON'T SHOOT, KNOWING A CONCUSSION BLAST KILLS THEM, TOO. INSTEAD, THEY GO INTO MELEE MODE, BEATING ON YOU WITH THE RIFLE.

4. Secret Area

Follow the ledge back to this small alcove where you find an armor vest and two power cell packs. Exit, hop down, and relieve the dead Trandoshan of his weapon so you can blast his foul species all the better. Then continue east along the walkway.

5. Locked Door (Need Yellow Key)

Your natural inclination: Go to this door. It's a good inclination. Unfortunately, the door is locked. You need the yellow key (see 8) to open it. Move along the wall and climb the rust-colored grate. A small alley runs to the right. Follow it.

6. Remote Door

Crouch to enter this small opening in the grate. Follow the passage.

7. IR Goggles

As you exit, an Ugnaught sits to your left, a spare battery to your right. Grab the battery, ignore the creature, and continue on your merry way.

8. Observation Post (Yellow Key)

Careful here. A Trandoshan with a concussion rifle has taken up a position across the gap (back where you started the mission). Pick him off quickly; then climb the ramp into the first level of the observation post. You find a bacta tank, two batteries, and the yellow key. Climb to the post's second level. There you find another Ugnaught sitting on a fuel canister, and a pair of shield recharges.

Now you must return to the door at 5. The wall you hopped down blocks that route, but use Force Jump (if available) to hop back up. Or you can just take a running leap off the observation post ramp to your start position and continue around to the door at 5. Open the door and enter the multilevel primary fuel tank area.

OVERVIEW: HOW TO REACH THE CARGO SHIP

LET'S REVIEW YOUR MISSION 9 OBJECTIVES. REMEMBER, YOUR ULTIMATE GOAL IS TO REACH THE CARGO SHIP (WHERE 8T88 PARKED HIS SHUTTLE) BEFORE IT DEBARKS FOR THE VALLEY OF THE JEDI. THE CARGO SHIP IS CURRENTLY REFUELING. TO REACH IT, YOU MUST WORK YOUR WAY THROUGH THE PRIMARY FUEL TANK— THAT HUGE ORANGE THING, AROUND WHICH DESCENDING RAMPS RUN—INTO THE STATION'S MASSIVE FUEL PIPES. THESE PIPES, IN TURN, PROVIDE ACCESS TO THE FUEL GANTRY TOWER NOW ATTACHED TO THE CARGO SHIP.

BUT TO GET THROUGH THE PRIMARY FUEL TANK, YOU MUST EMPTY IT OF FUEL. TO DO THIS, YOU MUST FLIP THE CORRECT FUEL-PUMP SWITCH. THE FIVE SWITCHES APPEAR IN ONE SPOT ON THE MAP—AT 10, 16, 18, 25, AND 27—BECAUSE THEY'RE STACKED ON TOP OF EACH OTHER. THEY TRANSFER FUEL BETWEEN THE PRIMARY FUEL TANK AND A SECONDARY TANK, WHICH YOU CAN SEE BEYOND THE WINDOW ABOVE EACH PUMP SWITCH.

FINALLY, YOU MUST FIND A STRIPED WRENCH AND USE IT TO OPEN THE PRIMARY TANK AND FUEL PIPES.

9. Imperial Presence

A Trandoshan opens fire with his big gun as you move forward. Stay away from the fuel canisters just inside the door! If you duck behind them and the Trandoshan hits them, they explode, taking you with them. The station has Imperial overseers, too. Two stormtroopers and an officer join the fray here.

10. Fuel Switch, Level 1

Careful—another Trandoshan launches big blasts at you from a ramp across the way. Flip the switch on this control panel. Watch through the view port as the fuel in the secondary tank rises to this level; this empties the primary fuel tank. (See "How the Fuel Switches Work.")

How the Fuel Switches Work

Each fuel switch fills (or drains) the secondary tank to the level of the switch. This, in turn, changes the level in the primary tank to an "opposite" amount. Thus, if you flip the fuel switch on Level 3, the fuel in the secondary tank becomes three levels deep, and the fuel in the primary tank becomes two levels deep.

But enough coy chatter. The simple solution: Flip the fuel switch on Level 2. Then leave all four of the other fuel switches alone—or, if you do flip them, be sure you go back to the Level 2 switch and flip that one last before you head down to the base of the primary fuel tank for step 30.

UNSOLVED

SOLVED

11. Attack Post

A field stormtrooper with a repeater rifle scowls (and shoots) at you through the window of an observation post. Near the window sits a pile of fuel canisters. If you don't have Force Jump ability, don't hit the canisters! You'll need them in the next step. Pick off the trooper through the window. Don't use anything explosive, like your rail detonator or concussion rifle, or the canisters will blow for sure.

FIGURE 9-2. FUEL CANISTER.
BROWN CANISTERS ARE BRIMMING
WITH EXPLOSIVE ROCKET FUEL.
SHOOT THEM FROM A DISTANCE.

12. Secret Area

Use Force Jump or the fuel canisters at 11 to hop onto the post roof. Grab the pack of sequencer charges, hop back down, and enter the observation post. An officer and an Ugnaught may be just inside the door, so be careful. Pick up the ammo in the window room (where you shot the stormtrooper) and head to the back room.

Tip

Fuel canisters can be nifty weapons. Each is full of highly explosive engine fuel. Whenever you see canisters, shoot at them from a distance. Chances are they'll wipe out bad guys. But remember they can hurt innocent Ugnaughts—and you, too. Stay away from fuel canisters in a firefight.

13. Watch Your Aim

More troopers stand in front of three huge fuel canisters, and Ugnaughts huddle in the corner. Precision shooting is necessary; if you blow up the canisters, you'll get hurt, and the Ugnaught is doomed. After the battle, examine the schematic of the two fuel tanks on the wall: "This looks interesting!" It shows the relative fuel levels in the primary tank (right) and the secondary tank (left). See the diagram on page 221.

Ignore the turbolift in the north wall for now unless you want to check out the secret area at 26a. (It runs down to the lowest ramp area.) Exit through the nearby door and turn right to face down the ramp.

14. Can Shooting (Second Level)

A Trandoshan and a stormtrooper camp near the fuel canister at the bottom of the ramp. Shoot the canister. It explodes, eliminating the stormtrooper. Don't get cocky, though. The Trandoshan may survive and open fire.

Now move down the ramp—you've descended to the second level now—and look ahead. If you see an Imperial officer and a stormtrooper near the big fuel canisters at 15, what's the next step?

> **Note**
>
> Actually, you can get through the primary fuel tank with this configuration. The catwalk you use to cross the tank is low, but you can still hop up to the tank hatch and throw its switch. (See step 31 later in this walkthrough.) The ideal configuration, however, leaves the fuel tank catwalk at hatch level so you can easily reach the hatch switch.

15. Imperial Pyrotechnics (Second Level)

You got it. Blow up the canisters. Continue along the walkway until you reach the fuel switch.

16. Fuel Switch, Level 2

Flip this pump switch to set the fuel level in the secondary tank to this level—that is, four levels full, leaving the primary tank one level full. This raises the catwalk inside the primary tank to the optimal level. This fuel switch is the only one you need to flip in this building! Turn around and head for the turbolift just up the walkway.

Note

Remember, the fuel switch at 16 is directly below the fuel switch at 10, and directly above the ones at 18, 25, and 27. Thus, these numbers are listed together on the map.

17. Turbolift (Connects Levels 2, 3, 4)

This turbolift drops down two levels, but doesn't stop at the intermediate level (3). Let's check out Level 3 first: Get ready to hop off a moving lift. Press the call button and face the lift, gun poised (an Imperial officer may ride up). Step on the lift and prepare for some furious action. Just as the lift lowers below the Level 2 floor, run forward. You end up on Level 3, snout to snout with a concussion rifle in the hands of a Trandoshan grunt.

18. Fuel Switch, Level 3

After you reduce the Trandoshan to lizard meat, continue forward to the fuel pump switch. Nice, isn't it? Don't touch it! If you flipped the switch on Level 2, your switch-flipping work is done. Go back past the turbolift to the edge of the ramp.

19. Vantage Point (Level 3)

Lots of guys down there. Hit those fuel canisters near the lookout post and two or three Imperials go up in rocket smoke. Finish off any other guards you see. This makes future exploration so much more pleasant.

Now go back to the lift at 17. The lift platform sits down on Level 4 and you can't call it up from here, so hop into the hole.

20. Drop Into Hell (Level 4)

When you hit bottom, Imperials open fire. (A poor little Ugnaught wanders through the crossfire; it's difficult to avoid hitting him.) The firefight's tough enough, but one Imperial officer may take a position behind a pile of fuel canisters. If these cans blow when you're nearby, not even 200 percent shield power can keep you alive.

Our advice: Sprint immediately around the wall behind the lift (marked as 20 on the map). A gleaming super shield keeps you invulnerable for 30 seconds as things get ugly. Clear the guard station and quickly head north around the curve in the hall to the lookout post just outside.

21. Lookout Post (Level 4)

If you move fast, you'll still have invulnerability time left. Three stormtroopers stand guard. Violently relieve them of their duties. (If you followed directions in step 19, this may be a ghost post when you arrive.) Turn around and go back into the guard station.

22. Door to Crawl Space

Open this door, crouch, and enter the low room. This is where the handy, hardworking Ugnaughts do repairs. Just inside the door-way, turn right and step into the first alcove.

Secret Area

23. Secret Area

Facing the wall, jump up to a small closet stuffed with two health packs. Most expeditious. Hop back down, crouch, and continue down the low corridor. You find a shield recharge on the way.

24. Drop

Drop down this small hole, crouch again, and crawl out onto the metal platform. Turn right and go to the fuel switch.

25. Fuel Switch, Level 4

Another fuel pump switch to admire but not touch. (Again, this assumes you flipped the switch on Level 2 last.) Turn right and step onto the turbolift.

26. Turbolift to Wrench

Ride this turbolift up to a small catwalk. Grab the power cells and, more importantly, the wrench. As Kyle says, "*This* should come in handy."

FIGURE 9-3. WRENCH, STRIPED. YES, THIS IS EXACTLY WHAT YOU NEED. THIS TOOL OPENS THE PRIMARY FUEL TANK AND EACH OF THE MASSIVE DOORS THAT SEGMENT THE FUEL PIPE SYSTEM.

Ride the turbolift back down, walk past the Ugnaught to the west end of the platform, and hop down to the next level. We also suggest you move to the edge of the walkway, look down, and pick off the pair of field stormtroopers guarding the base of the primary fuel tank.

26a. Secret Area

From 26, continue west walking around the tank clockwise. This will bring you to another room with Imperials and Ugnaughts (and a lift that goes back up to 13). To the right of the lift is a dark secret area you must jump up to. It contains two power cells. Return counterclockwise to the fuel switch at 27.

27. Fuel Switch, Level 5

Look, another fuel switch to ignore—this is the last one, if you're following this walkthrough. Proceed around the corner and through the next doorway to the turbolift.

28. Turbolift Down to Fuel Tank Base

Press the call button and ride the turbolift down. If you didn't nail the tank base guards back at 26, do so now. Hop over to the tank base.

29. Supply Depot

Turn left and pass through Ugnaught's control room. Two more stormtroopers are posted just around the corner on the other side. Go get them; They stand guard over two shield recharges.

30. Tank Hatch Controls

Return to the control room. Look at the schematic of the fuel tanks. If the right (primary) tank is empty or has just one level of fuel, turn the wrench switch (if you have the wrench from 26, of course) to open the hatch behind you. Enter the tank and use the switch just inside to close the hatch behind you.

FIGURE 9-4. OPTIMAL TANK SETTING. HERE'S THE BEST SETTING FOR THE FUEL TANKS—ONE LEVEL OF FUEL IN THE PRIMARY TANK. (NOTE HOW THIS LIGHTS UP THE GREEN CATWALK INDICATOR IN THE TANK.) NOW TURN THE HATCH SWITCH.

31. Mission Objective: Primary Fuel Tank

What a nice smell. Heed Kyle's observation: "Engine fuel. Could get a little hot in here. I'd better be careful with blaster fire." One shot into the fuel, good-bye. Turn the wrench-switch to open the far hatch and exit the tank. (This hatch won't open unless you closed the other hatch door.) Two troopers guard the other side. Kill them.

32. Turbolift to Pain

Ride this lift down. When you hit bottom, an ugly Trandoshan lays into you with big blasts of his concussion rifle. Don't miss the power cells on the console. Return to the lift, push the button to bring it down, and hop aboard. Ride up one level and wait; after a moment, the lift continues up to a secret area!

33. Secret Area

Grab the three shield recharges on the shelf; then proceed into the fuel canister storage room.

34. Secret Area

(Upper)

Hop atop the three stacked fuel canisters. Then leap up onto the tall canister on the left. Continue jumping up the canister stack to the high alcove and retrieve the armor vest.

35. Secret Area (Lower)

Hop back down to the floor. Another secret area is tucked behind the fuel canisters; you must blow them up to get it. Problem: An Ugnaught sits in the room. If you're a true Jedi, push the little fellow to the edge of the lift at 32. Now blow up the canisters and enter the secret niche to grab the concussion rifle full of power cells.

Ride the lift back down to the second stop below, where you killed the Trandoshan. Go through the door, down the stairs, and follow the corridor to the wall button.

36. Ramp Button

Push this button; the floor beneath you drops slowly to form a ramp down. Immediately, a bank of turret guns opens fire across the open space. Another gun-toting Trandoshan waits beneath the east half of the ramp. Look across the vast room. You stand atop the huge pipes that lead to the gantry where the cargo ship (with 8t88) is docked for refueling. Your job: Get down into the pipes.

37. Gun Dodge

That platform way across the room has eight robotic guns that pump turbolasers into any tres-passer atop the pipes; they open fire immediately, so it's a long run across the pipe under heavy fire. You could just launch rail charges or concussion rifle shots from a distance, but you'd kill the Ugnaughts posted under the guns. So turn right and cross over to the easternmost pipe. Get over as far to the right as you can without falling off; this cuts off the turret gun fire. Then sprint north across the pipe to the alcove at 38.

38. Secret Area

Wow! Grab the power boost stashed in this remote alcove. You now have 30 seconds of deadly double fire, so sprint directly to 39 and train some fury on the turret guns.

39. Guns and Ammo

Eight robotic guns spew energy blasts from this platform. After you take them out, hop into the back alcove and grab the bonanza—thermal detonators, health pack, bacta tank, and two shield recharges.

40. Secret Area

The exploding gun turrets probably blew out this wall section, revealing a secret area with power cells and another bacta tank. If not, slash it open with your lightsaber and feast on the goods.

41. Fuel Pipe Switches

Another moral choice: An Imperial officer attacks you here, but two Ugnaughts flank him. Watch your aim! Then throw the wall switches, moving left to right. This empties the fuel pipes so you can enter them below. (The yellow indicators flick off when the pipes are empty.) Proceed to the lift.

42. Turbolift to Pipes

Ride this lift down to the fuel-pipe level. Be ready with weaponry; a Trandoshan guard waits at the bottom. Grab the health pack in the first alcove on the left; then go to the first grate on the right.

43. Secret Area

Slash this heavily-scored wall grate on the west wall closest to the turbolift. Inside the niche sits a bacta tank. Go to the wall switch and flip it to open the pipe access door to your left.

44. Mission Objective: Fuel Pipe Access

Let the door open completely before you step into the huge pipe. Move up to the switch on the right (south) side of the door slot and turn that switch so the door closes to your left. (By the way, you're now inside the pipe you crossed back at 37.)

Move south. Don't walk or swim in the fuel! It causes damage. Instead, walk along the pipe's side walls. Open the next door, go through, and close it behind you. When you reach the door to the next pipe section, pause for a second and read the next step.

45. Remote Danger

Save your game here! A pair of remotes hover on the other side of this flow control door. Normally, taking out a remote is easy. Unfortunately, here its laser stingers can ignite the fuel, blowing everything to kingdom come. Here's the safest approach:

▼ Put away your lightsaber to avoid richochets.
▼ Open the door.
▼ Sprint past the remotes down the pipe to where it forks.
▼ Take the left fork. Continue sprinting to the next door.
▼ The remotes may or may not follow you. If they do, battle them as far from the fuel pool as possible.

The door back at 45 closes automatically. After you eliminate the remotes, turn to the door at 46 and get ready for another tough challenge.

46. Open and Shoot

Turn the switch to open the door. Just down the pipe, the hatch to a guard station slides open. Immediately fire a heavy weapon (concussion rifle or

rail detonator) into the station; alternatively, you can fire a blaster shot into the fuel below the station to ignite a firestorm. (Make sure you shoot from the other pipe.)

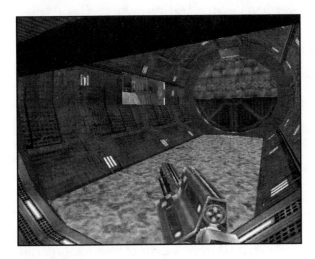

FIGURE 9-5. PIPE GUARD STATION. APPARENTLY, THOSE STORMTROOPERS DON'T CARE IF THEY IGNITE THE GALLONS OF FUEL UNDER THEIR NOSE. TAKE THEM OUT FAST, AND KEEP BACK FROM THE PIPE AHEAD IN CASE IT BLOWS.

47. Mop Up

Chances are at least one of the stormtroopers will survive your long-range assault. Move down the fuel pipe to the station; then pop up and finish off survivors.

48. Guard Station (Upper Level)

Explore the station to find the stormtrooper backpack and a bacta tank on this shelf. Walk around the corner to the turbolift.

Note

You can continue south down the fuel pipe if you wish, but it leads to a dead end.

49. Turbolift

Ride the turbolift down to the lower level of the station, where you receive a hearty stormtrooper welcome. Move with a vengeance through the main floor of this level. You won't find many power-ups on the floor level, but there's a nifty secret that level designer Reed Derleth revealed to me:

50. Healing Station!

A small tunnel (with checkerboard stripes) links the two main rooms. Step into it. Notice the slight blue glow? Now look at your health meter. It's rising! Yes, this is a miracle healing station. Stay here as long as you like. Come back as often as you like.

Return to the turbolift when the guard station is disinfected of Imperial scum.

51. Hop up

Push the call button, step aboard, turn right, and hop into the opening that appears about a third of the way up the shaft. Move down the low corridor and take the first right turn.

52. Health

Continue down the corridor to reach this health pack. Then turn and go to the other end of the corridor.

53. Shield Recharges

Before you reach the drop-off, turn right to score two shield recharges. Now you can go all the way back to the turbolift shaft or just return to the drop-off.

54. Clear a Path Down

Look down before you leap. A fuel canister blocks the passage below. Blast it and hop down. Go to the wall switch at 55.

55. Hatch Control

Pull this switch to open the protective hatch that seals off the room from the fuel pipe. Pull the switch left of the doorway to open the left (south) flow control door in the pipe. Now hop down and sprint through the open door.

56. Remote Danger

Why sprint? Because another pair of tiny remotes dogs your steps. Remember, one stray laser shot into fuel and you're flamed. So lure the remotes deeper down the pipe, away from the fuel. Turn and swat the annoying gadgets out of the air. Then continue down the pipe.

57. Another Remote

Yes, I we another remote. Lead it away from the fuel pools and slay it. Continue.

58. Bracing Swim

Nothing like a backstroke through engine fuel to put a little hair on your chest. You can't avoid a bit of damage here, so try to enjoy it, will you? Unless, of course, you have Force Jump ability. Then take a flying Jedi leap over the gas.

59. *Yaaaaaaaaghhh!*

You can't avoid the free fall here, Jedi or no. Think of it as an amusement park ride. Or don't. Your plummet drops you into another pipe, which forks vertically, with one opening above, one below.

60. Fork Up

Back up and take a running Force Jump into the upper opening here. Follow the pipe to the drop-off: See the alcove across the chasm? Back up and take a running leap to it.

61. High Stash

Interesting place for a supply depot. Grab the revive pack (for full health), bacta tank, and thermal detonators. Then plunge off the precipice into the cistern of fuel miles below. That's right—dive off the edge. Go for it. Show some Jedi trust in the Force.

Swim up and hop out of the fuel. You make another dizzying slide downward, ending up in a massive chamber with some sort of platform in its center.

62. Mission Objective: Out of the Pipes

Step onto the platform, wield your lightsaber, look down … and slash away. You cut through to another pipe leading down. What the hell. Take the plunge yet again. Guess what? Your long pipe nightmare is over. This time you slide out a spillway into a small area with stairs (and a Trandoshan) on either side. At the end of the spillway is a massive fuel reservoir.

Secret Area

63. Secret Area

Hop up to the small niche and gather the sequencer charges and shield recharge. Explore the area, battling Trandoshans and snagging health packs; then head down the narrow hallway to the south. Climb the stairs to the control room.

64. Control Room

Field stormtroopers with repeater guns camp above you on a raised platform around the corner. Ride the lift up to their level. Use the platform to make a running leap across to the three nutritious health packs on the high shelf across the room. (Or, much easier, you can Force Jump up from the floor.) Take the lift back up and continue down the corridor.

65. Firing Slot

Stop here and shoot the fuel canisters through the slot to wipe out some stormtroopers. (It's OK, Light Jedi, no Ugnaughts are nearby.) Move through the door just ahead. More troopers storm in from other rooms. Kill them.

66. Dark or Light?

If you shoot the canisters in this room, you can grab a bacta tank in the back corner—but you'll wipe out a pair of innocent Ugnaughts. Your Light Jedi task: Herd the little guys out of the room to safe positions. (Better yet, shoot at the ground near them. They tend to panic and run.) *Then* blast cans.

Move north into the next room, where Trandoshans make things difficult: They're up on a platform, firing rail charges down into your face.

67. Turbolift

This turbolift (like the one at 32) makes two stops above. Ride it to the Trandoshans' platform; after you step off, the lift rises to another level and stops. A health pack sits in a corner and a pair of shield recharges rest on a high shelf. Grab them, hop back down to the main floor, then press the call button at 67. This time, ride the lift up to its second stop.

68. Twin Turrets of Death

Stormtroopers and deadly sentry guns make this room a truly painful experience. Don't go blasting indiscriminately; a crew of Ugnaughts mans the gantry controls up the ramp.

69. Nonsecret Secret Area

Hop up to the crisscrossing struts and work your way to the west end of the webwork. Then make a rousing Force Jump up to this hidden raised platform. Help yourself to the armor vest and three energy cell packs.

70. Lift to Gantry Level

Take this long, long lift ride to the top of the fuel gantry. If you look south as you ride up, you see the cargo ship attached to the gantry. Prepare for a stormtrooper skirmish at the top.

71. Almost There

Boy, this is a big level, isn't it? Here, the air fairly buzzes with rail charges. Clear the area of field stormtroopers, grab the two shield recharges tucked in the struts and other assorted ammo items, and climb the stairs to the refueling pipes. The gantry has three sets of fuel pipes (stacked vertically) running out toward the cargo ship.

72. Remote Shield (Middle Pipe)

Hop over the middle pipe to this shield recharge on the other side. Yet another little remote hisses down the pipe to meet you.

73. Passage to Lower Pipe

Hop back over the middle pipe, drop down here to 73, and follow the passage. You end up atop the gantry's lower fuel pipe. Follow it south.

74. Bomb Bonus (Lower Pipe)

Hop off the pipe here to score some sequencer charges and thermal detonators on the walkway. Either Force Jump back onto the pipe or continue south down the walkway.

75. Hop Up

The walkway rises a step here. Use this raised section to get back atop the lower pipe. Return to 73, hop back up onto the middle pipe, and head south.

76. Corridor to Cargo Ship

Run south the entire length of the middle pipe; hop down here. Follow the dark corridor around the corner.

77. Mission Objective: All Aboard the Cargo Ship

Aha! That's the cargo ship taking fuel. But when you hop down onto the fuel connector pipe, the cargo ship disconnects. It's leaving! Quick, sprint to the ship and make a heroic leap onto the boarding ramp.

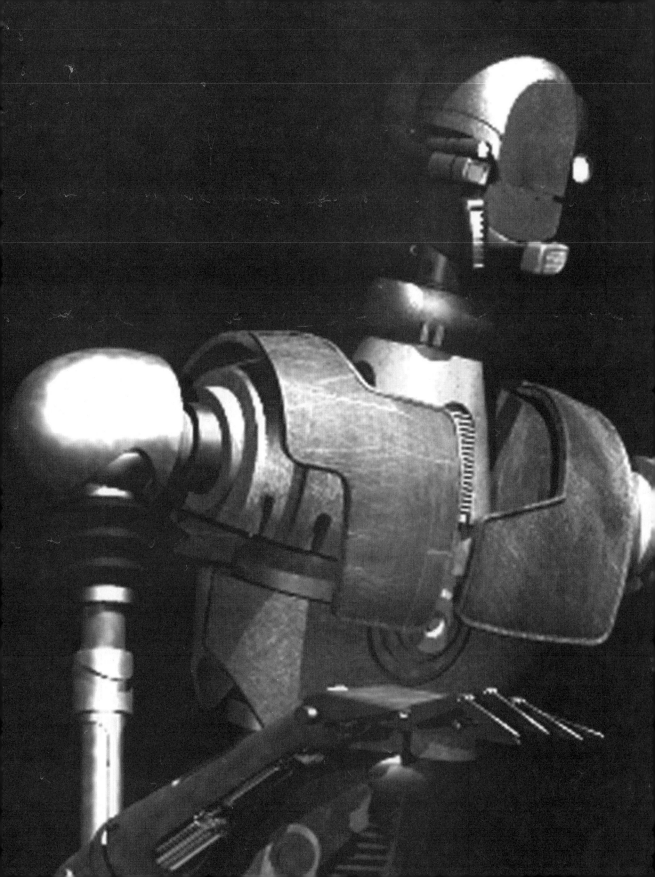

Mission 10

8t88's Reward

THAT LAST, DESPERATE LEAP FROM THE GANTRY PROPELLED YOU aboard the departing cargo ship. But now you have to get below deck, find the shuttle docking bay, and track down 8t88 once and for all. You know he can't get that map out of his head. You'll have to do it for him. With pleasure.

Mission Objectives & Secret Areas

Open the cargo doors and enter the cargo ship.
Find the main reactor duct, which leads to the reactor core.
Follow the reactor core vent to 8t88's shuttle.

Secret Areas: 6

Enemies

Stormtrooper
Field Stormtrooper
Imperial Officer
Probe Droid

Legend for Maps

1. START

2. SECRET AREA: SHIELD RECHARGES

3. CARGO DOOR SWITCH

4. SHOOT CIRCUIT (OPENS DOOR)

5. HOLD

6. DOOR

7. SENTRY GUN TURRET

8. SENTRY GUN TURRET (UNDER WALKWAY)

9. SHIELD RECHARGES

10. ELEVATOR CENTRAL

11. RED KEY (OPENS 12, 13, 16), SHIELD RECHARGE

12. RED KEY ROOM: RAIL CHARGES, THERMAL DETONATORS, SHIELD RECHARGE

13. RED KEY ROOM: PISTOL, POWER CELLS, HEALTH PACK

14. ELEVATORS

15. SECRET AREA: SHIELD RECHARGE, THERMAL DETONATORS, RAIL CHARGES

16. RED KEY ROOM: SEQUENCER CHARGES, STORMTROOPER BACKPACK, POWER CELLS

17. UPPER BALCONY (JUMP FROM CATWALK)

18. TURBOLIFT

19. THERMAL DETONATORS, SHIELD RECHARGE

20. DOOR

21. SWITCH FOR LOWER FORCE FIELD (AT 22)

22. TWO FORCE FIELDS (UPPER, LOWER)

23. BLUE KEY (OPENS 34)

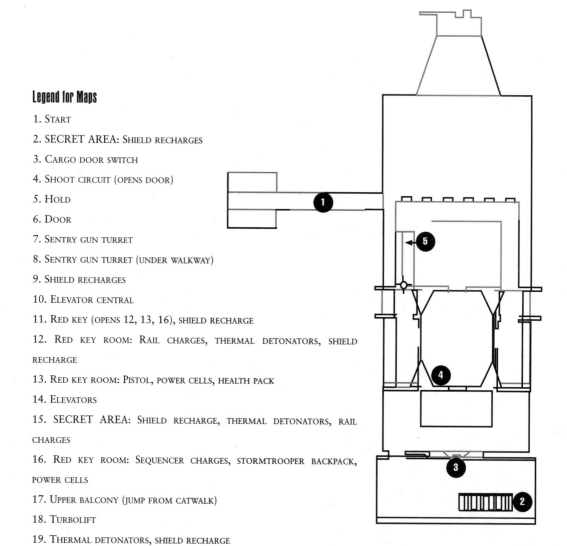

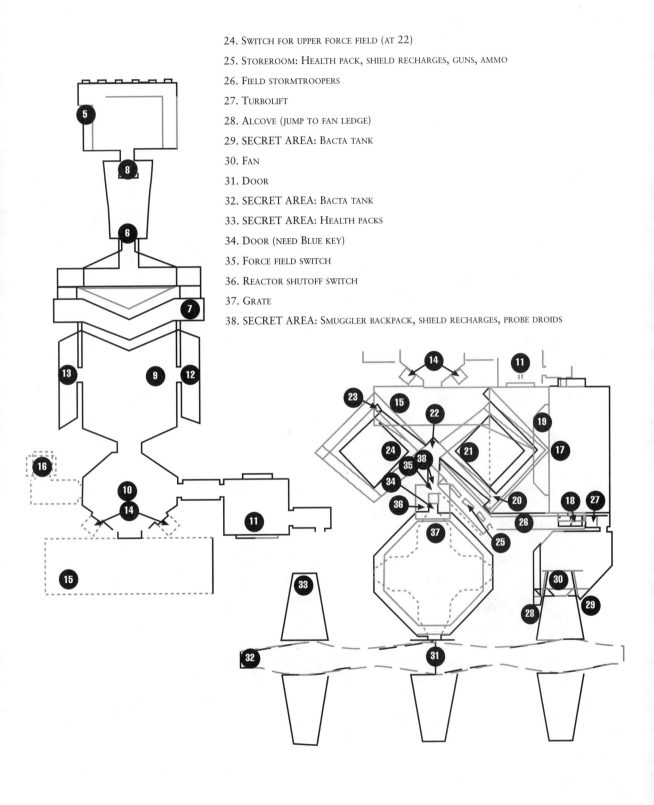

24. SWITCH FOR UPPER FORCE FIELD (AT 22)

25. STOREROOM: HEALTH PACK, SHIELD RECHARGES, GUNS, AMMO

26. FIELD STORMTROOPERS

27. TURBOLIFT

28. ALCOVE (JUMP TO FAN LEDGE)

29. SECRET AREA: BACTA TANK

30. FAN

31. DOOR

32. SECRET AREA: BACTA TANK

33. SECRET AREA: HEALTH PACKS

34. DOOR (NEED BLUE KEY)

35. FORCE FIELD SWITCH

36. REACTOR SHUTOFF SWITCH

37. GRATE

38. SECRET AREA: SMUGGLER BACKPACK, SHIELD RECHARGES, PROBE DROIDS

Walkthrough

You stand on a cargo loading ramp as the ship debarks. Move up the ramp to overlook the main cargo doors at the top of the massive, whale-shaped vessel. You can bet Jerec's ship is crawling with crack Imperial troops. Expect some mechanoid menace, too—probe droids, sentry gun turrets, and other forms of robotic evil.

1. Start

From here, blast the Imperials just below. Move forward and launch rail charges at the sentry gun turrets—left first, then right. Then fire your rail detonator at troopers by the far door. Switch to a weapon more suited for close-in fighting and go to the door.

2. Secret Area

Open the door and clear out the room. Then go behind the stairway and grab the shield recharges from the secret alcove. Climb the stairs to the control room.

3. Mission Objective: Cargo Door Switch (Upper Level)

Pull the switch on the control panel to open the exterior cargo doors that lead into the ship. Go back outside and hop down into the now-open cargo hold.

FIGURE 10-1. FIRST OBJECTIVE.
THERE, YOU OPENED THE
EXTERIOR DOORS. NOW HOP
INTO JEREC'S CARGO SHIP.

4. Circuit Breaker

Shoot this door circuit to open the west door in the
cargo hold. Enter the room and fight your way
past the pair of field stormtroopers to get the
stormtrooper backpack and battery. Continue
through the next pair of doors.

5. Lower Hold

From this ledge, pick off the pair of field stormtroopers
below. Hop down and proceed up the ramp on the far
side. Through the pair of doors you find bad guys and a
shield recharge. Return to this room and go through the
door in the back wall.

6. Red Room

Follow the walkway to the door on the far side of this room. Open it, kill the trooper, and move ahead to the edge of the upper deck. Use it as a sniper post to pick off stormtroopers below. Then hop down to the next deck—not all the way to the floor, yet—and go through the door to the left.

7. Sentry Guns

The moment you open this door a robotic sentry gun opens fire from the ceiling. Blast it and move to the next corner. Another sentry opens fire down the hall. Kill it and clean the area of Imperial troops.

8. Sentry Gun (Under Walkway)

Note

If you go down the ramp on either side of the walkway in the red room, a deadly sentry gun (see 8) hidden under the walkway blasts you at close range.

One more sentry gun hangs in the flashing red room, just below the walkway you crossed at 6. You can ignore it if you want. But it's kind of fun to demolish these robotic baddies. Retrace your route past 7 to the deck.

9. Box-Top Goods

From the second deck, hop across to the pair of shield recharges atop this box. Hop down to the floor and scoop up dropped weapons. Both side doors from this room are locked, so you must find the key. Exit through the

big double doors to the south, prepared for another robotic sentry gun and a squad of Imperial troops.

10. Central Room

Welcome to Elevator Central. A couple of turbolifts run down into the depths of the cargo ship from here. Peek over the striped precipice. Three probe droids rise to greet you; say "Hey" back with your weapon of choice.

We'll check out the elevators in a minute. But first, go through the side door to the east. A hallway leads to a control room.

11. Catwalk Access

This control room overlooks a vast central atrium crisscrossed by catwalks. Clear out the room, grab the shield recharge, and, more importantly, the red key on the shelf.

We'll check out the catwalks in a minute. First, let's return to 9 and open the two previously locked side rooms. Then we'll check out the elevators at 10.

12. Cache Number 1 (Need Red Key)

This room holds rail charges, thermal detonators, and a shield recharge. You need the red key from 11 to unlock this room.

13. Cache Number 2 (Need Red Key)

This room holds a pistol with energy cells, power cells, and a health pack. You need the red key from 11 to unlock this room.

14. Elevators to Docking Bay Observation Room

Return to Elevator Central (at 10) and take either of these elevators down. (They both lead to the same place.) At the bottom, slaughter a trio of Imperial officers; a sentry gun hangs in the open passage to the south, too. Look through the observation window to see 8t88's shuttle in the docking bay. Unfortunately, you can't reach it from here.

Secret Area

15. Secret Area

Two shield recharges sit atop boxes in the cargo hold; three more sit on the floor. Note how the box at 15 is tucked tight under the ledge. Jump on top of it to grab the shield recharge; you might need a Force Jump, but don't hurt yourself by smashing into the ledge. Then look up. See that dark niche? It's a secret area. Jump into it and grab thermal detonators and rail charges.

FIGURE 10-2. SECRET BOX. THE LEDGE ABOVE THAT FAR BOX IN THE CARGO HOLD MAKES IT HARD TO HOP UP FOR THE SHIELD RECHARGE. BUT IF YOU MAKE IT, YOU CAN JUMP INTO A SECRET NICHE IN THE LEDGE.

Use boxes or Force Jump to hop back into the docking bay observation room. Open the side door and blast the Imperial trio; then enter the next room.

16. Resupply Room (Need Red Key)

Stock up! You find sequencer charges, a stormtrooper backpack, and a pack of power cells. (You can't get in without the red key from 11.) Return to the observation room and ride either elevator back up to 10. Go to 11 and open the door to the catwalk area.

17. Jump Point

Cross to the middle of the upper catwalk and hop across to the upper balcony. At the left end of the balcony is a thermal detonator; a shield recharge sits at the other end. Hop back over to the catwalk and follow it to the end. Hop down to the middle catwalk, and then to the lower catwalk. Go to the south end of the lower catwalk.

Note

Pick off any stormtroopers you see below. Doing this should be second nature by now, but I'll mention it again. Life as a Jedi is so much easier if you take *every* opportunity to thin the enemy's ranks from a distance.

18. Turbolift

Ride the lift down. A couple of nasty troopers, including one with a Rail Detonator, patrol here. If you did your dirty work from above, however, the area may be deserted.

19. In the Red Zone

Grab the thermal detonators and shield recharge in this triangular, red-lit area. Then take the lift back up to the lower catwalk, go to the middle of the catwalk, and hop across to the lower balcony.

20. Door to Reactor Control Area

After you land on the balcony, turn left and go to this door. Pause and take a deep breath, save your game, and then burst through, blasting. Four field stormtroopers and an Imperial officer man the control consoles, and man, they really hate to be disturbed. Watch for more officers sniping at you from the ramps that run up around the room.

21. Force Field Button (Lower Field)

Push this button to deactivate a force field up one level of ramps, located at 22 on the map. (See 22 below for clarification.)

22. Force Fields (Two Levels)

This location on the map represents two force fields—one on the lower level and one on the upper level of the ramps. These fields block access to the other reactor control room, which contains an important item. Push the button at 21 to deactivate the lower force field.

23. Blue Key

Climb the ramp to the first landing. Then cross over into the other reactor control room, which, like the first one, is heavily guarded. After you clear the room, snatch that blue key from its niche in the corner.

> **Note**
>
> You see a green indicator light at the bottom of the button panel when the force field is active. Also note the obvious power-down and power-up sounds when you push the button.

24. Force Field Button (Upper Field)

In the same room, push the button in this corner to deactivate the force field on the upper level at 22. Climb the ramps around the room to the upper level, and approach the door there.

25. Stormtrooper Storeroom

Six vicious troopers of various stripes guard this well-stocked storeroom. Gun them down and grab a health pack, four shield recharges, and a bunch of guns and ammo. Then get ready to exit through the far (southeast) door.

26. Field Day

Two brutal field stormtroopers wielding Imperial repeater guns patrol this corridor. Blast past them and continue to the lift.

27. Turbolift to Reactor Fan

Step onto this lift and don't turn around. You end up facing an Imperial officer at the bottom. Fire as you step off the lift. Go through the door into the reactor fan room. A few stormtroopers and a probe droid welcome you. After you dispatch them, cross the room.

28. Jump to Fan Ledge

Climb up to the small alcove in this corner, on the west side of the fan. Then spot the narrow ledge on the side of the fan housing. (See figure 10-3.) Hop onto the ledge and carefully inch your way to the red glowing circuit. Shoot out the circuit and continue along the narrow ledge to the other side of the fan. Shoot the circuit on that side, as well. Shooting both circuits stops the fan so you can slip between the fan blades and enter the duct.

But wait! Before you enter the duct, continue along the end of the ledge.

FIGURE 10-3. THINK THIN. THAT LEDGE IS PRETTY NARROW, BUT NOTH-ING A JEDI CAN'T HANDLE. WALK IT TO A SECRET AREA. THEN DISABLE THE FAN BLADES BY SHOOTING CIRCUIT BOXES; HOP INSIDE THE FAN HOUSING FOR ANOTHER WINDY RIDE.

29. Secret Area

A refreshing bacta tank sits in this small niche. From here, inch back down the narrow ledge to the front of the fan.

30. Mission Objective: Fan Ride

Step through the unmoving fan blades into the reactor air duct. Even with the fan deactivated, the airflow sucks you down the duct. Go with the flow, but keep your gun ready.

31. Door to Reactor Core

Eventually, you end up in the gunsights of a pair of probe droids hovering near this door leading into the reactor core. Blast the droids and continue floating along in a westerly direction.

32. Secret Area

Somehow, a bacta tank got sucked into this end of the ductworks. Grab it and claw your way back up to the intersection.

33. Secret Area

And a pair of health packs ended up in this dead-end duct. From here, work your way back to the door at 31. Enter and hustle around the walkway to the door on the far side. Hurry, this room hurts.

34. Door to Main Reactor Control Room (need Blue key)

Enter and ride the turbolift up to the main control room. An Imperial contingent awaits your arrival. Disabuse them of certain notions of government; then grab the pair of health packs stashed behind the console.

35. Force Field Button

The button on this wall deactivates the force field blocking the doorway into this room. (Push it if you want, but if you're following this walkthrough, you don't need to leave the room at this point.)

36. Reactor Shutoff Switches

The switches on either side of the window overlooking the reactor core actually shut down the reactor for about 45 seconds. Pull one! Then hustle out to the reactor core. (Don't bother using the turbolift call button; just hop into the shaft to save time.)

37. From Core to Shuttle Bay

Hop down into the core and sprint north to the grate, pulling out your lightsaber as you go. Slash open the grate and run through. The vent behind the grate leads to a pair of intake valves next to the shuttle bay. But there's also a secret area; just beyond the grate, veer left into a small passage.

38. Secret Area

Jump up the step and slash the ceiling to access a big, odd room. As secret areas go, this one's dangerous. Although a smuggler backpack and two shield recharges offer some reward, three Imperial probe droids want to make you pay.

When you arrive in the shuttle bay, a trio of probe droids opens fire. Shoot them down; then cross the bay and push the green button on the far wall, next to the door.

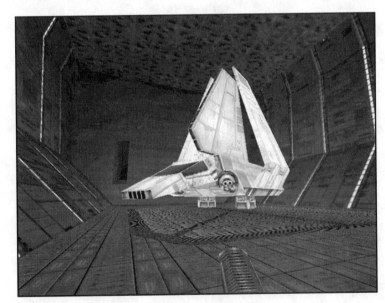

FIGURE 10-4. 8T88'S SHUTTLE. OH, *THERE* IT IS. AND AS KYLE SUGGESTS, 8T88 CAN'T BE FAR.

Mission 11

The Brothers of the Sith

Qu Rahn's assessment of Gorc and Pic: "It is a mystery why one would call Gorc and Pic twins. Even though one is a miniature version of the other, they look nothing alike. They also don't battle alike. Pic is the energy, and Gorc the power. They are the clashing balance of opposites, one the voice, the other the body. This combination is deadly."

Gorc Statistics

Health: 800
Resistance: 50% Impact, 50% Energy, 90% Fire
Special Instincts: Jump, Hit & Run
Force Powers: Grip

Pic Statistics

Health: 600
Resistance: 50% Impact, 50% Energy, 90% Fire
Special Instincts: Jump, Special Attack (jump attack), Circle & Strafe, Hit & Run
Force Powers: Persuasion

Combat Tips

By now you should have Force Seeing, which counters Pic's rabid use of Force Persuasion. ("You really need to use Seeing for Pic," says LucasArts tester Matthew Azeveda. "He's hard as hell without it.")

The lumbering Gorc, on the other hand, likes to immobilize you with Force Grip, allowing his spry brother to attack you with impunity.

Here are some fighting tips for your battle with Gorc and Pic, the Brothers of the Sith:

▼ Note the three bacta tanks on the balcony where you start.

▼ Focus on Gorc first. He's easier to defeat.

▼ Use your secondary fire button against Gorc. He's slow and easy to hit with this more powerful swing.

▼ Until one of the brothers falls, try to keep them separated. Whenever they team up, run. Don't let them get you cornered.

▼ If Gorc immobilizes you with his Force Grip, you must hurt him to break the spell. Pull out a blaster if you're too far away to whack him with your lightsaber.

▼ Again, use Force Seeing to offset Pic's ready use of Force Persuasion.

Mission 12

Escape with the Map

FEEL THE FORCE YET? YOU SHOULD. You've conquered three Dark Jedi and acquired numerous Force Powers. In fact, by now you should have added Force Seeing and Force Health to your considerable abilities. And you've finally gotten a head in this world—8D88's head, to be precise. Now it's time to head home.

Mission Objectives & Secret Areas

Find the main cargo hold and enter the control room.
Manipulate the key-activated catwalk system to work your way topside.
Return to the main deck to meet Jan and the *Crow*.

Secret Areas: 4

Enemies

Stormtrooper
Field Stormtrooper
Imperial Officer
Probe Droid
Sentry Droid

Legend for Maps

1. CARGO AREA
2. BALCONY (JUMP TO 3)
3. HEALTH PACKS
4. CONVEYOR BELT
5. CARGO BOX (JUMP TO 6)
6. BACTA TANKS
7. HEALTH PACKS, BACTA TANKS (FORCE JUMP ONLY)
8. SECRET AREA: THERMAL DETONATORS, SHIELD RECHARGES
9. FORCE FIELD SWITCH
10. TURBOLIFT
11. SECRET AREA: HEALTH PACK, BACTA TANKS, SHIELD RECHARGE
12. SECRET AREA: ENERGY CELLS, BACTA TANK
13. SECRET AREA: REPEATER GUN
14. TURBOLIFT
15. SHIELD RECHARGE, HEALTH PACK

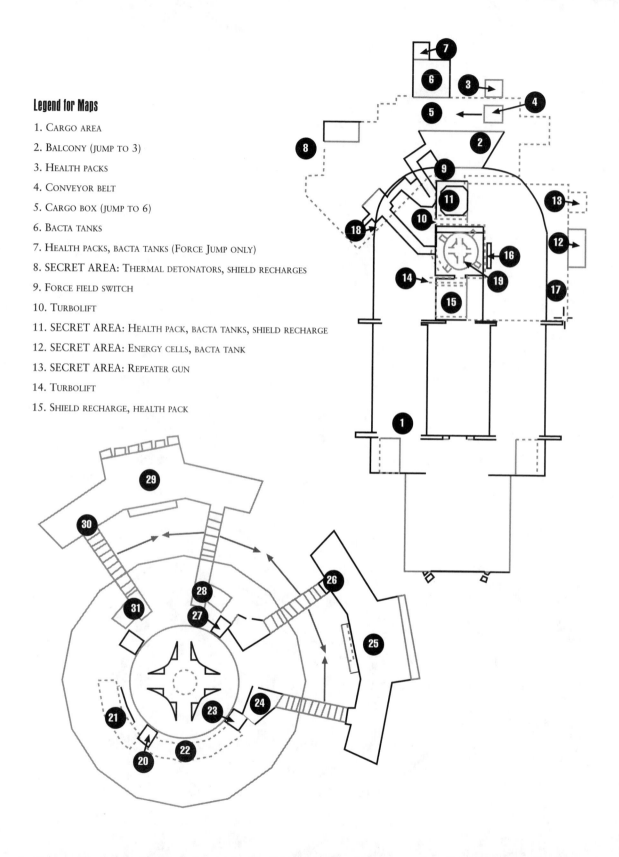

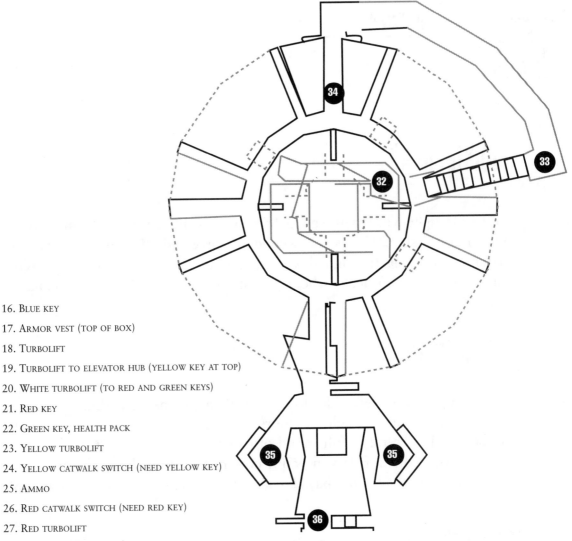

Walkthrough

You start right where you ended Mission 10—the shuttle docking bay of Jerec's cargo ship. Here's the second of three Jedi Knight missions that require navigating through this vast, labyrinthine vessel. Your goal: Get back up to the top deck (where you started Mission 10) via an exhaust venting port.

1. Cargo Corridor

Go through bay's west side door, then through the next door to face a probe droid. Fight through the doors, blasting stormtroopers and another probe droid—careful, a full squad of troopers is stationed at the curve of the **U**-shaped corridor. If you want, continue around the curve until you end up back in the shuttle bay. Then return to the big door at the curve of the corridor.

Note

You don't have to make the following jump. You can exit through the door at left, fight your way down the ramps to the lift at 18, ride down to the conveyor floor, and then Force Jump up to 5.

2. Scenic Overlook

Watch for probe droids here. This balcony overlooks a large cargo storage area with a heavy cargo conveyor belt moving boxes below. See those items in the box niches across the way?

3. Big Leap

Take a running jump from the balcony into this alcove. (Use Force Speed plus a regular jump, if necessary.) It hurts, but two health packs help make it all better. Go to the edge of the alcove and watch the boxes move past on the conveyor belt. See the big box (at 5 on the map) where the belt makes a 90-degree turn? That's your next destination.

FIGURE 12-1. NICHE OF PAIN. YES, IT'S A LONG JUMP. BUT YOU CAN DO IT. OR NOT. (YOU COULD ALSO JUST RIDE THE LIFT DOWN AT 18 AND FORCE JUMP UP INTO THE NICHE.)

4. Box Ride

Hop down onto one of the boxes moving down the conveyor belt and quickly turn right to face the box (see 5) at the curve in the belt just ahead.

5. Force Jump?

When the box you're riding reaches the turn in the conveyor belt, hop across to the big box. This is a tough leap. (If you have a strong enough Force Jump, you can skip the conveyor ride-'n'-jump and just hop up onto 5 from the floor.)

> ### Note
>
> If you don't have Force Jump available and just can't make the moving leap described in step 5, hop down to the floor, go back up to the balcony at 2 via the lift at 18 (see step 18 below) and make a regular running leap from 2 across to the ledge at 6.

6. Force Jump!

You need Force Jump for the next two steps. To hop onto the first box ledge, activate Force Jump, sprint forward to the ledge, and tap F just before you get there. A pair of bacta tanks is your Jedi reward.

7. Jedi Lords A-Leaping

There's yet another hidden alcove way up high. You won't reach this stash without using a sequencer to blast yourself up there—two health packs, two bacta tanks— unless you have four full stars of ability in your Force Jump. Even then, it's difficult. It's so high up, you'll need a shot of bacta after you drop back down! Then hop down to floor.

8. Secret Area

Maneuver around cargo boxes to this small alley. Thermal detonators and two shield recharges sit here. Grab them and come back around the boxes to the conveyor belt.

9. Force Field Button

Watch for dangling probe droids! They're everywhere. A force field bars you from riding the conveyor belt through the passage to the rest of the cargo storage area. Fortunately, the button here lets you deactivate it and follow the boxes. Careful, though—a sentry gun turret hangs from the ceiling inside the passage.

10. Turbolift

Head down the narrow corridor and ride this turbolift up to a small balcony nearly filled by a huge cargo box.

11. Secret Area

Walk halfway down the back side of the box. Look up. See that rust spot on the box, just above your head? Whack through it with your lightsaber; then jump in and marvel at the healthy goodies—a health pack, two bacta tanks, and a shield recharge. Exit and move around to the edge of the balcony.

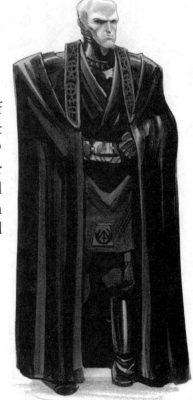

FIGURE 12-2. SECRET BOX STASH. GO BEHIND THE CARGO BOX AT 11 AND SLASH THE RUSTY SPOT JUST ABOVE YOUR HEAD. THEN HOP IN AND STUFF YOUR POCKETS.

12. Secret Area

Start hopping across boxes. It's kind of dark, so be very careful. (We recommend you save your game after each successful jump.) From the ledge, hop east, east, east, south, then east down to this ledge at 12 to get two energy cell packs and a bacta tank. Now Force Jump back up to the last box.

Note

If you can't Force Jump, drop down to the floor, take the lift at 10 to the ledge, and hop back east across the boxes.

13. Secret Area

Jump one box north and hop down into the alcove to the east. Some careless Imperial automaton dropped a lovely repeater gun full of power cells. Hop onto a moving box and ride it to the other lift at 14.

14. Turbolift

Take this lift up to another small balcony dominated by a huge cargo box. Something good's on top of it.

15. Hidden Stash

First, find the shield recharge at the far corner of the balcony. Then Force Jump to the top of the cargo box to find a health pack cleverly tucked away. (If you can't Force Jump, you're out of luck on this item.) Drop back down to the balcony. The door leads to a room we'll visit soon, but for now, hop to the first box to the east, turn left, and Force Jump to the catwalk edged with red lights.

16. Conveyor Control Room (Blue Key)

Two stormtroopers are reluctant to turn over their assigned post, so do some fast talking with your heat. And grab that blue key. You'll need it soon enough.

17. Armor Vest (Top of Box)

Before we leave this area, one more useful item remains. From the right (south) side of the catwalk, take a running leap onto the tall box to the east. Just ahead, on the next box, is an armor vest.

Go back to the catwalk and jump to the box just south. From there, hop back over to the balcony at 15 and open the door to the room at 19. (Skip the next step; it's for reference only in this walkthrough.)

18. Turbolift

This lift leads to a small, guarded balcony. If you must go back up to the big balcony at 2, head straight across the balcony through the set of doors

> **Note**
>
> If you can't Force Jump, go back to the lift at 11. From the balcony there, hop across boxes going east, east, south, then west. From that last box, you can make a regular running jump across to the catwalk.

and fight your way up the ramp. Otherwise, turn right and head down the corridor leading southeast. It leads to the room at 19.

19. Lift to Key Elevator Hub (Yellow Key)

Clear the room, grab the shield recharges hidden behind the box, and step onto the lift in the center. Ride up to a central elevator hub guarded by an Imperial officer and a field stormtrooper. The dying officer drops a yellow key. Scoop it up.

Look around the hub. Four turbolifts run from here. Each lift's doorway is lit—one red, one yellow, two white.

FIGURE 12-3. HUB ROOM. BOY, THAT'S A LOT OF ELEVATORS. WHERE DO THEY ALL GO? TRY THE LEFT WHITE ELEVATOR FIRST. YOU MUST ACQUIRE KEYS OF RED AND GREEN TO GO WITH THE TWO KEYS (BLUE AND YELLOW) YOU ALREADY FOUND AT 16 AND 19.

20. White Turbolift (To Red and Green Keys)

Hop aboard the left white turbolift. It makes two stops on the way up.

21. Red Key

Hop off at the first stop to grab the red key. Press the call button to bring the lift back. Step aboard and ride up to the next stop.

22. Green Key

Hop off at the white lift's highest stop to grab the green key. You also find a mini-medical center—one health pack. Continue down the short corridor to the shaft.

23. Yellow Turbolift

This is the yellow lift's shaft. Press the call button and ride the lift down to its first stop.

24. Yellow Catwalk (Need Yellow Key)

Flip the yellow wall switch. (You need the yellow key; see 19.) A catwalk slides into place on the other side of the door. Open the door and hurry across; this is the glowing exhaust venting port. Sentry droids patrol this godforsaken space, because humans (like you) take slow, painful damage here. And Imperial troops open fire through a window across the port.

25. Guard Room Number 1

Gun down the Imperial officer and two stormtroopers stationed here. Then add insult to injury by taking their big ammo stash.

26. Red Catwalk (Need Red Key)

Flip the red wall switch. (You need the red key; see 21.) The catwalk slides into place on the other side of the door. Open the door and hurry across the catwalk.

Caution

There is only one cat-walk for all four color-coded doors on this level! Each time you flip a colored switch, the catwalk slides around the venting port to that door. Thus, if you go back across to previously traversed doorways, don't forget to push the switch again to bring the catwalk to that door.

27. Red Turbolift

Here's where you catch the red lift. Step aboard and ride it up to the next stop.

28. Blue Catwalk (Need Blue Key)

Hop off the red lift and flip the blue wall switch. (You need the blue key; see 16.) The catwalk slides into place on the other side of the door. Open the door and hurry across the catwalk.

29. Guard Room Number 2

Three stormtroopers and an officer await you here. Drop them and rifle through their shelves—one health pack, one bacta tank, two shield recharges. Continue down the hall.

30. Green Catwalk (Need Green Key)

Flip the green wall switch. (You need the green key; see 22.) The catwalk slides into place on the other side of the door. Open the door and hurry across the catwalk.

31. Mission Objective: Catwalks Traversed

Congratulations, you've cleared the catwalks. Now you must reach the top of the venting port. Step into the turbolift and ride up to the next level. Climb the ramp to the red glowing room at the top.

32. Red Room

Enter the red room, turn right, and walk over the center ridge to the exit (marked '32' on the map) on the opposite side. Follow the ramp down to another catwalk across the venting port.

33. Ramp to Top of Port

Take this ramp up to the door. Open the door and gun down the stormtrooper waiting for you.

34. Lighted Path

Climb this red-lit strut to the top of the venting port. Follow the circular walkway around the port; watch for stormtroopers on the way. Approach the door on the opposite side.

35. Topside Store

You're very close to escape now. But some troopers and an Imperial officer just can't let go. Help them. Then take their health goods in each side storage area. Nail the last two field stormtroopers who stand below on the lift. Then hop down and emerge through the door into the light.

36. Meet the *Crow*

All you have to do is walk forward. There's Jan and the *Crow*.

Mission 13

The Lost Planet of the Jedi

JEREC HAS HIS HOOKS IN THIS PLACE, ALL RIGHT. Massive fortifications, including powerful magnetic shields, block passage to the base of the sacred valley. Not to mention all the crack Imperial infantry, assassin droids, and thundering AT-ST walkers. Thank goodness you're a Jedi Knight. Otherwise you might consider wimping out. Meanwhile, unmitigated evil would grip the galaxy and shatter star systems.

Mission Objectives & Secret Areas

Locate the first bunker that guards the magnetic field.
Find and destroy all the circuits powering the first magnetic shield.
Sneak past the second magnetic shield and find the main cargo lift to the base of the valley tower.

Secret Areas: 7

Enemies

Stormtrooper
Field Stormtrooper
Imperial Officer
Imperial Commando
Mailoc
Drugon
Probe Droid

Legend for Maps

1. START

2. HEALTH PACK, BACTA TANK

3. RAMP

4. THERMAL DETONATORS, ENERGY CELLS

5. SECRET AREA: HEALTH PACK, BACTA TANK, CONCUSSION RIFLE

6. UNDERWATER PASSAGE

7. HEALTH PACKS, POWER CELLS

8. POWER CELLS, HEALTH PACK

9. MAGNETIC SHIELD CIRCUIT

10. STORMTROOPERS

11. SHIELD RECHARGES, RAIL CHARGES

12. MAGNETIC SHIELD CIRCUIT

13. SECRET AREA: ENERGY CELLS, HEALTH PACK

14. WILD FIGHT!

15. MANY POWER-UP ITEMS

16. WALL GRATE

17. ARMOR VEST, OTHER ITEMS

18. SECRET AREA: ARMOR VEST

19. TURBOLIFT

20. MAGNETIC SHIELD CIRCUIT

21. MAGNETIC SHIELD CIRCUIT

22. MAGNETIC SHIELD (SLASH CIRCUITS AT 9, 12, 20, 21)

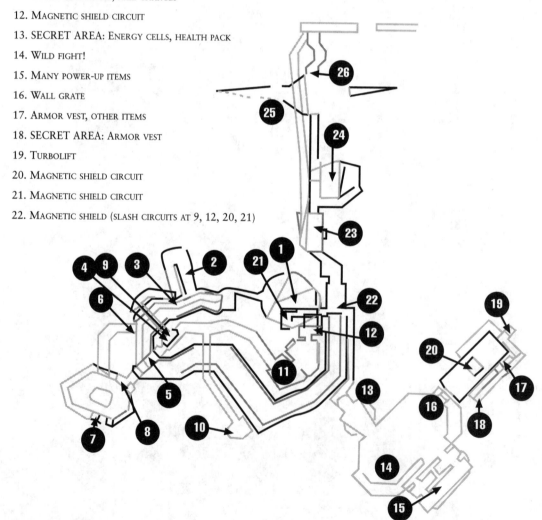

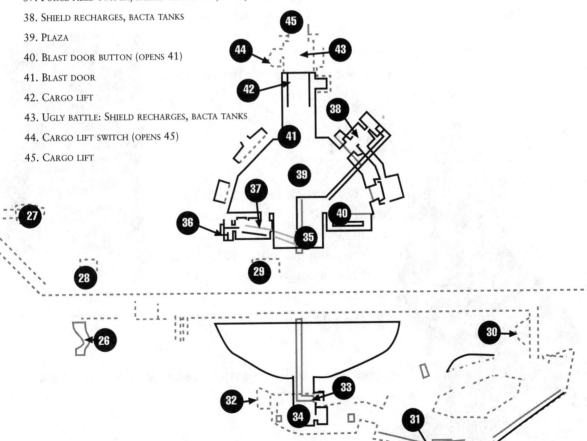

Walkthrough

Intricate canyons and waterways spread out before you. Jerec's men have erected force fields and cut impregnable command posts out of rock walls. On the Force power front, you may have applied your earned ability stars to Force Pull (light side) or Force Throw (dark side) after completing Mission 12.

1. Start

Follow the rocky path until it splits; then take the right fork. Continue to the first passage and enter.

Note

Watch for sniper attacks high and low throughout this entire canyon area. Mailocs flit through the passes and Drugons prowl the waterways, as well.

2. Good Start

Follow the rock ramp down to the health pack and bacta tank. The ramp leads farther down to a water passage, but return to the path. Continue to the next alcove on the right.

3. Ramp Up

Turn right here and climb up the steep ramp to the rock bridge and head across.

4. Conduit Station

Ammo! Some thermal detonators and energy cells make this dead end a worthwhile stop. Grab them and go back down to the path at 3. Look downstream at the river. See that rock arch over the water, just past the narrow triangular crevice in the wall? (See figure 13-1.) Dive into the water and swim under the arch.

FIGURE 13-1. GAP MARKER.
JUMP IN THE RIVER AND HEAD STRAIGHT FOR THE ARCH OVER THE RIVER, JUST DOWNSTREAM FROM THE TRIANGULAR CRACK IN THE ROCK WALL. WHEN YOU GET THERE, HOP UP INTO THE SECRET LEDGE BENEATH.

5. Secret Area

Under the arch, look up. A secret ledge! It's quite hard to jump up into it without using Force Jump. Hey, it's hard with Force Jump. But you'll make it eventually, acquiring a health pack, bacta tank, and concussion rifle full of power cells.

6. Against the Current

Swim upstream to the triangular crevice—it's on your left, now—and enter it. Then dive down and follow the underwater passage to the pool.

Note

Two stormtroopers guard the pool at 7. If you have enough air, shoot them from underwater. They can't see you, so they won't fire back! What idiots!

7. Canyon Goods

After you dispatch the stormtroopers, raid their store of health packs and power cells. Dive straight down to the bottom of the pool for a shield recharge. Then resurface and climb the winding path to the top. Watch out for the two sequencer charges planted on the path!

8. Tough Jump

At the top of the winding path, hop to this jutting ledge for some power cells and a health pack pick-me-up. Proceed over the rock bridge.

9. Mag Shield Circuit Number 1

Enter the power conduit station and slash the circuit with your lightsaber. One objective of this mission is to slash four of these circuits to deactivate the magnetic shield at 22. One down; three to go. Continue down the path to the next passage on the right.

FIGURE 13-2. CIRCUIT SWORDSMANSHIP. SLASH ALL FOUR OF THESE CIRCUITS IN THE POWER CONDUIT STATIONS AROUND THE CANYON TO CUT POWER TO THE MAGNETIC SHIELD AT 22. TRACK YOUR PROGRESS ON THE POWER METER NEXT TO EACH CIRCUIT.

10. Combat Interlude

Fight down the passage to eliminate three field stormtroopers, potential snipers later. Then return to the main path, turn right, and continue.

11. Guard House

Three field stormtroopers are so very unhappy to see you. Dispose of them and grab the pair of shield recharges behind the boxes. Push the button to open the door. Another trooper. End his military career and raid his room of rail charges. Hurry into the back room.

12. Mag Shield Circuit Number 2

Slash a trooper and another circuit in the power conduit room. The power meter on the wall (next to the circuit) says two down, two to go. And three bacta tanks in the cupboard say yes, you're feeling much better, thank you.

13. Secret Area

I really hate those sentry gun turrets. But you can't avoid them. This one guards a secret stash in a niche behind it. Blast it and grab the goods—four energy cell units and a health pack.

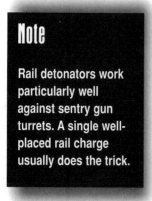

Note

Rail detonators work particularly well against sentry gun turrets. A single well-placed rail charge usually does the trick.

14. Killing Zone!

A large squad of field stormtroopers, including several nasty rail gunners, congregate in this rock plaza. Another sentry gun turret hits from a high arch behind you. This is a tough fight. Lob thermals and fight fire with fire; zing rail charges into Imperial ranks. Good luck.

15. Power Up!

Your reward for surviving 14 is this big room full of items. Exit and climb the ramp to the second level. Two upper rooms contain more stuff and a couple more troopers.

16. Grate Entry

Slash open this grate, shoot up the stormtrooper squad inside, and hop to the catwalk below. Follow the catwalk; turn right just before the lift and enter the lower control room.

17. Shelf Life

This shelf holds some beautiful items, including a much-needed armor vest. From here, blow up the fuel canisters ahead. Then proceed to the end of the room.

18. Secret Area

The canister explosion ripped apart a floor grate here, revealing another armor vest below. (Because you just grabbed a vest at 17, leave this one for later use.) Don't swim in the water! It's reactor coolant and, boy, does it hurt—bad. Hop back up and exit the control room.

19. Turbolift

Take this lift up to the second level. If you're playing Hard mode, do a few deep knee-bends. Loosen up, man. You've got a big jump ahead of you.

20. Mag Shield Circuit Number 3

See that circuit on the center podium? In Easy and Medium mode, you get a ramp to the circuit. In Hard mode, you must execute the infamous leap-and-slash technique, falling with a thud to the catwalk with each try. May the Force be with you.

Oh, speaking of that—it's probably much easier to Force Jump up from the catwalk below. That's our opinion, anyway. Once the circuit is cut, go down the catwalk to the door. Open it by pressing the button. Go back to the metal bridge and turn right, following the path down.

21. Mag Shield Circuit Number 4

Two field stormtroopers guard this final power conduit shack. Up ahead is an unsettling sight—mailocs! They want you bad, but something's holding them back. It's a magnetic shield (at 22), the one to which you've been cutting power with such diligence. Regrets? No way. Go in and slash that last circuit.

Note

Before you slash the last circuit, bringing down the magnetic shield (and unleashing the mailocs), use the Z key to place a row of sequencer charges along the shield. When the shield comes down, the mines might take out a mailoc or two.

FIGURE 13-3. ENTOMOPHOBIA. DO
YOUR BUG NIGHTMARES LOOK LIKE
THIS? MINE DO—NOW, ANYWAY.
SLASH THAT LAST CIRCUIT TO BRING
DOWN THE MAGNETIC SHIELD AND
FACE YOUR FEARS.

22. Magnetic Shield

This magnetic shield blocks access to the canyon beyond. Deactivate it by slashing the circuits at 9, 12, 20, and 21 (which you've already done in this walkthrough). Then proceed to the pool, goring mailocs as you go.

23. Pool

Dive into the pool of water, swim down and left into the trench, turn, and score the underwater items under the rock ledge—power cells, energy cells, health pack. Get another lungful of air and come back; then swim down the trench into the grotto on the right.

24. Grotto

Swim up the grotto and hop out. Follow the path up and around to the dropoff overlooking a seemingly bottomless pit with two mailocs far below. From there, hop across to the steep slope below 25.

25. Secret Area

Run up the steep, slippery slope to the niche in the rocks. (Force Speed helps here.) Grab two bacta tanks, two power cell packs, and a shield recharge. Go back down the slope.

26. Continue On

Save your game. Then hop to this ledge and continue north to the river. Jump in the water and swim upstream. (The current is swift, so Force Speed helps.)

Warning

If you slide too far downstream, you rouse sleeping drugons from their river nests.

27. Secret Area

After you round the bend and see the waterfall ahead, dive down and swim into the underwater passage on the right. You emerge in a hidden water cave packed with power-ups—three health packs, three shield recharges, three energy cell units, and a concussion rifle.

Swim back out and ride downstream.

28, 29. Drugon Nests

Watch out for drugons! Several underwater nests line the river bank. Ride the length of the river until you reach the tributary that branches to the right.

30. River Niche

A stormtrooper guards this small niche in the tunnel full of useful items—armor vest, power and energy cells, and two bacta tanks. Continue south into the pool, where much menace lurks. Wage war with four probe droids, two drugons, and a mailoc. And if that's not bad enough, a pair of sentry gun turrets opens fire when you cross the pool. Wow. How can you survive all this? Check the next step.

31. Secret Area

Make a beeline to the high alcove in the rocks here. A mighty Force Jump can hurl you out of the water into the alcove. There, you find a super shield, giving you 30 seconds of invincibility—enough to clear the pool area.

Swim over to the foot of the path and climb it to the top of the canyon, where another turret gun opens fire.

32. Bunker

Fight your way through troopers into the heart of this bunker. (If you have Force Throw, a dark side power, some nice movable rocks lie scattered through the bunker.) At the far west end you find a cache of arms, including rail charges, energy cells, and three bacta tanks.

33. Elevator (Tunnel)

Take this elevator down. In Easy mode, the elevator goes back up. In Medium and Hard modes, it stays down. Why is this important? You'll see in the next step. First, swing around into the next room, drop the stormtroopers, and grab the three shield recharges.

34. Secret Area

Next, use the single crate to hop onto the two stacked crates. A little niche holds three more bacta tanks, energy cells, and a repeater gun. Now go back into the elevator at 33.

You must get to something under the elevator. So push the button and hop off as the lift rises. Step into the shaft and use the lightsaber to slash open the floor grate to enter a secret tunnel. Drop down, hop up a step to another grate, and slash that open, too. Follow the tunnel across the pipe to the far side.

35. Either Way

At this fork, you can go either way. For this walkthrough, We flipped a coin and went left. Continue to the tunnel's end.

36. Hack 'n' Slash

Use the lightsaber on the grate above your head. Hop up into a room with lots of health items and a number of unhealthy ones, too—fuel canisters and stormtroopers, for example.

37. Force Field Control

The next room is even more impressive. An immense store of military items includes three shield recharges and a rail detonator with three units of rail charges. (These are most useful if you feel like taking out that big AT-ST walker you've heard stomping around the last several minutes.) The wall switch here turns off the big force field outside.

38. More Stuff

This side has a lot of power-up items, too. You can find three shield recharges and four—count 'em, four—bacta tanks in the connecting hallway.

39. Central Plaza

This area is a killer, surrounded by gun turrets and an endless stream of stormtroopers. Combat nuts might want to hang around to fight and fight and fight, but we recommend you make a straight line to 40.

40. Blast Door Button

Push this button to open the blast door at 41.

41. Blast Door

Push the button at 40 to open this huge blast door. Important: Shut it by pushing the button on the other side. If you wait for it to close on its own, you'll stand there battling a stream of stormtroopers.

42. Cargo Lift

Enter the small lift control room (staffed by a single stormtrooper) and push the button to bring down the cargo lift. Then step aboard the lift and push the button there to ride up into an Imperial maelstrom.

43. "Do Not Go Lightly..."

An elite guard consisting of Imperial commandos and Jerec's finest field stormtroopers patrol this final area. Survival chances are aided by some shield recharges and bacta tanks in the side room.

FIGURE 13-4. DID YOU
WANT TO SEE JEREC?
SORRY, HE'S NOT AVAIL-
ABLE. BUT THESE GUYS
WOULD LIKE TO HELP
YOU.

44. Lift Switch

Pull this switch to open the lift doors at 45.

45. Main Cargo Lift

Access this lift with the switch at 44. Then step
aboard and ride up to the base of the valley tower.
What's at the top? I'll give you a clue: It's dark.

Mission 14

Maw: The Revenge

Qu Rahn's assessment of Maw: "To the one called Maw— a bitter individual who loathes all and holds loyalty to few. A strong and formidable foe. For every cord of muscle, there is hatred. It is this hate that keeps his aging body strong."

Maw Statistics

Health: 900
Resistance: 50% Impact, 50% Energy, 90% Fire
Special Instincts: Jump, Open Doors, Circle Strafe, Special Attack (charge attack)
Force Powers: Throw, Grip

Combat Tips

By Mission 14 you've acquired the ability to develop all the neutral Force Powers—Speed, Jump, Pull, and Seeing—plus Healing and Persuasion on the light side, and Throwing and Grip on the dark side. Use whatever you have, frequently. Maw himself employs Force Grip and Force Throw. He also has a wicked spin move that looks pretty cool.

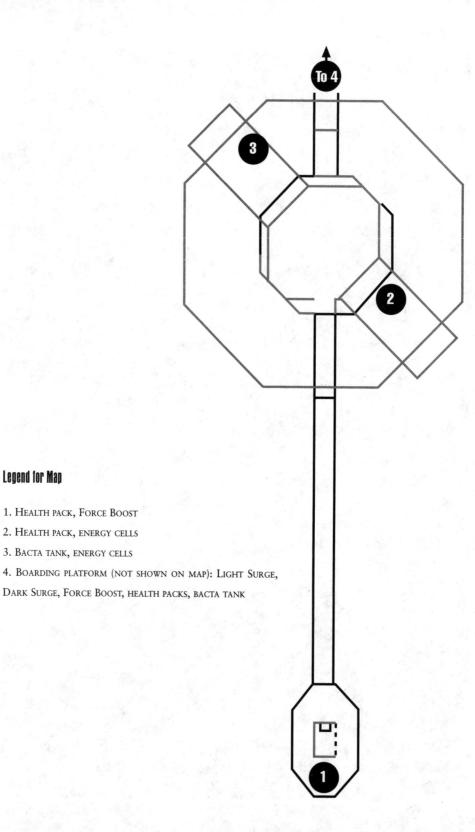

Legend for Map

1. HEALTH PACK, FORCE BOOST

2. HEALTH PACK, ENERGY CELLS

3. BACTA TANK, ENERGY CELLS

4. BOARDING PLATFORM (NOT SHOWN ON MAP): LIGHT SURGE,
DARK SURGE, FORCE BOOST, HEALTH PACKS, BACTA TANK

Know that Maw fights in three stages, beating a tactical retreat twice during your duel. If you engage Maw immediately on the elevator platform and hurt him badly enough, he rushes away to the central tower to wait for you. When you fight him in the tower and wound him again, he runs to the staging platform next to the cargo ship.

Here are some fighting tips for your battle with Maw:

▼ Keep an eye out for the many power-ups in this combat arena, particularly the Force Boost on the first elevator platform, and the Light and Dark Surges and another Force Boost on the staging platform by the cargo ship. (See 1 and 4 on the map.)

▼ **Important:** After Maw retreats the second time and runs to the boarding platform at 4, the north door out of the central tower will lock behind you if you chase him. Thus, you can't return to any of the power-ups (particularly the Force Boost at 1) once you pass through the door. Gather what goods you can before you give chase to the wounded Maw.

▼ If you have Force Throw ability, use the central tower. The small boxes there become deadly projectiles when you target Maw with Force Throw. (Remember, to slam a Force Throw target with flying debris, both the target and the debris must be in your view.)

▼ Stay away from Maw when he does his spin move. Wait until he finishes and then try a few quick thrusts.

▼ Use Force Persuasion if you have it! Maw won't be able to see you (because he doesn't have Force Seeing), so you can get in some excellent cheap shots against muscle boy.

Mission 15

The Falling Ship

JEREC'S CARGO SHIP IS FALLING, AND YOU'RE TRAPPED INSIDE. Your only avenue of escape is the landing bay, where the *Moldy Crow* hangs suspended. If you can reach the bay, lower the *Crow*, then raise a boarding ramp to it, you can fly out of this deathtrap. But you don't have much time.

Mission Objectives & Secret Areas

Race to the *Moldy Crow* in the landing bay before the cargo ship crashes.

Secret Areas: 1

Enemies

Probe Droids
(All other enemies won't attack)

Legend for Maps

A, B, C, D, E, F, G,: REFERENCE WAY POINTS IN WALKTHROUGH

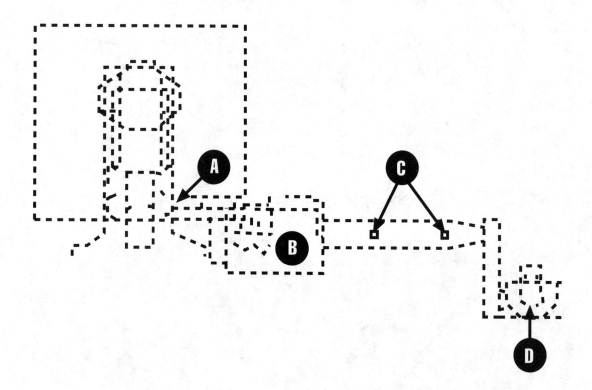

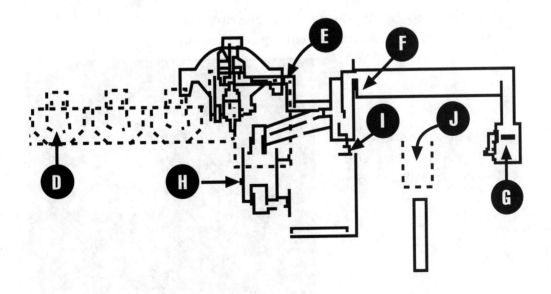

Walkthrough

Get ready to rock—literally. Warning lights flash, ceilings become walls, walls become floors. The cargo ship is falling, so most human enemies are panicked and won't shoot at you. Thus, you can ignore most Imperial soldiers. However, probe droids will attack. Be prepared to blast a few.

Four routes lead down to the landing bay area. The airshaft route is the "secret" path that earns you a star for finding a secret area. It's also the most direct route, so I highly recommend it. All four paths eventually converge in the final area near the landing bay.

Two things to watch for in all routes are the emergency braking thrusters and emergency direction indicators.

> ## Tip
>
> Generally, each route funnels you toward where you need to go, except in a few places I note in the walkthrough. So the best overall tactic is to "go with the flow." If you can't move in a certain direction, chances are good you *shouldn't* move in that direction.

EMERGENCY BRAKING THRUSTER BUTTONS GIVE YOU A 30-SECOND TIME BONUS.

EMERGENCY DIRECTION INDICATORS SHOW YOU WHICH WAY TO GO.

FIGURE 15-1. START POSITION. THE FOUR PATHS THROUGH THE CARGO SHIP ALL BEGIN HERE. FOR THE SECRET AIRSHAFT ROUTE, JUMP UP INTO THAT AIRSHAFT AT UPPER LEFT. FOR THE LOADING DECK ROUTE, HOP DOWN THAT STRIPED OPENING AT LOWER LEFT. FOR THE TWO ELEVATOR ROUTES, PROCEED STRAIGHT AHEAD THROUGH THE DOOR.

Route 1: The Secret Airshaft Path

As the mission begins, the ship's exterior hatch closes in front of you and Rahn tells you to seek the *Crow* in the landing bay. Turn around to face the door and take the following steps:

1. Run up the wall left of the door and hop into the air shaft opening. (See figure 15-1 and point A on the map.)

2. Slash open the grate with your lightsaber (although explosions may have done this for you already).

3. Go to end of the shaft, slash the grate on the right side, and jump through.

4. Slide down the air shaft into the fan room. (See point B on the map.)

5. Go through the pair of fans (at C), slashing the grates behind each to get through.

6. Continue down the air duct to the big open room. This is one of three connected rooms with big, round, red-lit exhaust ports.

7. Jump down any one of three round ports to end up in the large trench (at D). Again, all three ports empty into this same trench.

8. After you land, turn left and follow the trench through a light-rimmed passage into a room with side trenches.

9. In the right-hand trench you find a health pack and a bacta tank. But you're in a big hurry here, so unless you really need health, dive directly into the left trench.

10. Turn left and follow the side trench down another shaft. You end up in a room facing a big circle with cross-struts. (See figure 15-2.)

FIGURE 15-2. CROSSING GUARD. WHEN YOU REACH THIS ODD CROSS-SHAPED STRUCTURE, HOP UP INTO THE UPPER-LEFT QUADRANT TO FIND ANOTHER SHAFT.

11. Jump into the upper left alcove and follow the red-lit shaft (at E) to the end. You hop out into a room with two boxes.

12. Go down the ramp and through the lower door (at F), and then follow the corridor. Soon you see a mouse droid—and red emergency direction arrows pointing the way!

13. Enter the landing bay control room (at G).

14. First, push the emergency braking thruster switch on the left to add a 30-second time bonus.

15. Second, press the switch under the viewing port to lower the *Moldy Crow*. Through the window, you can see it dropping slowly in the bay.

16. Exit the control room and follow the passages to the big loading room (at H), where the red directional arrows split, or point in two different directions.

FIGURE 15-3. ARROWING EXPERIENCE. IT LOOKS CONFUSING, BUT IT'S NOT. FROM HERE, RIGHT LEADS TO THE LANDING BAY CONTROL ROOM, WHERE YOU LOWER THE *MOLDY CROW*. LEFT LEADS TO THE LANDING BAY ENTRY ITSELF, WHERE YOU RAISE THE RAMP AND BOARD THE *CROW*. THIS ROOM WITH THE "SPLIT-ARROWS" IS WHERE ALL FOUR PATHS CONVERGE, SO IT'S A MAJOR LANDMARK IN EACH PATH.

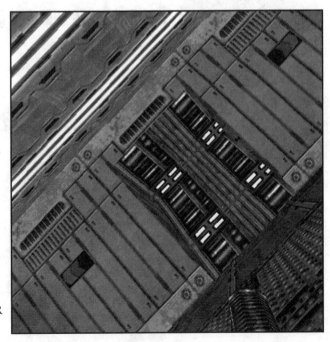

17. Continue past the "split-arrows" down the passage on the other side. Follow the red arrows to a ramp leading down a trench.

18. Go down the ramp. See the green direction arrows? You're almost home. Keep going to the next door (at I).

19. Go through the door. There's the *Crow*! But don't get crazy and make a run for it. First, press the switch at right to raise a ramp to the *Crow*.

20. Cross the ramp to the *Crow* (at J). Done!

None of the other three routes to the landing bay earns you a Jedi ability star. We go the extra mile. The following are brief descriptions of the other ways to reach the *Moldy Crow*.

Route 2: Cargo Loading Path

Face the door. Jump into the stripe-edged opening at left. Watch out for sliding boxes! Continue left through the opening; an unusually composed stormtrooper opens fire. Ignore him and hustle left, because a huge box sliding in behind you blows the guy to bits. (And you, too, if you don't get out of the way.)

Move east across the huge cargo area; all the boxes have slid to the right side. Watch for sequencer charges. One is planted just below the opening at the far east end; unfortunately, that's where you need to go. Hop through the

opening into a room lined with fuel canisters. In the next passage, turn right and sprint, because another box slides right behind you! You end up in a trench with green emergency direction arrows pointing the way west.

In the next room, watch for another sliding box. Let it go first; then follow and hop down on its right side into a passageway. Follow more green arrows. A probe droid attacks here. Kill it and continue past a loading crane. Stay far right; more arrows point ahead, so you're on the right track. Go to the end of the loading room and hop into the stripe-edged opening.

Follow the green arrows down the narrow passage to the right; continue through the door into another crane room. This is the big cargo loading room with the "split-arrows" shown at H on the map. To find them, go past the crane and hop down; then turn around. There they are! First, go right and follow passages to the landing bay control room at (G on the map) and lower the *Crow.* Then follow steps 16 through 20 in the foregoing secret airshaft route instructions.

Route 3: The ''Green'' Elevator Path (via the Bridge)

Go forward through two doors to the bank of six elevators. Hop into the second shaft on the left (one of four shafts marked by green arrows pointing down). At the bottom, step out of the shaft, turn left, and follow the green arrows to a room with

spilled fuel pooled in a trench. (Stay out of the fuel; it hurts.) Proceed to the door, push the button to open it, and go through.

Follow more green arrows to another pair of elevator shafts. Take the second one down; at the bottom, turn right and follow a long narrow passage around several turns until you end up in the massive, colorful bridge of the ship. Step onto the raised platform and push both braking thruster switches for a bonus minute of time. Then proceed to the pair of elevators (with green arrows pointing up) at the far end of the bridge.

Enter the right shaft, turn around, and hop onto the wall of the shaft above the doorway. Walk up the shaft! (Boy, it's fun.) Exit at the top, turn left, and follow the arrows to a ramp. Climb the ramp and move carefully through a room full of fuel canisters until you reach the big cargo loading room with the "split-arrows" shown at H on the map. To find them, go under the crane to the right. There they are!

At the split-arrows, go right and follow passages to the landing bay control room at (G on the map) and lower the *Crow*. Then follow steps 16 through 20 in the foregoing secret airshaft route instructions.

Route 4: The "Yellow" Elevator Path

Go forward through two doors to the bank of six elevators. Hop into the third shaft on the left (one of two shafts marked by yellow arrows pointing down). At the bottom, follow the white-lit passage. Skirt all the holding bins (square holes in the floor); yellow arrows point the way in the next passage. Ahead, three corridors lead east; all end up in the same room, but the middle opening harbors a probe droid.

Continue through the next corridor. It leads into the interior of the big fin of the cargo ship. Work your way down to the opening off the first "story" of the fin. This leads to a big cargo storage room full of boxes stacked to the right. Stay on the boxes! (If you walk along the floor, two big boxes overhead fall and crush your Jedi bones.) Work your way up to the narrow, red-lit shaft at the far eastern end of this room. When you emerge from that shaft, green arrows lead you to the left.

Follow the green arrows down the narrow passage; continue through the door into a crane room. This is the big cargo loading room with the "split-arrows" shown at H on the map. To find them, go past the crane, hop down, and then turn around. There they are! First, go right and follow passages to the landing bay control room at (G on the map) and lower the *Crow*. Then follow steps 16 through 20 in the foregoing secret airshaft route instructions.

Mission 16

Sariss (or Yun): Jedi Battleground

I F YOU'VE CHOSEN THE GOOD PATH—THE LIGHT SIDE—THEN YOU FACE THE DEADLY SARISS IN THIS MISSION. If you take a walk on the dark side, however, you face a rematch with Yun, who's disappointed in your Force choice.

QU RAHN'S ASSESSMENT OF SARISS: "OF ALL THE DARK JEDI I HAVE MET, SARISS IS THE ONE I CAN SAY I FEAR. POWERFUL AND STRONG IN BOTH THE PHYSICAL AND MENTAL ARENAS OF THE FORCE, SHE IS A MASTER, A PERFECTIONIST, QUIET AND RESERVED. THIS MAKES HER A VERY DANGEROUS FOE."

Sariss Statistics

Health: 1900
Resistance: 50% Impact, 50% Energy, 90% Fire
Special Instincts: Jump, Special Attack (jump attack), Circle Strafe
Force powers: Pull, Deadly Sight

Combat Tips

You want a challenge? You got it. Take a look at those Sariss stats—1900 health points! And her Force Pull ability means any weapon but your lightsaber flies out of your hands almost immediately. If even Qu Rahn fears her, maybe you'd better dredge up some healthy dread yourself.

Here are some fighting tips for your battle with Sariss:

▼ Keep a sharp eye out for health and other power-up items. You'll need them here.
▼ Forget using any weapon but your lightsaber. Her Force Pull ability is too advanced.
▼ Run down the rock ramp to the Light Surge in the cave, activate as many Force powers as you can (Persuasion and Blinding together, if you have them), and then go directly for Sariss, using your full double swing (secondary fire button) for big hits while the Force powers last.
▼ Don't run too far from Sariss! She'll train her Deadly Sight on you and you'll fry fast.
▼ But if you must run, sprint at Force Speed for the wreck of the cargo ship to cut off her line of sight. Inside, two health packs sit high on a platform (see 4 on the map), but it takes a considerable Force Jump to reach them.

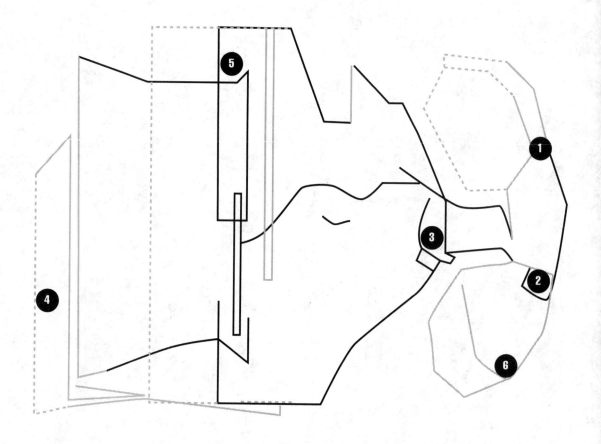

Legend for Map

1. HEALTH PACK

2. LIGHT SURGE

3. HEALTH PACK (IN WATER)

4. HEALTH PACKS

5. BACTA TANK

6. BACTA TANK, HEALTH PACK

Yun (Rematch) Statistics

Health: 1000
Resistance: 50% Impact, 50% Energy, 90% Fire
Special Instincts: Jump, Circle Strafe, Special Attack (jump attack)
Force powers: Blindness, Persuasion, Pull

Combat Tips

In this rematch, Yun is very tough and
Sariss-like. With 1000 hit points, a mean
jump attack, and three Force powers at
his disposal, he's grown considerably in
his abilities since last you met. He also
doesn't like your new attitude.

   One tip: When Yun performs a
Force Jump, don't be near him when
he lands!

Mission 17

The Valley Tower Ascent

YOUR STUNNING VICTORY OVER SARISS LEAVES ONLY BOC AND JEREC himself (and a few regiments of Imperial troops) in your way. But many physical obstacles remain between you and your goal of securing the legendary Jedi burial site. The valley perimeter is tightly sealed; you must solve many puzzles and fight many battles before you can face the final pair of Dark Jedi and save Jan.

Mission Objectives & Secret Areas

Activate the internal cargo conveying system to reach the outer perimeter of the valley.

Near the main exhaust port, find a vent leading into the mountain mining operations.

Suspend the airflow from the main exhaust port long enough to break into the exhaust monitoring station.

Find a way into the maintenance room high above the exhaust monitoring station. There, an elevator will take you to the main superstructure.

Secret Areas: 6

Enemies

Stormtrooper
Field Stormtrooper
Imperial Officer
Imperial Commando

Legend for Map

1. START
2. DOOR SWITCH (OPENS 3), SHIELD RECHARGE
3. OUTER DOOR
4. ELEVATOR
5. DOOR
6. RAMP DOWN TO WATCH POST (BATTERY, THERMAL DETONATORS)
7. RAMP UP TO FORCE FIELD SWITCH (TO 8)
8. ELEVATOR (TURN OFF FORCE FIELD AT 7)

9. HOLE (BATTERIES BELOW)
10. CONVEYOR SWITCH
11. SHIELD RECHARGE, GRATE
12. EMERGENCY ELEVATOR BUTTON (GRATE)
13. SHOOT SENTRY GUNS, HOP TO CATWALK
14. THERMAL DETONATORS, SEQUENCER CHARGES, RAIL CHARGES, BATTERY
15. SECRET AREA: BATTERY, PISTOL, STORMTROOPER BACKPACK
16. SIDE PASSAGE
17. SECRET AREA (TOP OF SHAFT): RAIL DETONATOR

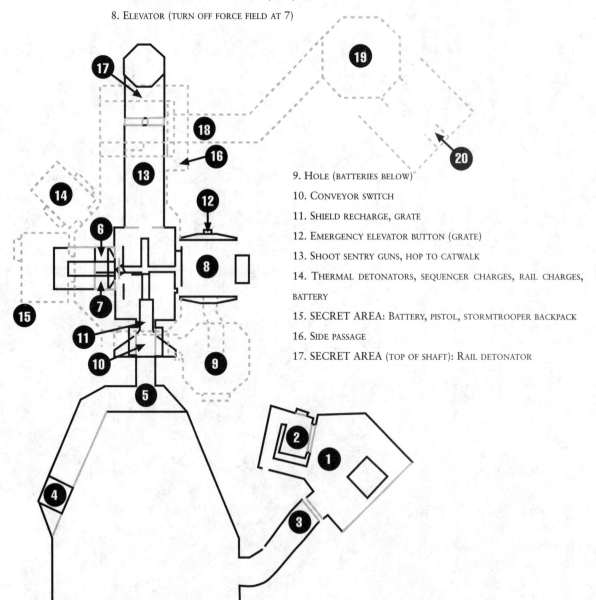

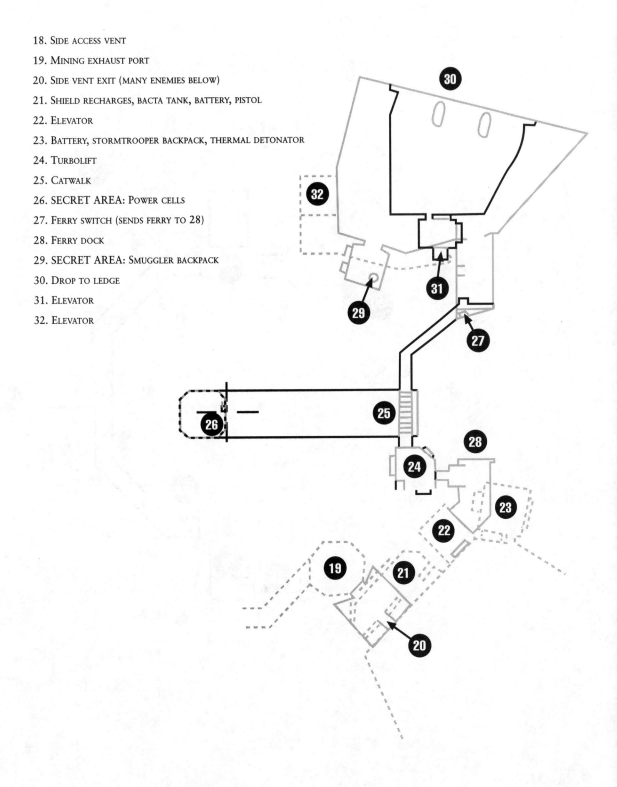

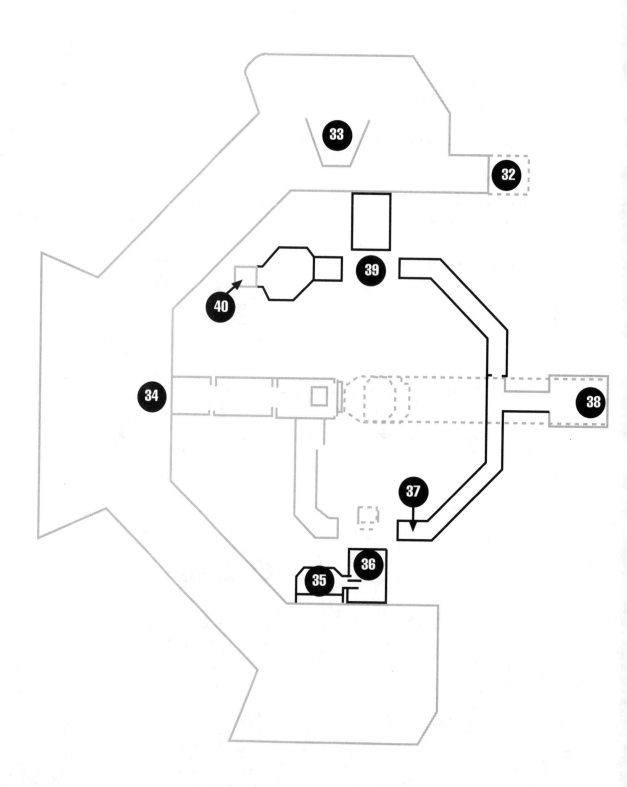

33. STORMTROOPER BUNKER, SENTRY GUN TURRETS

34. EXHAUST VENT, SENTRY GUN TURRETS

35. TURBOLIFT (THERMAL DETONATORS, BACTA TANK, BATTERY)

36. EXHAUST PORT (DOWN TO 37)

37. SIDE VENT (LIVE SEQUENCERS!)

38. BATTERY, HEALTH PACK

39. EXHAUST PORT (HEALTH, SHIELD ITEMS)

40. TURBOLIFT

41. VENT CONTROL BUTTON

42. VENT CONTROL BUTTON

43. ACCESS PORT (FLOOR HATCH)

44. CORE EXHAUST PORT BUTTON

45. ELEVATOR

46. ELEVATOR

47. MONITORING STATION

48. SHIELD RECHARGES, HEALTH PACK

49. CORE EXHAUST PORT BUTTON

50. CORE EXHAUST PORT (OPEN AT 44 AND 49)

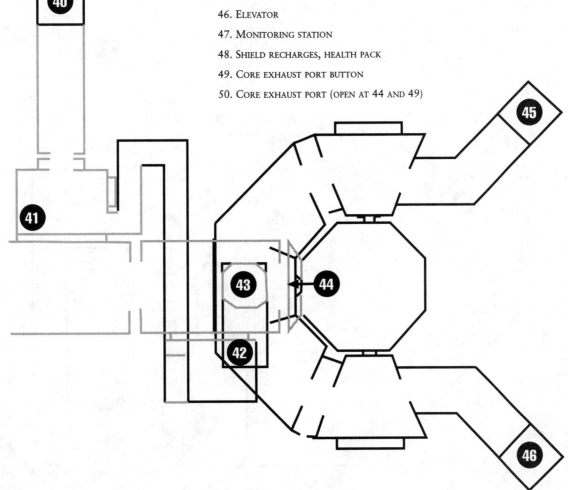

51. SECRET AREA (TOP OF PORT): ARMOR VEST

52. SECRET AREA (TOP OF PORT): BACTA TANK, SMUGGLER BACKPACK

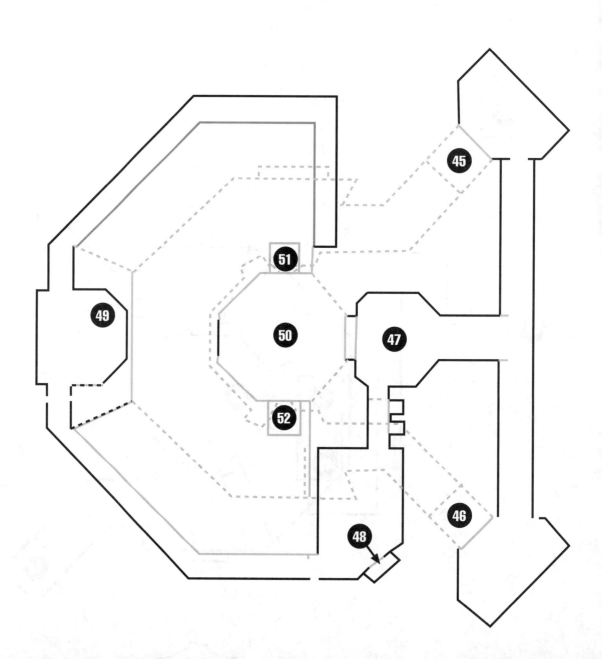

Walkthrough

Jerec's little cargo ship mishap—*oops!*—tore away the main cargo lift to the valley tower. The only way up now is via the internal cargo conveying system. And that only gets you to the outer perimeter of the valley. After that, you must find a way through the dangerous mining exhaust ports into the Imperial excavation area.

1. Start

Here's where Mission 17 begins. Head straight for that open doorway and up the ramp to the main entry control room.

2. Door Control

An officer and a stormtrooper keep watch over the main entry door button. End their watch and grab the shield recharge. Then push the button to open the door at 3 and sprint down. You have only a few seconds, so hurry!

3. Exterior Door

The button at 2 opens this outer door. Hustle through before it closes. A huge AT-AT walker looms around the corner. Don't worry, it's unmanned. But watch for a sniper above as you slalom between the walker's legs to the elevator.

4. Elevator

Push the call switch on the outside wall to bring down the elevator. Step aboard, push the "Up" switch inside, and ride up to the balcony.

5. Door

Two shelves just beyond this door hold power-up items. Grab what you can. The elevator on the right has a force-field barrier, so you can't get aboard yet. Instead, proceed to the second passage on the left. There, a ramp leads down.

6. Ramp to Watch Post

Go down the ramp. Two field stormtroopers keep watch over an empty shaft; looks like a pretty boring job. Eliminate them now for an easier time later at 11. Pick up a battery and thermal detonator belt and head back up the ramp. Return to the main entry and go up the ramp in the next passage.

7. Force Field Switch

A couple of Imperials guard the force field switch in a room at the top of the ramp. Battle to the switch and turn it off. Now you can use the elevator at 8.

8. Cargo Elevator

This big elevator moves cargo boxes. Ride it all the way down—that is, keep pushing the "Down" button at each stop. (It takes three stops to reach the bottom.) At bottom, you must get under the elevator, so hit the "Up" button and run east to the alcove. Hop down to the strut, walk to the strut intersection and go left to the hole.

9. Bomb Drop

Toss some detonators down the hole. Then hop down. You drop onto three batteries sitting atop the box. Exit through the only door.

10. Mission Objective: Activate Cargo Conveying System

This is the control area for the low-gravity cargo lift. It's pretty cool. Push the wall switch to activate the conveying system; crates begin to rise up. Hop onto a rising crate, and ride up to the platform at the top.

11. Grate Crasher

Grab the shield recharge and then slash through a pair of grates. Step onto the strut. (Remember the watch post back at 6? It's to your left. This is why you eliminated those guards.) Turn right at the strut intersection and walk to the elevator shaft.

12. Emergency Call Button

Hey, this is the same elevator you rode at 8. The elevator is far below, where you left it when you sent it up a stop and then jumped under it in step 8. Hop to the left ledge in the shaft, slash the small grate, and push the elevator call button to bring up the lift. Then ride up two stops to the conveyor area. (Boxes are moving down the belt now.)

13. Twin Turrets/Box Hop

Move to the striped center strip of conveyor, turn right, and take out the pair of sentry gun turrets. (Shoot through the force field.) Then hop atop a cargo box and use it to leap onto the catwalk that rims the area.

14. Rail Gunner

An annoying field stormtrooper with a rail gun stalks this first room on the catwalk. Inside, loot shelves lined with goods—thermal detonators, sequencer charges, rail charges, and a battery. Exit and go to the next room down the catwalk.

15. Secret Area

This room has some guys and a shield recharge. But wait, there's more. Move just out of the room and blow up the fuel canisters that block your path into a secret area with another battery, a pistol with energy cells, and a stormtrooper backpack.

16. Route Around

Hop off the catwalk and run to this small doorway on the other side of the conveyor belt. Follow the passage around and grab the shield recharge. Then step to the edge of the anti-gravity shaft (where the cargo boxes are rising) and look up.

FIGURE 17-1. WAY OUT. SAVE YOUR GAME, HOP ON A BOX, AND RIDE UP THE ANTIGRAVITY CARGO SHAFT TO THAT HEXAGONAL SIDE ACCESS VENT AT UPPER LEFT. (THERE'S ALSO A SECRET LEDGE IN THIS SHAFT.)

Refer to figure 17-1 here. See the hexagonal access vent on the left (east) side of the shaft? You'll go there in a minute. But first, find the ledge on the side opposite you, just slightly right and up from the side vent. There's another one like it on your (north) side of the shaft, directly above you. It's a secret area, and it's your next destination.

17. Secret Area

The antigravity shaft is pretty benign, but it's probably a good idea to save your game here, anyway. Hop onto a crate, turn around, and ride up to the ledge on the north side. You get a rail detonator full of rail charges. Now look down. The side access vent (at 18) is on the left (east) side, far below.

18. Side Access Vent

Easiest method to get here: From the ledge, just float down to the bottom of the shaft, hop onto another box, and ride up to this side access vent. Move down the vent and open the door.

19. Mining Exhaust Port

The vent leads to a mining exhaust port. You must ride a blast of exhaust up to an opening above. Save your game first! The antigravity ride was easy and gentle; this is not. You have less control, and if you miss the opening, the drop down can hurt. Note: There's a ledge about halfway up you can use as a waypoint. But it's possible to make it all the way to the opening in a single exhaust ride.

20. Exhausting Ride

When you reach the opening, step forward warily. Below, two big sentry gun turrets and a passel of troopers (including several rail gunners) wander a rock-ledge area. Toss down detonators, pick off the turrets, hop down to the long ledge, and good luck.

21. Armory

This is a tough firefight. If you survive, you earn a mess of power-ups in this room. Tip: Blast fuel canisters to take out some of the troopers. Then gather up the shield recharges, a bacta tank, battery, and pistol.

22. Elevator

Lean over the ledge and pick off any soldiers you see below. Then hit the elevator call button to bring up this lift. Ride it down with gun ready.

23. Elevator Control Room

The elevator call button for the lower level is in this room, should you need it. (In this walkthrough, you don't.) You also meet a couple of friendly Imperial officers who need a rest. Give it to them. In return, take their battery, backpack, and thermal detonator.

Now go back to the elevator at 22 and ride up past the first stop to the top. There, hijack the elevator guard. Look out across the open chasm. See

that black platform across the way? That's a ferry. You can ride it across the chasm. But first, you must bring it back over to this side.

Proceed through the door to your left.

FIGURE 17-2. FERRY CHASM. THAT BLACK PLATFORM ACROSS THE CHASM IS AN ANTIGRAVITY FERRY. FIND THE BUTTON THAT SENDS IT TO THIS SIDE AND THEN RIDE IT ACROSS. (AT LOWER LEFT IS THE MINING EXHAUST PORT YOU CROSS AT 25.)

24. More Melee

Four tough field stormtroopers congregate in this room. Waste them, call up the lift, and ride down to the room directly below, where four more guys block your passage. Don't go rushing out across the catwalk leading north until you read the next step!

25. Mining Exhaust Port

Stand at the edge of the catwalk and view the source of that rhythmic pounding you've heard since 21. See the white particles flying past? That's exhaust from the Imperial mining operations deep below. To get across the catwalk, wait for the exhaust particles to start to die down. Then sprint across the walkway. (Don't wait until the exhaust completely stops, or you may get caught.) Of course, Force Speed helps a lot.

Secret Area

26. Secret Area

Speaking of Force Speed, try this maneuver. Activate Force Speed and wait for the exhaust to fade. Step into the exhaust port, turn left, and sprint up into the dark, pulsing heart of the thing. Why? Because it's there! Also, it happens to be a secret area. You won't find much—just a couple of discarded weapons full of power cells. And getting back onto the catwalk without getting blown into the canyon beyond is very difficult—almost impossible, in fact, without using Force Jump. But remember, you earn Jedi ability stars by finding all secret areas in each mission. So it's worth it.

27. Ferry Switch

From the catwalk, across the exhaust port, move up the path to the switch. Note that the ferry platform is directly above you. Push the switch to send the ferry across the chasm. Now retrace your route back through 24 to the other side of the chasm.

28. Ferry

Step onto the ferry platform and push the button to ride the ferry across.

29. Secret Area

Fight across the open area to this storeroom, blast the fuel canisters, and get the smuggler backpack hidden in a secret floor hole. Some thermal detonators and a shield recharge sit on the shelves, too.

30. Jutting Ledge

Go to the edge of the cliff and drop to the ledge jutting out below to get to the lower level. Be ready—lots of bad guys wait below. Then cross the room to the elevator.

31. Elevator

Take this elevator to the top of the shaft; then climb up a rock ramp to another lift.

32. Elevator

Take this elevator up, too. You end up at the edge of a huge rock ledge that runs around the mining core.

33. Trooper Stream

This bunker produces endless pairs of stormtroopers. Best tactic: Quickly take out the sentry gun turrets—two on the ground and one overhead, hanging under the rock arch. Then gun down any troopers and run southwest.

34. Mission Objective: Exhaust Vent

Three more gun turrets guard this exhaust vent. It's your avenue into the mountain, but you can't enter yet because of the strong air thrust. Continue southeast along the wide ledge. Look for shield recharges atop cargo boxes.

35. Turbolift

Take this lift up to the next level. At the top, two troopers protect a stash of thermal detonators, a bacta tank, and a battery. Continue

through the doorway. A pair of shield recharges sit on a ledge to the right; it's a tricky jump, so be careful. Hop back to the balcony overlooking the main exhaust port.

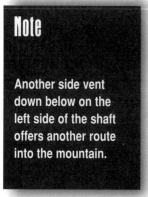

Note

Another side vent down below on the left side of the shaft offers another route into the mountain.

36. Ride the Exhaust Again

Look down the shaft. See that side vent just above you on the right side? That's your destination. Wait for the thrust to spout. Wait a second; then jump across to the vent.

37. Side Vent

Here's where you leap from the balcony at 36. When you arrive, follow the dark passage. (It helps to use your field light or IR goggles here, or keep your lightsaber lit.) Watch for a pair of sequencer charges planted on the way.

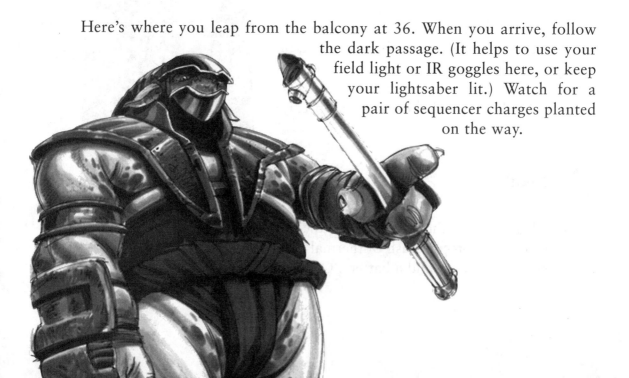

38. Small Treasure

Veer right here and grab a battery and health pack. Then come back to the dark passage and follow it to the end.

39. Exhausted Yet?

That's right, another exhaust port leap. First, ride the exhaust across to the opening at right (overlooking the stormtrooper bunker at 33); grab some health and shield power-ups. Then hop across to the right again; you end up in a control room full of consoles.

40. Double Lift

Take this lift down to a heavily guarded room; four Imperial commandos guard health and ammo power-ups. Take the elevator down again. Follow the narrow passage through the door into an exhaust vent control room.

41. Vent Control Button Number 1

Two officers and an Imperial commando watch over the exhaust vent. Take over their post and look out the window. See the vent doors moving in and out? These control the exhaust flow. You must shut off that flow to break into the main exhaust monitoring station below. Now push the nearby wall

button; an alarm sounds, the vent doors stop moving, and the lights turn green. Interesting, but what does it mean?

It means you're one step away from an emergency airflow shutoff. Before you do that, you should remove an obstacle. Exit through the side door and follow the passage to the other exhaust vent control room.

42. Vent Control Button Number 2

You end up in the other exhaust vent control room. Two Imperial officers present your obstacle; eliminate them and look out the window. See that octagonal hole in the floor of the vent?

43. Access Port

This is an access port that leads down into the main exhaust monitoring station. You can't reach the port now because of the strong exhaust flow. To shut off the flow:

▼ Follow the passage back to 41 and push the button; again, the lights turn green.

▼ Sprint back to 42 and push the button there. The lights turn red and the vent doors close, shutting off the exhaust flow for a few seconds.

▼ Quickly leap through the window into the vent and drop into the access port.

▼ Prepare for battle and open the hatch beneath you.

44. Core Exhaust Control Button Number 1

You're now in the lower level of the reactor core. Clear the immediate area and push the switch here. This partially opens the big core exhaust port. Fight your way in either direction around the core; a lot of Imperial commandos find your presence most distressing.

45, 46. Elevators

Take either of these elevators to the upper core level. At the top, go down the corridor to the doors.

47. Upper Level: Exhaust Monitoring Station

Fight through the Imperial commandos and enter this room; then battle your way into and around the passage beyond.

48. Relief!

Grab the shield recharges and health pack in this wall niche. Continue through the doors to the narrow catwalk.

49. Mission Objective: Core Exhaust Open

Follow the catwalk to this control room and throw the final switch to fully open the "pie-slice" hatch over the core exhaust port. Now you must ride the exhaust flow up to a control room at the top of the port. But wait—two secret areas, very difficult to reach, lie near the top, too. So if you want to find all the secrets on this level, save your game here!

FIGURE 17-3. FINAL EXHAUST. THROW THE SWITCHES AT **44** AND **49** TO OPEN THIS CORE EXHAUST PORT. (HERE, IT'S PARTIALLY OPEN, SO ONLY ONE OF THE SWITCHES HAS BEEN THROWN.) RIDE THE AIRFLOW UP TO TWO SECRET LEDGES AND A GRATE THAT LEADS INTO THE FINAL PASSAGE OF MISSION 17.

50. Core Exhaust Port

Before you hop into the airflow, look up. Three vertical stripes (two red, one yellow) end at an octagonal opening at the top of the room. Just beyond the lip of that opening is a sloped ledge and a pair of secret side vents. To reach them, ride the exhaust past the lip and rush forward before the airflow pushes you up to the grate at the top. Once you reach that grate, you can't get back down.

51. Secret Area

This side vent to the north holds an armor vest.

52. Secret Area

This side vent to the south holds a bacta tank and a smuggler backpack.

After you gather the items from the secret areas at 51 and 52, hop back out into the exhaust flow and ride to the top of the shaft. Slash open the side grate there and follow the passage to the elevator guarded by three field stormtroopers. Push the button to end the mission.

Mission 18

Descent into the Valley

J EREC HAS CRACKED OPEN THE UNDERGROUND BURIAL CHAMBER. The power of the ancient Jedi flows through him. Boc holds Jan prisoner. The massive Imperial installation crawls with Jerec's troops. And you haven't even made it to the *excavation site* yet.

Things don't look so good, do they?

Mission Objectives & Secret Areas

Find the entrance to Sublevel 2.
Find the control room and lower the payload through the cargo doors.
Continue down to Sublevel 3, past the cargo staging area.
Find the ventilation system.
Drop into the air shaft leading to the valley interior.

Secret Areas: 7

Enemies

Stormtrooper
Field Stormtrooper
Imperial Officer
Imperial Commando

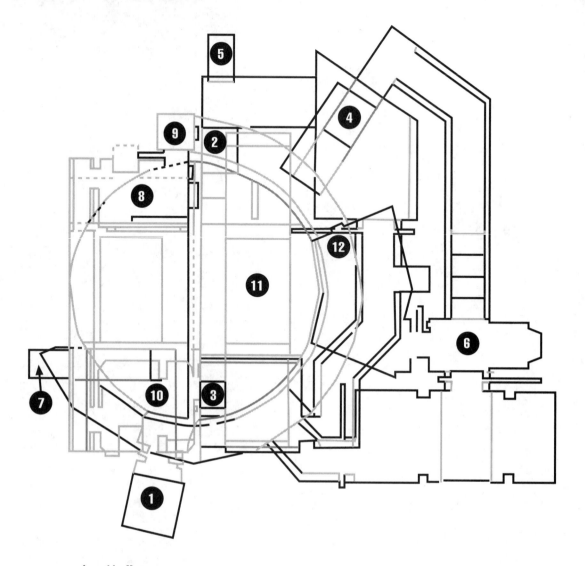

Legend for Maps

1. START

2. RAMP ACCESS

3. TURBOLIFT

4. SECRET AREA: RAIL DETONATOR

5. SECRET AREA: SMUGGLER BACKPACK

6. DOORS

7. SECRET AREA (UNDER RAMP): ARMOR VEST

8. SECRET AREA: RAIL CHARGES, SEQUENCER CHARGES

9. ELEVATOR

10. CONTROL ROOM KEY (OPENS 12)

11. CARGO DOORS

12. CONTROL ROOM (NEED CONTROL ROOM KEY), CARGO DOOR SWITCH

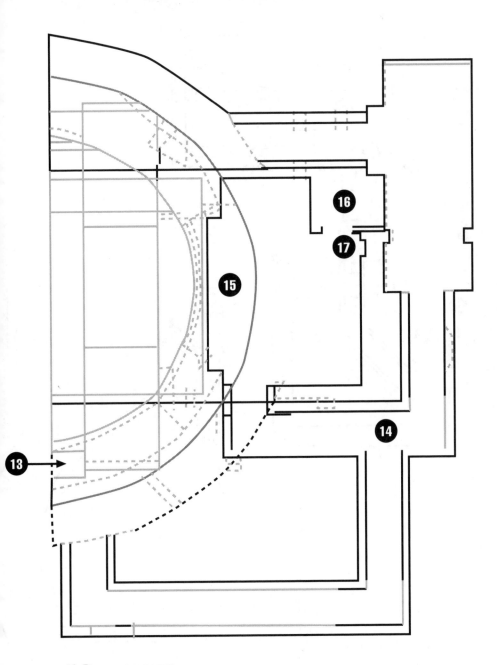

13. DROP TO NEXT LEVEL

14. INTERSECTION

15. CONSOLE ROOM (UPPER), OBSERVATION ROOM (LOWER)

16. ELEVATOR

17. PAYLOAD SWITCH

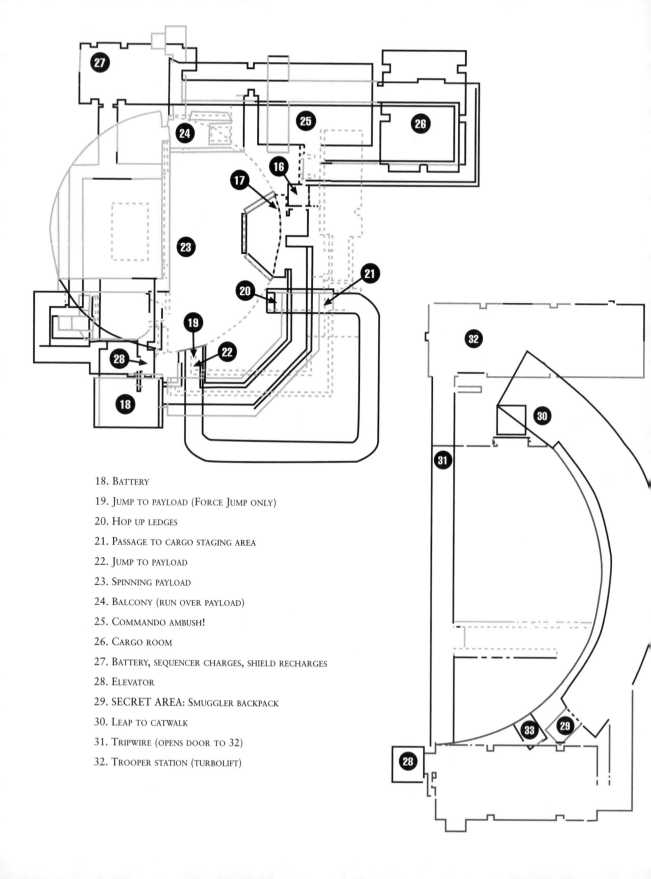

18. Battery
19. Jump to payload (Force Jump only)
20. Hop up ledges
21. Passage to cargo staging area
22. Jump to payload
23. Spinning payload
24. Balcony (run over payload)
25. Commando ambush!
26. Cargo room
27. Battery, sequencer charges, shield recharges
28. Elevator
29. SECRET AREA: Smuggler backpack
30. Leap to catwalk
31. Tripwire (opens door to 32)
32. Trooper station (turbolift)

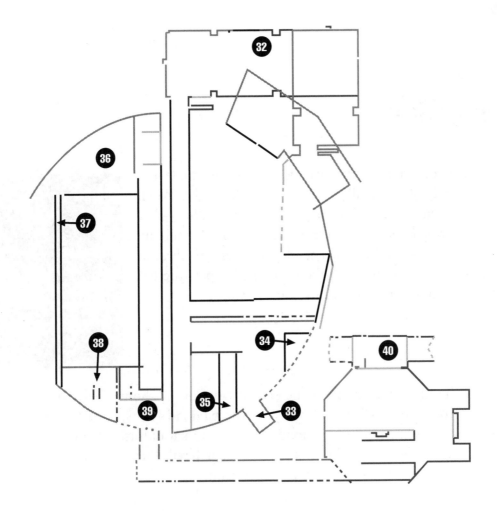

33. SECRET AREA: SMUGGLER BACKPACK

34. LEDGE

35. PLATFORM

36. RAMPS, PLATFORMS

37. NARROW BEAM TO 38

38. SECRET AREA: SHIELD RECHARGES, BBACTA TANK

39. RAMPS, LEDGES

40. AIR FILTRATION UNIT

Walkthrough

Your first objective is to get down to the sublevels. Unfortunately, all official passages are sealed tight. You'll just have to find an *unofficial* passage. One possibility—that massive payload suspended over the cargo doors. Somebody has to lower it. Let it be you. Then follow it into the breach and work your way through the unfinished superstructure of ramps, beams, open platforms, and catwalks.

> **Note**
>
> This is a dark, gloomy level. Use Force Seeing to save battery power when entering shadowy new areas.

1. Start

Step off the lift you rode up at the end of Mission 17. Some thermal detonators sit on a nearby box. Above you, the payload is suspended over the cargo doors. What kind of payload? Funny you should ask. I don't know what kind of payload. Nobody knows, except Jerec. But nobody wants to ask him, not even the Jedi Knight design team.

2. Ramp

So just cross the room, go down this ramp, and don't ask any more questions.

3. Mission Objective: Sublevel 2

Press the call button and ride the turbolift down one level. Ignore the guys in the control room. They forgot their window glass is blaster-proof. Watch them for awhile; it's amusing. Step off the lift, step back on to reactivate it, and quickly hop off. As the lift rises, hop into the hole beneath it.

Mission objective accomplished! You're now on Sublevel 2. Was that easy, or what? Follow the passage east through the doorway, battle the Imperials just around the corner, and continue north through the door. Fight your way up to the top of the ramp.

4. Secret Area

At the top of the ramp, turn right and hop across to the narrow ledge running along the wall. Turn around and hop up into the dark alcove above the ramp. (Both are tough leaps; use Force Jump for greater ease.) Scoop up the rail detonator and grin real big.

Hop down and return to the top of the ramp. Turn left and hop across into the low corridor.

5. Secret Area

This route to the secret area is for Force Jumpers only. (If you haven't developed Force Jump ability yet, use the lift at 10 to access this area.) From the end of the corridor, Force Jump up to this high alcove and grab the smuggler backpack. Return to the ramp at 4 and proceed down the passage to the doors.

6. Control Room Door (Need Control Room Key)

The door to the west is locked. Hmm. It leads to the control room, and you need the key at 9 to open it. Go through the south door for more Imperial fun; then head west through the next door. Fight your way down the ramp that circles the core.

7. Secret Area

At the bottom, skirt the striped opening; lots of gunners open fire from below, so pick off any you see. Then crouch, go under the ramp, and grab the rail charges. See the corroded door? Too bad the Empire uses such cheap materials in its new installations. Back out and shoot the corroded door from a safe distance. *Voila!* Secret area. An armor vest is your reward.

8. Secret Area

Move back around the stripe-edged opening. Use Force Jump or the black box to hop onto the ledge at 8 where you find rail and sequencer charges. Hop back down and go through the north door to the elevator.

9. Elevator

Ride this elevator down to the lower level. Exit and follow the passage past the open area on your left; it overlooks the cargo doors below.

10. Key Room (Control Room Key)

Open the next door by pressing the green button next to it—but prepare for heated combat. Four Imperial hard hats, including a commando, wait inside. After you clear the room, get the control room key. (See figure 18-1.)

FIGURE 18-1. CONTROL ROOM KEY.
THIS KEY OPENS THE CONTROL ROOM
AT 6 THAT LOWERS THE PAYLOAD.
THE LIFT AT RIGHT RUNS UP TO A
DARK BALCONY WITH POWER-UPS
(AND POWER-HUNGRY IMPERIALS).

Ride the nearby lift up to a small platform with a health pack and some thermal detonators. Ride back down and push the green button to open the door to a room with cargo doors on the floor.

11. Cargo Door Room (Turbolift)

Note the switch on the wall; nothing happens when you push it yet. Go to the turbolift in the back corner, ride it up, and hop over to the ledge at the top. If you didn't use Force Jump to reach the secret area back at 5, hop across to it now and grab the smuggler backpack. Otherwise, hop down, turn right, go to the ramp at 4, and then retrace your route around to the control room door at 6.

12. Mission Objective: Lower the Payload

Enter the very well-guarded control room. Spill some Imperial guts, and then punch the switch on the control console to open the cargo doors and lower the payload. (Watch it drop outside the window.)

Exit and continue to retrace your route down to the bottom floor at 11. Now you can throw the wall switch and lower the payload still farther. After the payload drops, hop onto it. Save your game and make a running jump south to the ledge.

13. Hole Drop

Go to this hole. Kill the troopers stationed below, drop down, and fight your way down the passage south and around to the center room.

14. Intersection

Turn left (west) at this intersection to reach the center room.

15. Console Room

Wipe out the guards and grab shield recharges and health packs on the shelf. Go to the elevator call button.

16. Observation Room

Call the elevator here; it arrives with a pair of guests. Gun them down and then descend in the elevator. You arrive at a room with big windows overlooking bored, scratching stormtroopers.

17. Control Switch (Lowers Payload)

Throw this console switch to lower the payload and start it twirling. Save your game. There's a nifty little jumping puzzle coming. Exit the room to the south.

18. Balcony

Follow the passageway to this dark balcony, which holds a battery—a useful commodity on this generally dark level.

19. Jump Option Number 1 (Force Jump)

You can move down the corridor and Force Jump onto the spinning payload from here. (If you want to solve the jumping puzzle without a big Force Jump, skip ahead to 20.) If you choose this method, skip ahead to 23.

20. Jump Option Number 2 (No Force Jump)

When you step out of the observation room, a trooper opens fire from a beam above you at 20. This guy was placed as a clue; how did he get up there? Gun him down and find out.

FIGURE 18-2. GUY HIGH. IF SOME GUY IN WHITE BODY ARMOR CAN GET UP THERE, SO CAN YOU. HOP UP NARROW LEDGES TO A PASSAGE THAT LEADS TO YOUR PAYLOAD DESTINATION.

Before you begin jumping, lean over the edge of the walkway and eliminate Imperial troops below, or they'll harass you unmercifully as you hop up the ledges. Then hop up to the ledge west of the walkway and turn right.

Hop up to the north ledge, then either hop south to the beam or just try a running leap up to the passage at 21. (I had better luck with the latter when not using Force Jump.)

21. Passage to Cargo Staging Area

Move down this well-guarded passage to the cargo staging area, where the payload is spinning.

> **Note**
>
> You should be able to perform all the jumps in 20 without Force Jump. Of course, a Force Jump from the walkway straight up to 21 is a simple and effective way to get up, too.

22. Jump Point (Upper)

From here you can execute a running leap to the payload without resorting to Force Jump. Here, you're directly above 19.

23. Payload Walkover

From your jump point (lower or upper), leap to the payload when it's just past horizontal so you can run across it, walk over the top, and down the other side.

24. Twin Balconies

Two balconies, upper and lower, wait on the other side of the payload. Hop from the payload to the upper balcony to grab some power-ups. As the payload flips over again and rises toward horizontal, hop onto it and run down

to the lower balcony, directly below. You can also hop over to a small platform to the side of the spinning payload from here; a bacta tank and shield recharge is your reward. It's a tricky leap back, though, so save your game first.

From the lower balcony, go through the door.

25. Mission Objective: Sublevel 3

Enter a cargo storage room full of boxes. Some Imperial commandos hop around in here; for some reason, they think they can challenge you. End their delusions; then hop onto the raised ramp and proceed into the next room east.

26. Average Room

Nothing of great interest here—just guys and their stuff. The guys are tough commandos, though. Fight well. Return to 25, exit south and head out the passage.

27. Door Switches

Follow the passage to this big room. Empty it of Imperials and power-ups, including a battery in a closet, some sequencer charges, and a pair of shield recharges. Then throw the three green switches to open the south door. Go through and follow the walkway to the elevator.

28. Elevator

Battle past two commandos and an Imperial officer onto this elevator. Ride down to the quarry level, exit into an Imperial hornet's nest, and battle down the passage.

29. Secret Area

Before you go down the curving ramp, turn left and shoot the corroded compartment door to find a hidden smuggler backpack. (See figure 18-3.) Then fight down the ramp to the big dropoff.

FIGURE 18-3. POOR MAINTENANCE. CORROSION LIKE THIS SHOULD MAKE YOU SO MAD YOU COULD JUST, YOU KNOW, SHOOT IT OR SOMETHING.

30. Big Leap

From the dropoff, take a running leap over to the catwalk across the room.

31. Tripwire Ambush

See the door to the north? You can't open it. But back away from it down the catwalk. When you hit the spot marked 31 on the map, you trip open the door and four field stormtroopers attempt an ambush.

32. Troop Room

Blast your way into their lair and scour it clean of Imperial troopers. We'll be back in a minute, but first, let's go find a secret area, shall we? Exit south down the catwalk and take the second left, a ramp leading upward. Watch it; an Imperial commando waits at the top.

33. Secret Area

Another corroded door. Somebody should call maintenance. In the meantime, shoot the door. Yes, another smuggler backpack. Now go back to room 32. Take the lift down to the lower level, blow away two field troopers and an Imperial officer, and exit south through the door to face a tough commando.

34. Hopscotch

Feel centered? Good. Leap across to this triangular ledge, turn right, walk across the narrow beam, and, finally, hop to the small ledge with the switch.

35. Platform Switch

Push the switch to raise the platform below to your left. Jump quickly to the platform and exit south before the platform drops again in a few seconds. Continue south, fighting through Imperial hordes across a dangerous catwalk. (Another annoying rail gunner on a high balcony tries to give you a charge.)

36. Ramp Warfare

Battle up this series of ramps until you reach what appears to be a dead end with a bacta tank and other power-ups. But turn around and look for a small catwalk behind the final ramp. Hop to it, and then hop back and forth from platform to platform to reach the upper platform. Clear out troopers, taking particular pleasure in dropping the ones with rail detonators.

37. Beamrider

Go to the edge of the platform and pick off all snipers in the vicinity. Your next move is a drop to the striped beam, where you are particularly vulnerable. (See figure 18-3.) Walk across to the far wall—but wait, don't turn yet!

FIGURE 18-4. FUN WITH VERTIGO. DROP DOWN TO THAT STRIPED BEAM JUST BELOW. DON'T BE AFRAID. IT'S GOT TO BE AT LEAST THREE OR FOUR INCHES WIDE.

38. Secret Area

Slip carefully around the wall to find this hidden niche full of shield recharges and a bacta tank. Then move back around the wall and drop down to the narrow ledge with a striped outer edge. Follow the ledge into the next room.

39. Ramps

Hop up the ramps and ledges until you hop through a hole onto the top platform. (Jump through the hole facing south or west; if you jump out the north side, you might fly over the edge and fall shrieking.) Clear the platform and head down the passage.

40. Mission Objective: Air Filtration Unit

A lot of troopers patrol the air filtration unit. After you deal with them, save your game. This is a tightly timed puzzle. Flip the filtration switch, immediately hop into the duct, and start running against the wind. If you wait for the airflow to die, you will, too; it's a long drop down the duct, and you need the residual wind to cushion your fall.

Follow the duct to the floor grate and slash it open. Finished!

Mission 19

The Valley of the Jedi

THIS IS YOUR LAST TRUE MISSION IN JEDI KNIGHT. So savor it. After this, your final challenge is to face Boc, and then Jerec, saber to saber, in Force Power combat. Jerec grows more powerful by the second. But you're almost there, now. All you have to do is battle through a bajillion more stormtroopers, solve some mind-bending puzzles, and slug it out with three massive, deadly super-enemies at the burial chamber threshold.

Mission Objectives & Secret Areas

Make your way to the excavation below the Imperial superstructure. Manipulate the ancient stone doors to open a passage to the valley core.

The main passage to the valley entrance is blocked. Find an alternate one.

Fight your way through the blast doors into the Jedi burial chamber.

Secret Areas: 8

Enemies

Stormtrooper
Field Stormtrooper
Imperial Officer
Imperial Commando
Kell Dragon
AT-ST Imperial Walker

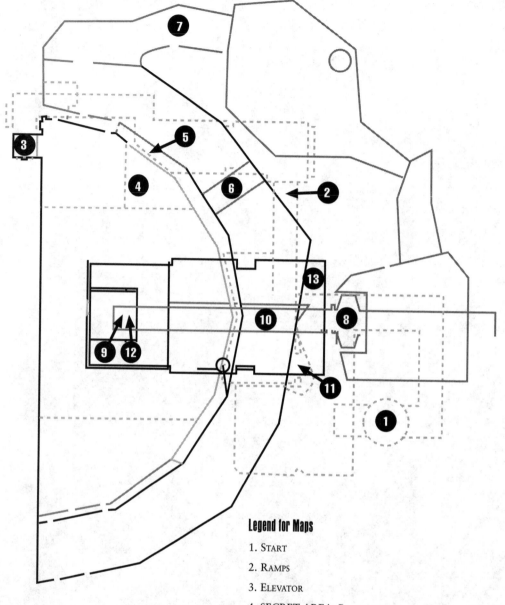

Legend for Maps

1. START

2. RAMPS

3. ELEVATOR

4. SECRET AREA: BACTA TANK

5. SECRET AREA (WINDOW LEDGE): SHIELD RECHARGE, THERMAL DETONATORS

6. SHIELD RECHARGE, RAIL CHARGES

7. ROCK TUNNEL

8. CATWALK TO ELEVATOR

9. GRATE (BACKPACK)

10. SECRET AREA: SHIELD RECHARGES, HEALTH PACK

11. SECRET AREA: SMUGGLER BACKPACK (FORCE JUMP ONLY)

12. SECRET AREA (UNDER ELEVATOR): BACTA TANKS, SHIELD RECHARGE

13. TURBOLIFT

14. EXCAVATED HOLE

15. BATTERY, SHIELD RECHARGE, HEALTH PACK

16. SECRET AREA: SMUGGLER BACKPACK

17. BACTA TANK, BATTERIES

18. SECRET AREA: ARMOR VEST

19. KELL DRAGON!

20. KELL DRAGON!

21. HOP DOWN TO NARROW LEDGE

22. CATWALKS, MANY TROOPERS

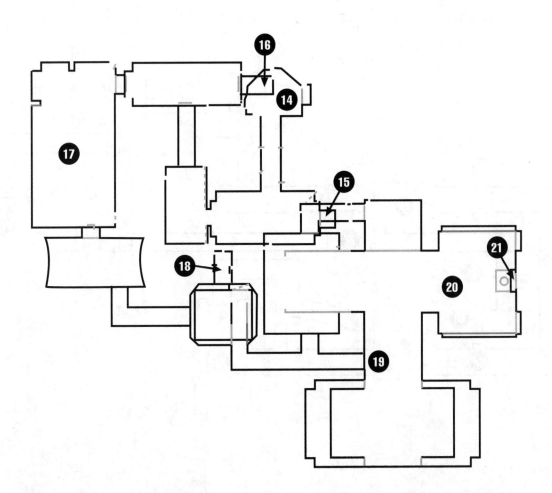

23. TROOPERS, POWER-UPS

24. DOOR ACTIVATION PANEL (MOVES 25, 32)

25. STONE DOOR

26. DOOR ACTIVATION PANEL (MOVES 25, 32)

27. DOOR ACTIVATION PANEL (MOVES 28, 30)

28. STONE DOOR

29. TROOPERS

30. COUNTERBALANCE TO 28

31. SECRET AREA: FORCE BOOST!

32. COUNTERBALANCE TO 25

33. DROP TO VALLEY ENTRANCE

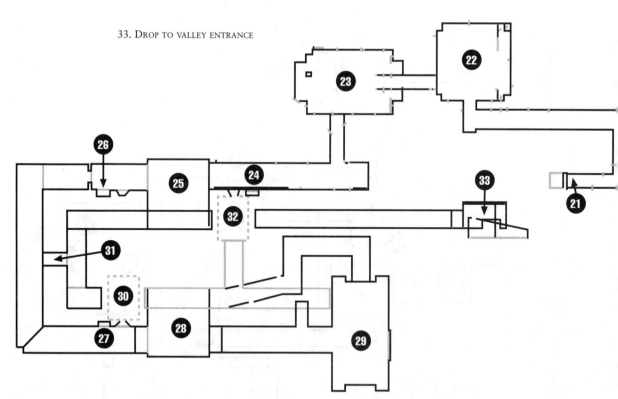

34. Triggers open blast door

35. AT-ST (commando with red key to 36)

36. Red key door

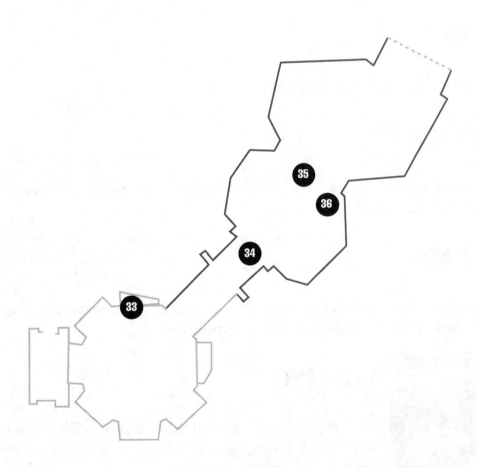

Walkthrough

Jerec's troops have excavated deep into the surrounding chambers that lead into the Valley of the Jedi. Make your way through the Imperial excavation to the valley core. Look for the usual hidden ledges and exploding walls, where secret stashes are kept.

1. Start

Your final exploration begins here.

2. To the Shaft

Go through the first door. Then fight your way down ramps until you reach the shaft cut into the rock.

3. Elevator

Take this elevator down to the next level. Scoop up the sequencer charges stashed on the floor and hop up onto the ledge.

4. Secret Area

Grab the bacta tank behind the black box. (What's in these weird black boxes, anyway?) Then get back on the elevator and push the down button.

5. Secret Area

As the elevator drops, look left. See the open window up high on the wall? That's a secret area, and goodies—a shield recharge and a thermal detonator belt—sit on the ledge there. Jump to it as the elevator raises or lowers. It's a tough hop, but you don't need Force Jump to reach it. If you miss, you drop hard to the floor—into the firing cone of two angry Imperials.

FIGURE 19-1. WINDOW LEDGE. THESE IMPERIALS ARE LIKE SQUIRRELS THE WAY THEY STASH EVERYTHING IN HIGH, INACCESSIBLE PLACES. HERE, LEAP FROM THE MOVING ELEVATOR TO THAT SECRET WINDOW LEDGE.

Note

Good alternative tactic: Ride the elevator down to the floor and terminate the Imperial threat—two on this side of the room, two more around the center structure at the far end of the room. Then ride back up and make the leap to the ledge at 5. This way you don't have guys sniping at you while you execute tricky maneuvers.

One other caution: If you make it to the ledge, a field stormtrooper launches rail charges at you from the top of the raised platform in the room. His first shot can blow you right off the ledge. So swivel and nail him the moment you land.

6. Another Tough Leap

If you manage to stay on the ledge, look down outside the room. Items sit on a small strut extending from the building into the rock wall outside the room. Hop to it from the ledge and grab the shield recharge and rail charges. If you miss, a quick Force Jump should get you back up.

Hop down. Follow the rocky path north as it curves along the structure.

Tip

Some Imperial troops, including a pesky field stormtrooper with a rail detonator, encamp far below at the bottom of the structure. Toss some thermal detonators off the catwalk to thin their ranks.

7. Quarry Room

Hop up the rock ledge and continue east through the tunnel, past the pillar with red stripes. (Look for a battery behind the pillar.) When you come to the catwalk, wipe out the guards (and don't miss the shield recharge on the ground, just around the corner).

8. Catwalk to Elevator

Hop onto the catwalk, open the door, and continue down the catwalk to battle the pair of commandos guarding the elevator.

9. Grate Slashing

Before you ride the lift, look above you. See the backpack through the grate in the ceiling? Slash open the grate and jump up through it. (Force Jump can make this an easier task.) Move down the walkway and hop through the tall window.

10. Secret Area

Two shield recharges and a health pack sit on a strut outside the window. But that's not all. From the strut, look up at the rock wall. See the dark alcove in the rocks above? Another secret area!

11. Secret Area

Use Force Jump to reach this rock alcove. Grab the smuggler backpack and hop back down to the strut at 10. Go back through the tall window and down through the grate; then ride the elevator down to 9. Be aware—killers lurk below (unless you eliminated the threat with thermal detonators earlier).

12. Secret Area

Push the button to send the elevator up; then quickly hop off. Beneath, you'll find a secret area with a couple of bacta tanks and a shield recharge. Now head for the lift over in the corner.

13. Jerec's Excavation Site

Ride this lift down; two troopers wait at the bottom. Duck under the beam to get below the Imperial superstructure. Look over the edge. That's the biggest drill bit you've ever seen. As Kyle says, "They must have unearthed the entrance to the valley down there." Do you feel a disturbance in the Force? It's all getting too intense, isn't it?

Your next goal: Get through the ancient doors to the valley core.

Follow the curving ramp down to the bottom. A tough Imperial trio guards the floor surrounding the drill bit.

14. Core Guard

Drop into the excavated hole—beware the commando posted there—and follow the ramp down to the south.

15. Alcove Clue

Turn left in the first room and grab the assortment—battery, shield recharge, health pack—in the small alcove. This alcove is visible, but note it well. More like it, also laden with goods, are hidden behind exploding walls in the ruins. Let's go to one now, shall we?

16. Secret Area

Follow the corridors to the room with the cracked wall. (See figure 19-2.) Shoot the cracked section to blow open

a secret alcove with a smuggler backpack. (It's a tight fit, so it might take a few hops to get in.) Exit west to the next room.

FIGURE 19-2. ANOTHER EXPLOSIVE FIND. WHEN YOU SEE A CRACKED SECTION OF WALL IN THE CATACOMBS, MOVE WAY BACK AND SHOOT IT TO TRIGGER AN EXPLOSION THAT EXPOSES A SECRET AREA.

17. Support Room

This room with the durasteel supports in the corner is home to four vicious field stormtroopers, including a rail gunner. Look for a bacta tank and two batteries, too, then exit south. Move through a dark room and down an ancient stone ramp.

18. Secret Area

The next room with a durasteel ramp has another cracked wall. Blow it open and grab the armor vest. Climb the ramp and continue east down the passage. Before you enter the next room, read step 19.

19. *Kell! Kell! Kell!*

We're shouting because we want to get your attention here. Before you go east or north into this big room, know that not one, but two Kell dragons wait hungrily inside. One aggressively chases you, but the second stands guard over the passage that leads down to the valley core.

FIGURE 19-3. PLEASE DON'T KELL ME.
TWO DRAGONS IS A LOT OF DRAGON,
BELIEVE US. ONE STAYS PUT, BUT THIS ONE
CHASES. STAY IN THE PASSAGE, THOUGH,
AND HE CAN'T REACH YOU. LAUNCH
RAIL CHARGES INTO HIM,
AND KEEP BACK!

Best tactic: The aggressive Kell can't enter the connecting passages, so lure him to 19 on the map and stay just out of his reach up the passage. Move back and blast him with rail charges and thermal detonators (save some detonators to use against the AT-ST), then move forward and take careful whacks with the lightsaber. Keep out of tooth range! Occasionally the Kell will move away. Step warily to the doorway, plant a couple of sequencer charges with the Z key, and hop back when he takes the bait.

20. Kell Guard

The Kell dragon guarding the passage won't chase you, but if you get too close, he'll happily gnaw on you. So gauge his range and blast him with any remaining rail charges or thermals. You can also run up close (to about 20 on the map), plant a sequencer with the Z key, and quickly back up. The dragon's proximity blows the charge and hurts the Kell. Repeat many times; then finish him off with the saber.

21. Passage to Lower Level

Jump down carefully here. You want to land on that little lip of ledge protruding from the east side of the hole. (If you miss, you must Force Jump back up or move across a dark room below, ride up the airshaft, and then return to 21 and try again.) Follow the passage to the big room with catwalks and lots of troopers.

22. Catwalk Room

Hop down the catwalks while battling the three Imperial commandos and three field stormtroopers (one with a rail gun) who man this room. Then exit through the lower door.

23. Strut Room

More guys, more power-ups. Nice support strut, though. Exit south.

24. Mission Objective: Stone Door Panel

Push this wall panel four times to completely open the door (a big stone block) at 25. You must leave the door completely open so the counterbalance at 32 is in the proper position when you reach it later.

FIGURE 19-4. STONE DOORS. PUSH THE WALL PANEL (LEFT) TO OPEN THE STONE-BLOCK DOOR. FOUR PUSHES FULLY OPEN THE DOOR. AT 27, PUSH IT A FIFTH TIME AND SPRINT PAST THE CLOSING DOOR.

25. Stone Block Door

A huge sliding block of stone forms a door here. Open it by pressing the wall panel at 24, which raises the counterbalance at 32 that moves the stone block.

26. Stone Door Panel

This panel manipulates the stone door at 25. In this walkthrough, however, you don't need to use it.

27. Stone Door Panel

Push this wall panel four times to open the door (a big stone block) at 28. Then push it one more time, which closes the door, but sprint past the sliding block before it seals the passage shut. Hurry or the stone will crush you. The stone door must be closed so the counterbalance at 30 is in the proper position when you reach it later.

28. Stone Block Door

A huge sliding block of stone forms a door here. Open it by pressing the wall panel at 27, which raises the counterbalance at 30 that moves the stone block.

29. Troop Room

A squad of troopers deploys in this room. Access east is blocked by cargo boxes. Head up the low passage to the north.

30. Counterbalance to 28

If you did not close the stone door at 28, its counterbalance blocks the passage here. If you did close door 28 behind you, then you can walk across the top of the counterbalance. (It's tempting, but don't cut the rope!) Continue down the passage.

31. Secret Area

Check the wall up high on the left as you round the corner just past the counterbalance at 30. *Aha!* Cracks! Move back and shoot to blow open another secret alcove. Inside you'll find a Force Boost, which adds 100 points to current reserve (maximum at this level is 400 points). Hop out and continue up the passage.

32. Counterbalance to 25

If you closed the stone door at 25, its counterbalance blocks the passage here. If you did not close door 25 behind you, then you can walk across the top of the counterbalance. Continue down the passage.

33. Mission Objective: Alternate Passage to Valley Entrance

Drop down this opening into a real hellhole. Your next objective: Survival. Swarms of soldiers guard the valley entrance. Fortunately, some power-ups lie scattered about, and you can duck behind boxes for cover and respite. When you've cleared the room, head down the ramp to the blast door.

34. Door Trigger

When you step across the threshold of the outer blast door here, it closes behind you. Meanwhile, the blast door in front of you opens. Guess who?

35. Final Foe

Yes, that's an AT-ST Imperial walker, piloted by an Imperial commando. Gun it down with rail charges, toss thermals, or just bash at its belly with your lightsaber. Whatever you do, bring it down. When the driver hops out, bring him down, too. He drops the critical red key.

36. Final Door (Need Red Key)

If you got the red key from the AT-ST driver in 35, use it on this control panel to open the blast door leading into the fabled Valley of the Jedi!

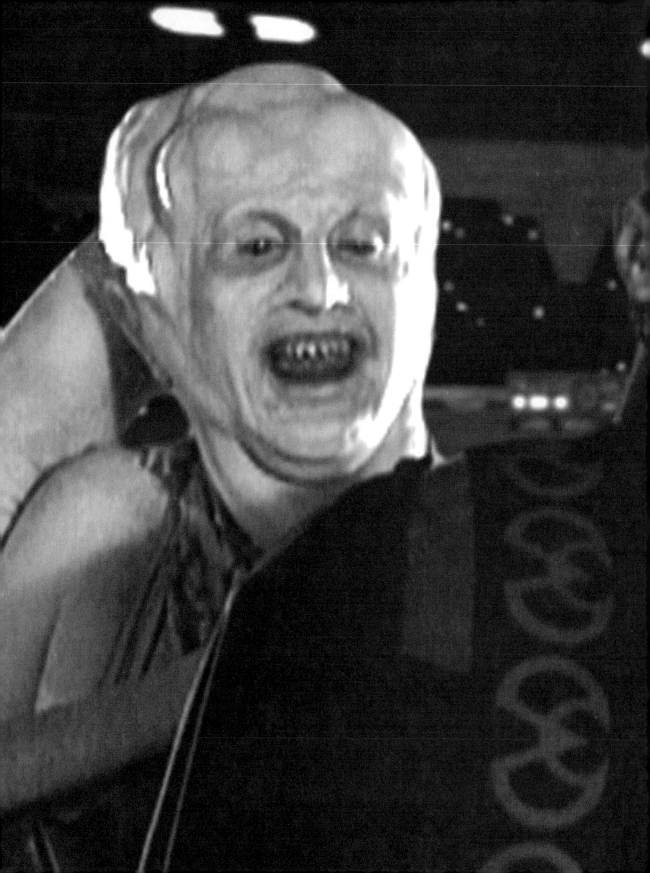

Mission 20

Boc: The Crude

Qu Rahn's assessment of Boc: "I can't abide this creature named Boc. He is one of the few who actually uses two lightsabers in battle. He is a crude individual who lacks both tact and teeth. Only a Dark Jedi can he be."

Boc Statistics

Health: 1500
Resistance: 50% Impact, 50% Energy, 90% Fire
Special Instincts: Jump, Open Doors, Hit & Run
Force Powers: Repel, Destruction

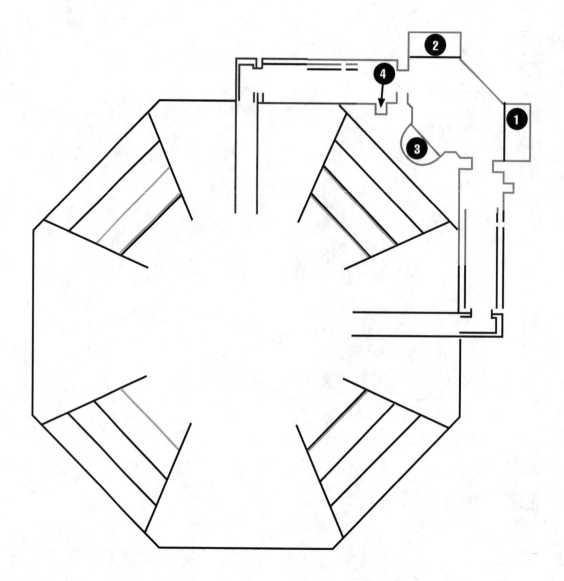

Legend for Map

1. Revive, bacta tank, Force Boost
2. Bacta tanks, health packs
3. Health pack
4. Bacta tank

Combat Tips

"You're an angry one, aren't you?"

Yes, this bouncing lunatic will drive you nuts. He can't help it, though; he's got that Twi'lek thing around his neck. Plus, he's the last line of defense between you and Jerec. That's a lot of pressure on a guy.

Here are some fighting tips for your battle with Boc:

▼ If you haven't already, press the F1 key to use the third-person view with Boc. Otherwise, it can be difficult to track him as he hops about like a demented durkii.

▼ By now, you will have developed your own fighting style. Stick with basic saberfighting techniques—block and counterstrike, keep close, keep moving sideways and circling, throw in an occasional rush or leap for variety.

▼ Use your Force Powers. You should have plenty by now. Force Absorb is fun; you can suck up Boc's Destruction blasts. And Force Protection adds a mighty dose to your shields.

▼ Don't miss the great hidden areas in the high alcoves (see 1 and 2 on the map). One holds a revive pack for a full health injection.

Mission 21

Jerec: The Force Within

SINCE THE TIME OF THE CLONE WARS, NO JEDI BATTLE HAS LOOMED QUITE SO LARGE AS THIS ONE. The fate of the galaxy sits like a rare Tumanian pressure-ruby in your hands. Jerec was already powerful enough to subjugate the other Dark Jedi to his designs; now he has tapped the power of a thousand Jedi ancients. Fortunately, you have interrupted him in midusurpation.

All you must do now is beat him. Have you been collecting your Jedi stars?

We sure hope so.

QU RAHN'S ASSESSMENT OF JEREC: "HIS HEAVY BROW OVERSHADOWS THE EMPTY RECESSES THAT NORMALLY EMBRACE EYES. JEREC HAS THE UNCANNY POWER TO ABSORB AND OVERSHADOW ONE'S CONNECTION TO THE FORCE, LIKE A DARK CLOUD. A DEEP, EMPOWERING GRASP OF YOUR WILL IS WHAT YOU NEED."

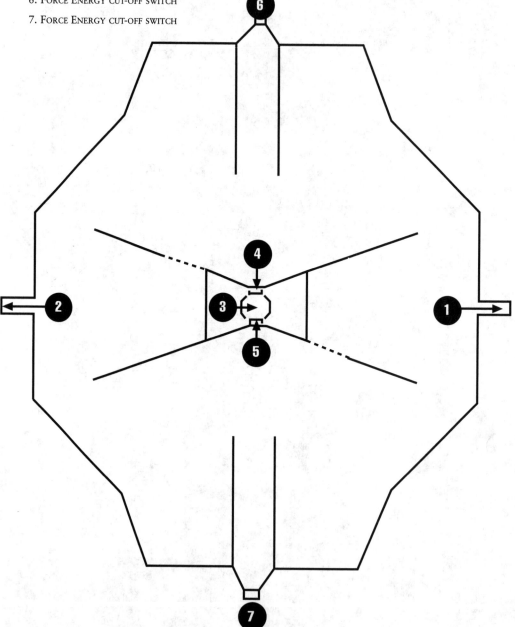

Jerec Statistics

Health: 2000
Resistance: 50% Impact, 50% Energy, 90% Fire
Special Instincts: Jump, Open Doors, Circle Strafe, Hit & Run
Force Powers: Destruction, Lightning, Pull

Mission Objective

Jerec is powerful enough already—just check his Health stat of 2000!—but now he has an eternal source of regeneration. The Dark Master has learned how to tap into the Force Energy flow at the core of the Valley. Whenever your attack hurts him badly, he retreats, rides the flow up the core, and regenerates full health while meditating within an impenetrable Force Protection cocoon fed by the Force.

How do you stop Jerec's regeneration? Take the following steps:

1. Fight Jerec until he retreats to the central tower and rides up in the stream for regeneration.
2. Sprint to the nearest wall panel (at 6 or 7 on the map).

Before Jerec's trip up the core for regeneration, big Jedi statues block these wall panels. But when Jerec starts tapping the Force flow, the statues slide forward toward the central tower. The power raises you, as well.

3. The moment you land, push the wall panel (6 or 7).

4. *Quick!* Activate Force Speed (if you have it) and *sprint* to the opposite wall panel and push it, too.

Warning

Don't let the Jedi statues slide all the way to the tower! If they do, Jerec chuckles—the full power of the ancient Jedi now infuses him—and you lose.

The statues stop moving. Pushing *both* wall panels cuts off the flow of Force Energy to Jerec, so his regeneration process stops, too. If you halt it soon enough, you leave Jerec is a weakened state. But Jerec doesn't know this, being deep in Dark Jedi meditation.

JEREC MEDITATES IN AN IMPENETRABLE COCOON OF FORCE PROTECTION, REJUVENATING BACK TO FULL STRENGTH. PUSH THE WALL PANELS BEHIND THE JEDI STATUES TO CUT OFF THE FORCE FLOW AND LEAVE THE DARK MASTER WEAKENED.

5. Sprint to the central tower, ride up the core stream, and whack Jerec out of his meditation. (He may be done already, though, which means he's close to fully rejuvenated.)

6. Lure Jerec down near one of the wall panels to continue the fight. If Jerec is weakened, you may be able to finish him off now.

7. Attack Jerec until he tries to run for the core again. Keep attacking as he runs; cut him off if you can.

If you lured Jerec far enough away from the central tower, you can finish him off before he reaches the core to heal himself again. But if he makes it up the tower, hustle back to the wall panels and repeat steps 3 to 7.

Combat Tips

Here's how to lock sabers with Jerec:

▼ Stay close to Jerec! If you get too far away, he can unleash his Force Destruction blast.

▼ But if you're low on health, use Force Speed to sprint to one of the several regenerating power-ups in the core area. (Check the map for locations.)

▼ Use the Force! Both Protection and Absorb are particularly useful in countering Jerec's mastery of dark side attack powers.

▼ Again, if you've cut off the Force flow to Jerec, leaving him weakened, lure him away from the central tower. That way, when he breaks off again to rejuvenate, you can chase him (or even cut him off) and get in enough saber hits to destroy him before he reaches the tower.

PART III

APPENDIX

The Jedi Knight Design Team

Plus an Interview with Justin Chin

ONE OF THE MOST SATISFYING ASPECTS OF MY WEEK-LONG STAY AT LUCASARTS WAS MEETING THE JEDI KNIGHT DESIGN TEAM. I arrived the day after code release, which means the final version of the software was frozen in place. Jedi Knight was essentially finished, and everybody was in a jolly mood. We feasted in a team celebration the first night. In the days that followed I met with most of the team members individually to discuss their contributions to the project.

The following team profile section concludes with an in-depth interview with project leader, writer, designer, and all-around Jedi visionary Justin Chin. Check it out if you're interested in the birth and development of the Jedi Knight story and its overall design.

Ray Gresko, Lead Programmer

Imagine spending your teen years working for robotics companies and NASA, like Ray Gresko. Jedi Knight's lead programmer went on to study computer science at Temple University in Philadelphia. "But I was always a big-time gamer," he says. After graduation, Gresko created some demos and sent them to game companies; he eventually landed a job at Spectrum HoloByte, working on simulation games and 3-D engine development.

That led directly to a LucasArts gig.

"Daron Stinnett [LucasArts project leader for Dark Forces and, recently, Outlaws] had been at Spectrum, and knew what I was doing," says Gresko. "So after he came here, he hired me, and that's how Dark Forces happened."

From there, it was a natural progression to Jedi Knight, where Gresko says the goal was to raise the technical level and "immersiveness" of the game. He and Justin Chin formed the original core team, and his primary task was to turn Chin's design ideas into reality.

"My job was to manage the design of all systems in the game—how everything flows, how the art path works," he says. "We hired programmers for engine development and the whole networking, multiplayer aspect."

Aside from managing the technical team, the bulk of Gresko's work was developing the 3-D engine. "The biggest challenge was getting stable toolsets in place," he says. "You can have the coolest 3-D technology in the world, but if you can't create ways for designers to make a game, all you have is a slick 3-D demo."

Che-Yuan Wang, Level Editor, Gameplay Programming

Che-Yuan Wang earned his degree in electrical engineering from the University of Illinois. A college interview led directly to a job at Parallax Software, where Wang found himself working on the level editor for Descent. After Descent shipped, he joined Justin Chin and Ray Gresko at LucasArts for work on Jedi Knight.

His primary task was to create Jedi's level editor, called "Leia."

"We wanted flexible ways to build geometry," he says, "to build and extrude sectors, for example."

A sector is simply a convex space—cubes or other arbitrarily shaped spaces—simulated on a computer. Wang's Leia allows level designers to lay out sectors, stack them, cleave them, sculpt them, and basically carve geometric spaces.

"And it lets editors run Jedi's run-time engine within it, in a window," he says.

Leonard Robel, Lead Character Animator

Need an inspiring, "find-what-you-want, go-do-it" kind of story? Consider Leonard Robel. He took a high school degree and then knocked around at a few jobs. He decided he liked art, he liked computer games, so why not do both? After a few Life Drawing classes, some self-training, and a little freelance work, he found The Secret of Monkey Island and decided, "I want to work for that company."

That company, of course, was LucasArts.

"It became my dream company, and I got in almost immediately after that," says Robel.

Soon he found himself creating the art for classic LucasArts titles such as Rebel Assault and Full Throttle. His 3-D animation work on Dark Forces, combined with an intense interest in Japanese martial arts swordfighting, pegged him as a natural for Jedi Knight.

Robel created most of the game's incredible 3-D animation. His favorite is the Boc death sequence.

"I had his death animation," he says. "Then Justin [Chin] came with this great sound file—the actor is laughing and choking and suddenly realizes he's dying. So I modified the animation to work with that."

Another personal favorite is the idle, scratching stormtrooper—which perfectly illustrates Robel's basic approach: "I'm always looking for ways to create the sense that this character has a real person inside."

Garry M. Gaber, Story Editor, 3-D Art

Garry Gaber took a somewhat circuitous route from NYU Film School through the world of industrial CAD work, then back into film, and, eventually, computer gaming.

"I was working at a company that designed chemical plants," he says. He adds, laughing, "So I was basically doing the same thing then as I am now. Hey, it's amazing how relevant all that stuff is."

Together with Ralph Gerth, Gaber provided most of the 3-D art for the game's cutscenes, building wire-frame models of objects (such as the stunning ships), giving them color and texture, and then putting them in motion. But his participation in the Jedi Knight project began at an even more fundamental level—one that put his film-school background to good use.

"Yeah, I helped Justin re-write his script," he says. "Many late pizza nights."

In particular, he remembers the evening they wrote Rahn's dream-sequence monologue on his computer, which then crashed. "We drove like maniacs from my place to work repeating the speech, line by line, back and forth," he recalls. "I think we were yelling it at each other. I'm pretty sure I'll never forget that monologue as long as I live."

Ralph M. Gerth IV, Lead 3-D Artist

Ralph Gerth's first profession was musician. While earning his art degree at Old Dominion University in his home state of Virginia, and for several years after graduation, Gerth played in a traveling band. Eventually, he earned a master's degree in computer art from the School of Visual Arts in New York City, then did TV production work, gaining valuable experience in computer graphics.

In 1993, Gerth came to LucasArts to work on Rebel Assault and help build up the company's expertise on SGI machines. "I was the first person here to use an SGI," he says. After working on classic LucasArts titles such as Sam & Max Hit the Road, The Dig, and Dark Forces, Gerth became lead  3-D artist for Jedi Knight. "Besides doing the 3-D art, I helped Justin art direct and manage the cut scenes," he says. "We took mock 3-D backgrounds down to the shoot in L.A., so we could layer the actors right into our set backgrounds on a monitor. It made the whole shoot a lot more precise, I think."

David Levison, Interactive Sound Effects

After studying music composition at Cal Arts, David Levison moved north to the Bay Area and did sound-related work at several places, including Rocket Science. He joined the Jedi Knight team at LucasArts in December 1996, creating all the in-game sound effects—weapons, Force Powers, enemies, ambient sounds, everything you hear when playing Jedi Knight.

"We had access to the Skywalker sound libraries, which is great, of course," says Levision. "But we went to a lot of sources beyond that."

In fact, the Jedi team built its own library, using field recordings and sampling techniques.

"I produced a lot of stuff using synthesizers," he says.

His favorite sound in Jedi Knight? "I love the rail detonator weapon," he laughs. "And I like our Force Destruction sound a lot, too."

Christopher Ross, Game Tuning/Enemy Placement

Marin County native Chris Ross left the rolling hills north of San Francisco to attend UC–Santa Barbara and study geography.

"It's all computer stuff," he says with obvious relish. "Satellite imagery, digital cartography, information systems." He wanted to pursue it after graduation, but took a job offer from LucasArts, where he'd done work during school as an art technician working on cutscenes for Rebel Assault. After a while, it struck him.

"You know, I play games more than I ever really liked geography in my life." Now he's there to stay.

Ross wore several hats on the Jedi Knight project. The first year he worked with the cutscene team, making sure color and compression for all

scenes were in balance—"compressed, but still looking good," he says—plus some general help with effects, lighting, and other tasks.

Then he moved into his primary roles—item placement and game tuning.

"I worked with Rob Huebner on the AI, helping him organize things, setting up test cases with characters so he could debug, and so on."

Then Ross worked with the level designers to tweak the gameplay in each mission, adjusting placement of characters and items for the various difficulty levels.

Item and enemy placement, of course, is a critical component of gameplay, one that's taken for granted by players lost in a good game. How did Ross approach the task?

"I spent a lot of time on the first mission," he laughs. "I tweaked it over and over, for a month. After a while, you start to develop an instinct, and a system. Then I learned to listen very carefully to the testers. Their feedback was crucial."

Ingar Shu, Lead Level Designer (missions 1, 2, 16, 20, 21)

Back in 1994, Dark Forces project leader Daron Stinnett called the architecture department at the University of California at Berkeley looking for students who could work on his new 3-D game for LucasArts. A professor referred him to Ingar Shu. Although still a semester short of graduating, Shu took the job. His Dark Forces experience led to the position of lead level designer on Jedi Knight.

"I'm still three classes short of graduating," Shu laughs. "I'm not exactly sure when it might happen. My parents are a little concerned."

As one of the first Jedi team members, Shu did a lot of preproduction design work, sketching out puzzle ideas and spatial concepts for the entire game. With Justin Chin, he selected the level design team; he also worked with the programmers in creating Leia, the team's proprietary level-editing tool.

While Shu oversaw the design of all Jedi Knight missions, he also personally designed the smuggler's haven of Nar Shaddaa in missions 1 and 2. "I conceived of Nar Shaddaa as someplace that grew organically over time, built piece by piece with no particular plan. I envisioned it sort of like Hong Kong—everything crammed into whatever space is available, with a random geometry. Lots of tall spaces, massive cargo areas and hangars, interspersed with a lot of weird little nooks and crannies."

Duncan Brown, Level Design (missions 3, 10, 11, 12)

As a practicing architect at a major New York firm for 10 years, Duncan Brown found that designing skyscraper space left something to be desired. Then one day near the end of 1995, while surfing the 'Net, Brown saw that LucasArts was looking for level designers with an architecture background. His fascination with the innovative spatial worlds of 3-D games like Doom and Descent inspired him to apply for the job.

"Level design is architecture with a twist," he says with a smile. "The added element of gameplay makes it much more interesting."

The understated Scot, educated at university in Edinburgh, received a roughly mapped plan of Mission 3, "The Return to Sulon," from project leader Justin Chin. "We talked about the character of the space we wanted," he says. "The Katarn homestead is pretty straightforward, in an architectural sense."

In missions 10 and 12, however, Brown was encouraged to push the limits of what could be done with the cargo ship's geometry—"warping the sectors, twisting them, then seeing how they could be put together." He particularly enjoyed creating the catwalk spaces in Mission 12.

Matthew Tateishi, Level Design (missions 4, 8)

Matt Tateishi benefited from the same call to the Cal-Berkeley architecture department that brought Ingar Shu to LucasArts. Shu, in turn, brought Tateishi to the Dark Forces project. Tateishi went on to work on Shadows of the Empire before joining the Jedi Knight team and creating missions 4 and 8.

"Mission 4 has all those waterways," he says. "I wanted to keep it really kinetic, always moving, like a roller-coaster. Mission 8 was more typical, with exploration the key."

Tateishi's favorite bit is the TIE bomber that makes all those devastating bombing runs across the tower roof in 8.

"I think it's a good example of how powerful the scripting language is," he adds. "Something like that wouldn't be possible in other games."

Reed Knight Derleth, Level Design (missions 5, 6, 9)

A former film student at San Francisco State, Reed Derleth let his love of both celluloid and computer gaming lead him naturally to LucasArts, spending his first two years in the testing department. His primary assignment was Dark Forces. "I knew that game like the back of my hand," he says.

So when DF's lead tester Brett Tosti was named producer for Jedi Knight, he asked Derleth to try level design on the new project. It was an interesting challenge; Derleth was a rabid gamer, but admits, "I had no architecture background like the other guys, and I'd never worked with a CAD program in my life."

Derleth's constant push to dramatize the dark/light moral choice aspect of Jedi Knight gives his missions an added cinematic twist. In Mission 5, "Barons Hed," for example, you face the challenge of gunning down Gran bullies who are literally beating up the populace. Streets are full of civilians who can get caught in your crossfire. In Mission 9, "Fuel Station," you discover a secret area behind fuel canisters. The only way to reach it is to blow them up; but an innocent little Ugnaught sits on one of the cans.

"I look for little scenarios to spin like that in each level," he says. "If I have one design philosophy, it's to script situations that constantly point back to the central theme."

The actual geometry of his levels drew from various real-world sources. "With Barons Hed, I had the pretty clear model of Mos Eisley," he says. "I also modeled after Turkish and Greek architecture—small squarish buildings, little humble houses, nothing technological at all."

In Mission 6, the palace area is "all about security."

"This is a heavily fortified tower, full of logical security systems," he says. "I really wanted you to feel like one man pitted against an entire fortress."

For Mission 9, "Fuel Station," Derleth actually spent a day at the Chevron plant in nearby Richmond, making sketches and noticing that "wherever you go, you see pipes. Pipes, tanks, pipes, more tanks. So for our fuel station, I took the basic shape of a cylinder and just played with it a million ways."

Steven Chen, Level Design (missions 7, 13, 17)

Steven Chen is another well-pedigreed architect, studying at Cornell University, then earning a graduate degree in both architecture and computer graphics from Columbia University. Chen worked four years at a

traditional architecture firm in Los Angeles, designing a wide range of projects, from houses to hospitals.

"But I got interested in real-time 3-D games because you can actually get into a world that has a story or agenda," he says.

In particular, Chen was a fan of Dark Forces; when he saw that LucasArts was looking for level designers for a sequel, he jumped at the opportunity.

Chen's two primary missions, 13 and 17, are both unique in that much of the exploration occurs outdoors.

"This genre is usually about tunnel hunts," he says. "But our engine supports a much bigger geometry, so we wanted to open up the space more."

Chen enhanced the open feeling by designing levels that weren't strictly linear.

"Balancing notions of gameplay with spatial design is always a challenge," he says. "I mean, as an architect, you're not usually thinking, 'How am I gonna play this building?'"

But, notes Chen, you do think in terms of function. You ask, What is the purpose of this space?

"That drives the design," he says. "In Mission 17, for example, we needed a military base, freshly dug out of the rock. The story drove the design, and the gameplay evolved from that. So it's not just a frag-fest. It's figuring out how the geometry and gameplay and puzzles make sense in light of the story. How do they move the story forward?"

Jacob Stephens, Level Design (missions 14, 15, assist on 18, 19)

After graduating from Penn State University with a degree in architecture, Jake Stephens sent his résumé to LucasArts and landed a job immediately. He's responsible for the maddening and entirely unique Mission 15, "Falling Cargo Ship."

"Justin pushed us to use spaces in ways that you normally wouldn't," he says. "That was the idea in the falling ship. Everything rotates back and forth 45 degrees—walls become floors, you walk up elevator shafts, that sort of thing."

For Maw's level (Mission 14), Stephens wanted something simple so that the complex fighting AI wouldn't get confused or hung up. He also took over the final stages of design in missions 18 and 19, after original designer Doug Shannon left the company.

"Doug did all the geometry and most of the puzzles," says Stephens. "I just finished up lighting and texturing, and wrapped up any bugs we'd find."

He explains that in those levels, Shannon started with a huge cylinder and started carving his way down to the core. In fact, 18 and 19 started out as a single level in the original design, but Shannon's cylinder was so huge, the Jedi team decided to cut it in half.

An Interview with Justin Chin

OK, so Justin Chin and I are old friends. We worked together at Accolade in the early '90s; he was art director and I was lead writer for a now-obscure adventure game, Lost in L.A. We also tried to start a software design studio in 1992. So when I received the assignment to write the official strategy guide for Jedi Knight, we were both pretty pleased. Fortunately, I am so unbiased by nature that I spent the entire week referring to Justin as (directly) "Mr. Chin," or (indirectly), "the alleged leader of this so-called project."

After our aborted entrepreneurial attempt in 1992, Justin went on to work as an artist for Sega of America, then joined LucasArts and became art director for Dark Forces. Toward the end of that project, he was appointed project leader for the planned sequel.

RICK BARBA: Let's talk about the birth of Jedi Knight. Where did the story come from?

JUSTIN CHIN: Toward the end of Dark Forces, I knew I was going to be project leader for Jedi, and I was developing a lot of ideas. I explored a number of different story lines. I was looking for something that was fundamentally a hunt or a chase. Two movies heavily influenced me at that time. One was The *Seven Samurai*—and all the Akira Kurosawa films, really, which I knew deeply influenced George [Lucas]. I was actually researching those because I wanted to see what influenced him, what he liked, what he was trying to do with *Star Wars*.

The other movie, and it sounds crazy maybe, was *The Good, the Bad, and the Ugly*. I liked the idea of searching for this legendary gold, which in my story became the Valley of the Jedi. I made it a Jedi burial ground

with lost, untapped power that could be exploited. It worked well, because Kyle as a character could go either way. He could either save it from Jerec or take it for himself. When that spark happened, I just jumped on it. I figured out how Kyle's father worked into the concept, added a Jedi Master, Rahn, and then the seven Dark Jedi, sort of like the evil seven samurai. That made for a good gameplay element, of course—seven Jedi you can fight as level bosses, each with different characteristics, and your victories allow you to progress in your own growth as a Jedi. So it seemed to work the best.

BARBA: Can you synopsize the story of the game? Although Jedi Knight has a remarkably well-rounded story and character development for a 3-D action game, limitations in the genre still leave some gaps that readers might want to see filled in.

CHIN: The Jedi Knight story is closely tied to the one we set up in Dark Forces. In Dark Forces, Kyle is initiated into the Rebellion. Originally, he was an Imperial soldier, and in fact became one because he thought his father was killed by Rebels. His revenge was to fully enlist in the Imperial army. He was at the Imperial Academy to get an education when Morgan Katarn's murder occurred, but the death pushed him into the military.

Jedi Knight starts off with Kyle looking for the true murderers of his father. He's since learned that it was an Imperial job, but that's all he knows. He goes to 8t88, who's well-known in Nar Shaddaa and elsewhere as a source of information. He's a manipulator who wants to be powerful. So when 8t88 does find out who killed Morgan Katarn, the droid also learns that the murderer, Jerec, can offer him a lot more in terms of a "well-deserved reward."

Meanwhile Rahn, the Jedi Master, who knew Morgan Katarn, also knows that Kyle will play a central role in the fate of the Valley of the Jedi.

Rahn, as a young Jedi, was a wanderer, sort of an orphan. He learned of the valley, which some thought mythic, like Atlantis, a place told of in old tales. The ancient Jedi, of course, were very secretive about it. Knowledge of such a valley could be exploited. Rahn was obsessed with the tale; it was his guide to the Force, in a way.

In the course of searching for the valley, Rahn meets Jerec, who seeks the same knowledge, but for his own nefarious purposes. Jerec tries to recruit Rahn into his fold. Rahn was still kind of borderline, but he chooses not to go down the dark path. And then he meets Morgan, who actually knows where the valley is.

BARBA: How does Morgan know?

CHIN: Morgan found the Valley by helping the Rebels. In the course of sneaking people out of Sulon and away from the corruption of the Imperials—Jerec, in fact, had built his palace there in Barons Hed— Morgan stumbles upon the valley on another planet, which we left unnamed, where he's been hiding Rebel sympathizers. So when Morgan and Rahn meet, and Rahn speaks of the valley he seeks, Morgan tells him, "I know the place. I've found exactly what you're describing."

Rahn is overwhelmed, but wise enough to know that Jerec is powerful enough to take the information from him. So he doesn't let Morgan tell him the valley's location, and convinces Morgan to hide the information and pass it on to his son, Kyle.

BARBA: So Rahn senses that Kyle Katarn will become strong in the ways of the Force.

CHIN: Yes. Exactly. He senses the Force in Morgan, too, but knows his son will be stronger still, and the focal point of the final confrontation, whatever that may be. And Rahn gives Morgan the lightsaber to pass on to Kyle, too.

THE OFFICIAL STRATEGY GUIDE

BARBA: It's so...biblical.

CHIN: (laughs) Isn't it?

BARBA: It's the Joseph Campbell myth stuff. Every deep *Star Wars* fan probably knows about Campbell's influence on George Lucas, his recognition of the resonating myths that underpin the *Star Wars* saga. He treated *Star Wars* as a serious piece of modern mythology. Father–son things always resonate deep.

CHIN: And the great creatures. The belly of the Death Star. All the ancient myths played out on another scale.

BARBA: And so that sort of mythic underpinning carries into Dark Forces and Jedi Knight?

CHIN: (laughs) Geez, I hope so.

BARBA: I have to say, I was actually moved by the final scene. I won't describe it, in case somebody reading this interview hasn't finished the game yet. But it worked in that weird primal sense, tapping into a deep vein, the way a myth should.

CHIN: Yeah, when I was writing it, I told Ray [Gresko, Jedi Knight's lead programmer] it was actually a very deep story for me. I mean, this is personal. It's about my own childhood, growing up with my father, then losing my father.

The funny thing is that Jason Court, the actor who plays Kyle, came up to me on the set one day and said, "So Justin, what's your story? Where'd this come from?" I told him how it was very personal for me, about my father, how I wanted those elements in. It turns out Jason had a very complicated, troubled childhood himself. So in the scene where

Kyle slays Maw, who taunts him about putting his father's head on a spike and all that, Jason's performance is truly amazing. Just watch that cutscene sometime. Before Jason played it, we talked about the anger, the fact that he's crossing the line to anger, the dark side, and in a sense betraying his father by using the Force and the saber for revenge, a dark side emotion. I mean, we were totally stunned by the real emotion Jason brought to that scene.

BARBA: This is a tough question, and our respective marketing departments might not want you to answer it, but do you feel satisfied with what you were able to do in this game?

CHIN: In general, yeah. I feel very happy with it. I mean, I'm so close to it, it's hard to say. As I explain all these elements, I look at the game and wonder, "Does anybody see this? Maybe I didn't say any of what I wanted to say." I did try to get the core story into the game. And I do like the medium, because I think it can be pushed, and made to serve good storytelling. Even this genre, the 3-D action game, can do more than just get your fast-twitch muscles jumping, I think.

BARBA: I guess the movie *Star Wars* itself proves that, in a way. A pure action film in the classic sense, and yet it resonates on all kinds of levels. My God, it works as myth, even.

CHIN: You can't do much better than that, artistically.

BARBA: Or commercially.

CHIN: (laughs) Yes!

BARBA: Along these lines, I have to say that one of the neatest, most involving aspects of Jedi Knight's gameplay is that whole light side–dark side element. I mean, you can indiscriminately slaughter Ugnaughts sitting on fuel canisters, or you can save them by herding or chasing them to safety. You can gun down anything that moves and take out a lot of innocent pedestrians and droids, or you can be careful, because being good always requires care, whereas being evil can be as simple as just being careless or doing what's expedient.

CHIN: Yeah, the banality of evil.

BARBA: And then these moral choices have consequences in the game.

CHIN: That situation you described with the Ugnaughts is a credit to Reed Derleth. He was adamant about putting those sorts of situations involving moral choice, dark versus light, into the missions he designed. It was so great, and I encouraged it all the way. He put a lot of effort into doing that. The whole dark–light meter is a great element, and it's a testament to the team, who all wanted to include this sort of thing in the game. I mean, in this game, you're a Jedi. Sure, everybody wants to be a Jedi. But what does it mean? What does it entail? What do you have to do to be a Jedi? Just kill a lot of stormtroopers? Maybe that's good enough for the dark side. But a true Jedi is more. A true Jedi uses the Force for good. We wanted that in the game. It took awhile, but we got it in.

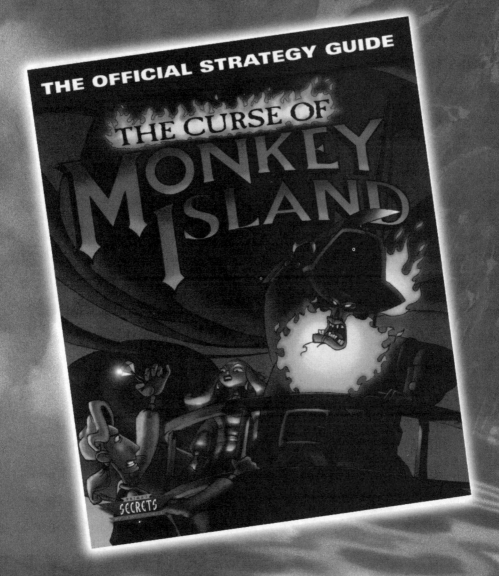

COMPUTER GAME BOOKS

688 (I) Hunter/Killer: The Official Strategy Guide	$19.99
Betrayal In Antara: The Official Strategy Guide	$19.99
Birthright: The Official Strategy Guide	$19.99
Blood: The Official Strategy Guide	$19.99
CD-ROM Classics Vol. 2	$19.99
Command & Conquer: Red Alert Secrets & Solutions—The Unauthorized Edition	$19.99
Command & Conquer: Red Alert—Unauthorized Advanced Strategies	$19.99
Command & Conquer: Red Alert-Counterstrike—Unauthorized Secrets and Solutions	$19.99
Dark Earth: The Official Strategy Guide	$19.99
Diablo: The Official Strategy Guide	$19.99
Diablo battle.net Advanced Strategies: The Official Strategy Guide	$16.99
DOOM II: The Official Strategy Guide	$19.95
Duke Nukem 3D: Unauthorized Secrets & Solutions	$14.99
Dungeon Keeper Official Secrets	$19.99
Ecstatica II: The Official Strategy Guide	$19.99
Fighters Anthology: The Official Strategy Guide	$24.99
Final Doom: Unauthorized Game Secrets	$19.99
Heroes of Might and Magic II: The Price of Loyalty—The Official Strategy Guide	$14.99
Imperalism: The Official Strategy Guide	$19.99
Interstate '76: The Official Strategy Guide	$19.99
Links LS 98: The Official Strategy Guide	$19.99
MDK: The Official Strategy Guide	$12.99
Microsoft Flight Simulator for Win95: The Official Strategy Guide	$19.99
Myst: The Official Strategy Guide	$19.95
NASCAR Racing 2: The Official Strategy Guide	$19.99
OddWorld: Abe's Oddysee—The Official Strategy Guide	$12.99
Online Games Guide: The Official Strategy Guide	$19.99
Outlaws: The Official Strategy Guide	$19.99
Pacific General: The Official Strategy Guide	$16.99
Phantasmagoria: Puzzle of Flesh—The Official Strategy Guide	$19.99
Quake Strategy Guide: Unauthorized	$19.99
Quake Unauthorized Map Guide	$14.99
Rebel Moon Rising: The Official Strategy Guide	$19.99
Shadows of the Empire, PC Version: The Official Strategy Guide	$19.99
Shivers Two: Harvest of Souls—The Official Strategy Guide	$19.99
Sid Meier's Civilization II: The Official Strategy Guide	$19.99
The Games Troubleshooting Guide: Simple Solutions to Common Problems	$7.99
The Last Express: The Official Strategy Guide	$19.99
Timelapse: The Official Strategy Guide	$19.99
Ultima Online: The Official Strategy Guide	$19.99
WarCraft II: Beyond the Dark Portal Official Secrets & Solutions	$14.99
WarCraft II: Tides of Darkness—The Official Strategy Guide	$19.99

To Order Call 1-800-531-2343

Warlords III: The Official Strategy Guide	$19.99
Wing Commander IV: The Unauthorized Strategy Guide	$14.99
X-COM Apocalypse: The Official Strategy Guide	$19.99

Video Game Books

Beyond the Beyond: Unauthorized Game Secrets	$14.99
Blast Corps Unauthorized Game Secrets	$12.99
Blood Omen: Legacy of Kain—Official Game Secrets	$14.99
Dark Rift: Official Secrets & Solutions	$12.99
Doom 64 Official Game Secrets: Official Secrets & Solutions	$12.99
Dynasty Warriors: Official Secrets & Solutions	$12.99
Game Boy Pocket Power Guide: Unauthorized	$7.99
GoldenEye 007: Unauthorized Game Secrets	$12.99
Hexen 64: Official Secrets & Solutions	$12.99
Killer Instinct Gold: The Unauthorized Guide	$12.99
MDK: The Official Strategy Guide	$12.99
Mortal Kombat 3: Official Power Play Guide	$9.95
Mortal Kombat Trilogy Official Game Secrets	$9.99
Nintendo 64 Pocket Power Guide Volume 2: Unauthorized	$7.99
Nintendo 64 Unauthorized Game Secrets Volume 2	$12.99
OddWorld: Abe's Oddysee—The Official Strategy Guide	$12.99
Ogre Battle: The Official Strategy Guide	$12.99
PlayStation Game Secrets Unauthorized Volume 4	$12.99
PlayStation Pocket Power Guide Volume 2: Unauthorized	$7.99
Shadows of the Empire Game Secrets	$12.99
Sports Pocket Power Guide—Authorized	$7.99
Star Fox 64: Unauthorized Game Secrets	$12.99
Super Mario 64 Game Secrets: Unauthorized	$12.99
Tomb Raider Game Secrets	$14.99
Twisted Metal 2 Unauthorized Game Secrets	$12.99
Vandal Hearts Unauthorized Secrets & Solutions	$14.99
Warcraft II: Dark Saga—Official Game Secrets	$12.99
War Gods Official Arcade Game Secrets	$9.99
War Gods Official Game Secrets	$12.99
WCW Vs. the World: Official Secrets & Solutions	$3.99
Wild Arms: Unauthorized Game Secrets	$12.99
Castlevania: Symphony of the Night—Unauthorized Secrets & Solutions	$12.99
Sega Saturn Pocket Power Guide Volume 2: Authorized	$7.99
GameShark Pocket Power Guide: Authorized	$7.99
Croc: Legend of the Gobbos: Authorized	$12.99

To Order Call 1-800-531-2343

To Order Books

Please send me the following items:

Quantity	Title	Unit Price	Total
_____	_____	$ _____	$ _____
_____	_____	$ _____	$ _____
_____	_____	$ _____	$ _____
_____	_____	$ _____	$ _____
_____	_____	$ _____	$ _____

Subtotal $ _____

Deduct 10% when ordering 3-5 books $ _____

7.25% Sales Tax (CA only) $ _____

8.25% Sales Tax (TN only) $ _____

5.0% Sales Tax (MD and IN only) $ _____

7.0% G.S.T. Tax (Canada only) $ _____

Shipping and Handling* $ _____

Total Order $ _____

*Shipping and Handling depend on Subtotal.

Subtotal	Shipping/Handling
$0.00–$14.99	$3.00
$15.00–$29.99	$4.00
$30.00–$49.99	$6.00
$50.00–$99.99	$10.00
$100.00–$199.99	$13.50
$200.00+	Call for Quote

Foreign and all Priority Request orders:
Call Order Entry department
for price quote at 916-632-4400

This chart represents the total retail price of books only
(before applicable discounts are taken).

By Telephone: With MC or Visa, call 800-632-8676 or 916-632-4400. Mon–Fri, 8:30-4:30.

WWW: http://www.primapublishing.com

By Internet E-mail: sales@primapub.com

By Mail: Just fill out the information below and send with your remittance to:

**Prima Publishing
P.O. Box 1260BK
Rocklin, CA 95677**

My name is _____

I live at _____

City_____ State_____ ZIP _____

MC/Visa#_____ Exp._____

Check/money order enclosed for $ _____ Payable to Prima Publishing

Daytime telephone _____

Signature _____